An Explanation of Muḥammad ibn ʿAbd al-Wahhāb's

Kashf al-Shubuhāt

A critical analysis of *shirk*

Translation and Commentary by
Abū Ammaar Yasir Qadhi

ISBN 1 898649 62 6

British Library Cataloguing in Publication Data.
A catalogue record for this book is available from the British Library.

Published: Al-Hidaayah Publishing and Distribution

Distributed by: Al-Hidaayah Publishing and Distribution
P.O. Box 3332
Birmingham
United Kingdom
B10 0UH

Tel: 0121 753 1889
Fax: 0121 753 2422
Website: www.al-hidaayah.co.uk
Email: mail@al-hidaayah.co.uk

An Explanation of
Muḥammad ibn ʿAbd al-Wahhāb's
Kashf al-Shubuhāt

Contents

Foreword

Verily, all praise is due to Allāh, the One Who has the Most Perfect and Beautiful Names, and the Most Noble and Lofty Attributes. He alone is worthy of worship. And may Peace and Blessings be upon Muḥammad ibn ʿAbdillāh (ﷺ), the final Prophet and last Messenger, who was sent to perfect the worship of Allāh.

Of the most fundamental matters of Islām – in fact, the most fundamental of all fundamentals – is the fact that only Allāh deserves our worship and veneration. This simple concept is summarised in our testimony of faith, the *shahādah*: *lā ilāha illa Allāh*, 'There is no deity worthy of worship except Allāh'. There is not a single Muslim except that he or she cherishes this phrase, and professes belief in it. This concept (known in Arabic as *tawḥīd*) is the basis of Islām, and differentiates a Muslim from a non-Muslim.

Yet, the sad fact of the matter is that there are some who ascribe themselves to Islām and claim to be amongst its adherents while they worship other than Allāh. They might verbalise the *shahādah*, but it has no meaning in their hearts, for they do not understand the implications of this simple phrase. So you find some of them making *duʿā* to a grave, and others undertaking a pilgrimage to a religious shrine other than the *Kaʿbah*, or making sacrifices to a 'holy saint', or seeking help from a prophet, and so on. These people all claim to be practising *tawḥīd*, yet their actions prove that they are guilty of *shirk* – the antithesis of *tawḥīd*. What is still more amazing is that, when such people are approached and advised to leave such acts, they become rebellious and arrogant, refusing to acknowledge the clear sin that they are guilty of. In fact, they might even misquote verses from the Qur'ān, and *aḥādīth* of the Prophet (ﷺ) in order to justify the greatest of all evils!

Therefore, it is imperative that the Muslim who wishes to call to the pure worship of Allāh arms himself with the knowledge of *tawḥīd*, and protects himself from the evils of *shirk*. Such a caller must equip himself with knowledge of the weaponry that his opponent uses as well, and also know how to defend himself against such weapons.

This book that is in the reader's hands is perhaps the most comprehensive work for the lay-Muslim with this goal in mind. It is an explanation of a book entitled *Kashf al-Shubuhāt*, which literally translates as: 'The Clearing of

Doubts'. In it, the author concentrates on explaining and refuting the 'evidences' that were used by certain Muslim groups of his time to justify acts of *shirk*. The author intended in this work to expose the falsity and speciousness of these arguments by proving that the pagan Arabs whom the Prophet (ﷺ) fought – known as the *Jāhilīyyah* Arabs – utilised the exact same arguments and fell prey to the same reasoning as these people did.

This is one of the most advanced works on the subject, and over a dozen different arguments and evidences used to justify *shirk* are presented and then refuted. In order to maximize the benefit of this work, I have taken the liberty of including introductory sections concerning other aspects of *shirk* not mentioned by the author. To this end, I have included a detailed discussion of the definition of *shirk*, the types of *shirk*, the history of *shirk*, the evils of *shirk*, the futility of *shirk*, and other related topics, in order that this work become a comprehensive study of this greatest evil known to man.

I have tried my best to conform to the original Arabic of the work. However, in order to make the reading of the translation more amenable, I have taken the liberty of interpolating phrases and words into the actual text of the work. No new concepts are introduced, nor is any idea expressed by the author ignored. Rather, small sentences and words were added in order to allow for a smoother reading of the text. Also, I added section titles, and numbered various points mentioned by the author. I pray that this facilitates a better understanding of the text. For the Arabic, I relied primarily on the text edited by ʿAbdullāh al-Qahtanī, with a forward by Dr. ʿAbd al-Raḥmān al-Maḥmūd. The text has been published in many different editions with slight, but frequent, word-variations, and I found this particular edition to be the best. This text, along with its translation, is delineated from the explanation by markings in the margin. The term 'TEXT' denotes the start of the actual work, and 'EXPL.' denotes the start of my explanation.

The introductory sections on *shirk* are based primarily on material that I studied at master's level in the Dept. of *ʿAqīdah* (Islāmic Theology) at the University of Madīnah. Many of these sections are merely summarised and edited versions of my personal notes. As for the explanation of the text of *Kashf al-Shubuhāt*, this is based on the various texts that I could obtain, most of which are referenced in the Select Bibliography at the end of this book. I also benefited from other sources related to the subject, which were referenced when used. Lastly, Dr. ʿAbdullāh Brown, and Br. Navaid Aziz, both kindly read the initial draft of the work, and offered suggestions for improvement.

This work is related to *al-Qawā'id al-Arba'ah* by the same author.[1] As this work is a more advanced work on the same subject, it is recommended that the reader study *al-Qawā'id al-Arba'ah* before proceeding to this one.

Since human endeavours are always prone to error, I would appreciate any sincere advice or constructive criticism from the reader.[2]

And finally, our success is with Allāh alone!

Abū Ammaar

The City of the Prophet (ﷺ) – *al-Madīnah al-Nabawiyyah*

1st of Ramaḍān, 1422 A.H. (16th Nov., 2001 CE)

---

[1] Available as *An Explanation of Muḥammad ibn 'Abdul Wahhāb's Four Principles of Shirk* (al-Hidaayah Publications, Birmingham, 2002 CE).

[2] The author may be contacted via the publisher, or at the following e-mail address: *yqadhi@hotmail.com*.

1. The Definition of *Shirk*

Linguistically, the word '*shirk*' is based on the three letter root (ش رك). The famous linguist Ibn Fāris defines it as meaning: '...to add or append, not being single or one'.[3] Therefore the word *sharīk* implies a partner or helper.

From an Islāmic perspective, various scholars have defined it differently, although these definitions carry the same theme.

Al-Rāghib al-Asbhanī (d. 425 A.H.) wrote: "*Shirk* is defined as affirming partners (*sharīk*) with Allāh."[4] Al-Shawkānī (d. 1255 A.H.) stated: "*Shirk* is to make a *du'ā* to other than Allāh in matters in which only Allāh should be asked, or to believe that a certain object has powers that only Allāh has, or to intend to please an object with an act that should only be performed for Allāh."[5] Muḥammad ibn 'Abd al-Wahhāb (d. 1206 A.H.) defined it as: '...directing an act of worship to other than Allāh, (such as) calling out to others as well as Allāh, or intending an act of worship that Allāh has commanded to other than Allāh.'[6] It has also been defined as: "...making a partner (*nidd*) with Allāh."[7]

Although these definitions are all similar, it appears that the most accurate one is the last: to attribute a partner, or *nidd*, with Allāh. The Qur'ān and Sunnah both describe *shirk* with these exact phrases. Allāh states in the Qur'ān:

فَلَا تَجْعَلُوا لِلَّهِ أَندَادًا وَأَنتُمْ تَعْلَمُونَ

> "So do not make, along with Allāh, partners (*andād*) while you know (that He is the true Creator)" [Sūrah *al-Baqarah*; 22].

Ibn Mas'ūd asked the Prophet (ﷺ), "What is the greatest sin?" He replied: "To take alongside Allāh a partner (*nidd*) even though it was He that created you." [8]

---

[3] *Mu'jam Maqāyīs al-Lughah*, 3/275.

[4] *Mufradāt al-Qur'ān al-Karīm*, p. 452.

[5] *Al-Durr al-Nadīd*, p. 34.

[6] *Mu'alafāt al-Shaykh Muḥammad ibn 'Abd al-Wahhāb*, 1/281.

[7] *Fatāwa al-Lajnat al-Dā'imah*, 1/516.

[8] Reported by al-Bukhārī (# 4477) and Muslim (# 87).

Thus, *shirk* involves believing in a partner along with Allāh. Such a 'partner' could be a partner in lordship (*rubūbiyyah*), or in worship (*ulūhiyyah*), or in attributes (*asmā wa l-ṣifāt*). In other words, the essence of *shirk* involves giving Allāh's rights to other than He. Therefore, to claim that a certain object or deity has the power to bless one with one's needs is *shirk*. Likewise, to prostrate or make *duʿā* to other than Allāh is also *shirk*. And the claim that any created object knows everything, or can hear any plea directed to it, is *shirk*. Whenever any specific right of Allāh's is given to any other object, whether that object be a living being or an inanimate object, real or imagined, *shirk* has occurred.

2. *Tawḥīd* Preceded *Shirk*

Historically speaking, *tawḥīd*[9] existed before *shirk*. Mankind was set upon the pure worship of Allāh before it deviated into the practice of *shirk*. The proof of this is manifold.

The First Evidence: *Fiṭrah*

Allāh created mankind with an innate nature, known in Arabic as *fiṭrah*. This innate nature, ingrained in every single human being, enlightens a person about the knowledge of right and wrong, and good and evil. It is because of this *fiṭrah* that every person believes that murder, lying and stealing are evil acts, and that taking care of orphans, and being kind to one's parents, are noble acts. The *fiṭrah* was placed by Allāh in every single person at the time of Adam's creation. When Allāh created Adam, He extracted from his loins all of his progeny, and caused them to be spread out in front of Him. He then made a covenant with them, asking, "Am I not your Lord?" They all replied, "Yes, we have testified [to this]."

The covenant – known in Arabic as the *mīthāq* – is mentioned in the Qur'ān and Sunnah. Allāh states:

وَإِذْ أَخَذَ رَبُّكَ مِنۢ بَنِيٓ ءَادَمَ مِن ظُهُورِهِمْ ذُرِّيَّتَهُمْ وَأَشْهَدَهُمْ
عَلَىٰٓ أَنفُسِهِمْ أَلَسْتُ بِرَبِّكُمْ ۖ قَالُوا۟ بَلَىٰ ۛ شَهِدْنَآ ۛ أَن تَقُولُوا۟ يَوْمَ
ٱلْقِيَٰمَةِ إِنَّا كُنَّا عَنْ هَٰذَا غَٰفِلِينَ ﴿١٧٢﴾

> "And when your Lord took, from the Children of Adam, from their loins, their descendants, and made them testify of themselves, [saying to them] 'Am I not your Lord?' They replied, 'Yes, we have testified.' [This] lest they should say, on the Day of Resurrection, 'Indeed, we were of this [fact] unaware'" [Sūrah *al-A'rāf* 172].

---

[9] *Tawḥīd* is the affirmation of the Perfect Existence of Allāh, along with the direction of all acts of worship to Him alone. Thus, it is the opposite of *shirk*. The concept of *tawḥīd* will be discussed in greater detail at the beginning of the text of *Kashf al-Shubuhāt*.

Ibn 'Abbās stated: "Allāh took the Covenant (*mīthāq*) at Nu'mān (a valley outside of Makkah), on the Day of Arafāt, from the loins of Adam. He extracted from his loins every soul that would be created, and He spread them before Himself, and spoke to them directly: 'Am I not your Lord?'"[10]

In another narration, 'Umar ibn al-Khaṭṭāb said, "I heard the Prophet (ﷺ) being asked about (the meaning of) this verse. He responded: 'Verily, Allāh created Adam, and then rubbed his back with His right hand, and caused all of his progeny to appear....'"[11]

The *mīthāq* is also referred to in another ḥadīth, in which the Prophet (ﷺ) narrated that Allāh said: "I have created My servants, all of them, pure (and inclined towards my worship), but the *Shayāṭīn* came and diverted them from their religion. They prohibited them from matters that I allowed them, and commanded them to associate partners with Me...."[12] Thus, Allāh states that all humans were created in a natural state of *fiṭrah*.

In these narrations, we are informed that Allāh made a covenant with every single person at the time of Adam's initial creation. This covenant specified that only Allāh is the *Rabb*, the true Lord, and thus only He deserves to be worshipped. Even though man does not remember this covenant, it is ingrained subconsciously in every person's *fiṭrah*. It is because of this *fiṭrah* that every human, whether Muslim or not, innately knows good from evil. And the greatest good is the pure worship of Allāh, whereas the vilest evil is the association of partners with Allah.

So if being kind to one's parents is ingrained in every person, then is not the right of worshipping Allāh alone more deserving of being ingrained? And if the evils of lying and stealing are agreed upon by mankind, then surely the evil of *shirk* has more right to be acknowledged.

Allāh's prophets all delivered the message of the pure worship of Allāh, which is embodied in this *fiṭrah*. Therefore, when a person hears the prophet's

---

[10] Reported by Aḥmad (1/272), al-Nasā'ī in his *al-Kabīr* (as mentioned by al-Mizzī in his *Tuḥfat al-Ashāf* (4/440)), al-Ḥākim (2/544) and others. Al-Ḥākim, al-Dhahabī and al-Albānī (in his *al-Ṣaḥīḥah*, # 1623) all declared it to be authentic. Although this statement was narrated by Ibn 'Abbās, it takes on the status of a ḥadīth of the Prophet (ﷺ), as it concerns the matters of the unseen. The scholars of ḥadīth state that when a Companion narrates from the matters of the unseen, it takes on the status of a ḥadīth.

[11] Reported by Mālik in his *Muwaṭṭa'* (2/898), and Aḥmad in his *Musnad* (1/44). It has a slight weakness in its chain, but it is possible to raise it to the level of *ḥasan* (acceptable) if the other narrations of this ḥadīth are taken into account. (For a more detailed discussion of the various *aḥādīth* pertaining to the *mīthāq*, one is referred to the book: *Akth al-Mīthāq* by Dr. 'Abd al-'Azīz al-'Uthaym).

[12] Reported by Muslim (# 2876).

message, he or she immediately inclines towards it, as it conforms with his or her *fiṭrah*.

So the primary message of every single human's *fiṭrah* is: there is only One Creator, and only He is worthy of worship. It is precisely for this reason that the Prophet (ﷺ) stated: "Every single child is born upon the *fiṭrah*. Then, his parents make him a Jew or a Christian." [13] In other words, every single child is born upon *tawḥīd*, and, had he been left without any outside factors, he would be a Muslim (hence the Prophet (ﷺ) did not say, '..or a Muslim', for the child is born 'submitting' himself to Allah). However, a person's parents then corrupt the child's *fiṭrah*, by making him a Jew or Christian, or a believer of any other faith.

Ibn al-Qayyim writes: "The *fiṭrah* is amenable to the knowledge of Islām and the love of Islām. The *fiṭrah* itself necessitates acknowledgment and love (of Allāh)...So every single child is born in a state in which he or she acknowledges the Lordship (of Allāh). So if the child were left without any preventive factors, he would not turn away from the *fiṭrah* to anything else."[14]

The existence of *fiṭrah* also explains why so many people convert to Islām. Once a person who sincerely desires the truth is exposed to the teachings of Islām, he immediately inclines himself towards it, as it reinforces the subconscious *fiṭrah* embodied in him.

So *fiṭrah* is one of the primary evidences that *tawḥīd* is the natural state of man, and, therefore, must have existed before *shirk*. Since *shirk* is a corruption and deviation from the original state of man (based upon *fiṭrah*), it must have crept in after *tawḥīd*.

The Second Evidence: The People of Nūḥ

It has been authentically narrated that the people of Nūḥ (Noah) were the first people that practiced *shirk*. Nūḥ was the first messenger (*rasūl*) sent to mankind.[15] Ibn 'Abbās narrates, "Between Nūḥ and Adam were ten generations, all of which followed the law (of Allāh), upon the truth. But they differed (amongst themselves), so Allāh then sent prophets, as bearers of glad

---

[13] Reported by al-Bukhārī (# 2758).

[14] Paraphrased from *Shifā al-'Alīl*, 2/309.

[15] Nūḥ was the first *rasūl* (messenger) sent to mankind, but Adam was the first *nabī* (prophet). The difference between a *rasūl* and a *nabī* is that a *rasūl* is one who is sent to a nation that does not believe in him, whereas a *nabī* is sent to a nation that believes in him. A *rasūl* thus occupies a status higher than that of a *nabī*.

5. The Futility of *Shirk*

Not only is *shirk* the most evil of all evils, it is futile and useless as well. In other words, any reason that a person who commits *shirk* might use to justify his actions will not materialise or be reached through *shirk*.

The evidences for the futility of *shirk* are numerous, and can be categorised as follows:

Evidences from the Qur'ān

The Qur'ān shows the futility of *shirk* in many verses. These verses can themselves be categorised as follows:

1. By Mentioning Allāh's Creations

Frequently, Allāh reminds mankind that it is He Who created them, and all that they see around them. Only Allāh provides man with all his needs. Therefore, why turn to other than Allāh for these very needs?

وَلَئِن سَأَلْتَهُم مَّنْ خَلَقَ السَّمَٰوَٰتِ وَالْأَرْضَ وَسَخَّرَ الشَّمْسَ وَالْقَمَرَ لَيَقُولُنَّ اللَّهُ ۖ فَأَنَّىٰ يُؤْفَكُونَ ﴿٦١﴾

> "And if you were to ask them who created the Heavens and the Earth, and put the sun and moon under (His) command, they would respond: Allāh. So how are they misguided?" [Sūrah *al-'Ankabūt*; 61].

If man acknowledges Allāh as the Creator and Sustainer, how are they then misguided in their worship of Him?

By reminding man of Allāh's Lordship (*Tawḥīd Al-Rubūbiyyah*), Allāh then shows them that only He deserves to be worshipped (*Tawḥīd al-Ulūhiyyah*). In another series of verses, Allāh states:

قُلِ ٱلۡحَمۡدُ لِلَّهِ وَسَلَٰمٌ
عَلَىٰ عِبَادِهِ ٱلَّذِينَ ٱصۡطَفَىٰٓۗ ءَآللَّهُ خَيۡرٌ أَمَّا يُشۡرِكُونَ ﴿٥٩﴾
أَمَّنۡ خَلَقَ ٱلسَّمَٰوَٰتِ وَٱلۡأَرۡضَ وَأَنزَلَ لَكُم مِّنَ ٱلسَّمَآءِ
مَآءً فَأَنۢبَتۡنَا بِهِۦ حَدَآئِقَ ذَاتَ بَهۡجَةٖ مَّا كَانَ لَكُمۡ
أَن تُنۢبِتُواْ شَجَرَهَآۗ أَءِلَٰهٞ مَّعَ ٱللَّهِۚ بَلۡ هُمۡ قَوۡمٞ يَعۡدِلُونَ ﴿٦٠﴾
أَمَّن جَعَلَ ٱلۡأَرۡضَ قَرَارٗا وَجَعَلَ خِلَٰلَهَآ أَنۡهَٰرٗا وَجَعَلَ لَهَا
رَوَٰسِيَ وَجَعَلَ بَيۡنَ ٱلۡبَحۡرَيۡنِ حَاجِزًاۗ أَءِلَٰهٞ مَّعَ ٱللَّهِۚ بَلۡ
أَكۡثَرُهُمۡ لَا يَعۡلَمُونَ ﴿٦١﴾ أَمَّن يُجِيبُ ٱلۡمُضۡطَرَّ إِذَا دَعَاهُ
وَيَكۡشِفُ ٱلسُّوٓءَ وَيَجۡعَلُكُمۡ خُلَفَآءَ ٱلۡأَرۡضِۗ أَءِلَٰهٞ
مَّعَ ٱللَّهِۚ قَلِيلٗا مَّا تَذَكَّرُونَ ﴿٦٢﴾ أَمَّن يَهۡدِيكُمۡ فِي
ظُلُمَٰتِ ٱلۡبَرِّ وَٱلۡبَحۡرِ وَمَن يُرۡسِلُ ٱلرِّيَٰحَ بُشۡرَۢا بَيۡنَ يَدَيۡ
رَحۡمَتِهِۦٓۗ أَءِلَٰهٞ مَّعَ ٱللَّهِۚ تَعَٰلَى ٱللَّهُ عَمَّا يُشۡرِكُونَ ﴿٦٣﴾
أَمَّن يَبۡدَؤُاْ ٱلۡخَلۡقَ ثُمَّ يُعِيدُهُۥ وَمَن يَرۡزُقُكُم مِّنَ ٱلسَّمَآءِ وَٱلۡأَرۡضِۗ
أَءِلَٰهٞ مَّعَ ٱللَّهِۚ قُلۡ هَاتُواْ بُرۡهَٰنَكُمۡ إِن كُنتُمۡ صَٰدِقِينَ ﴿٦٤﴾

"Say: Praise be to Allāh, and peace be upon His servants whom He has chosen. Is Allāh better or what they associate with Him? Is the One Who created the heavens and the earth, and sent down for you rain from the sky, causing to grow thereby gardens of joyful beauty, which you could not (otherwise) have grown its trees [not best]? Is there any god besides Allāh [who did this, and is thus worthy of worship?] Rather, they are a people who ascribe equals (to Him). Is He [not best] Who made the earth a stable ground, and placed within it rivers and made for it firmly set mountains, and placed between the two seas a barrier? Rather, most of them do not know. Is He [not best] Who responds to the call of the one in distress, and removes evil and makes you inheritors of the earth? Is there a deity with Allāh? Little do you remember. Is He [not best] Who guides you through the darknesses of the land and sea, and Who sends the winds as good tidings before His mercy? Is there a deity besides Allāh? Exalted is Allāh over what they associate with Him. Is He [not best] Who begins the creation, and then repeats it, and who provides for you from the heavens and earth? Is there a deity besides Allāh? Say: Produce your truth if you are truthful" [Sūrah *al-Naml*; 59-64].

How can man affirm that only Allāh creates and gives life, grants sustenance and controls everything, yet at the same time worship other than Him?

2. By Giving Analogies and Examples

Many different parables and examples are given in the Qur'ān which show the futility of *shirk*. In one such example, Allāh states:

مَثَلُ ٱلَّذِينَ
ٱتَّخَذُواْ مِن دُونِ ٱللَّهِ أَوْلِيَآءَ كَمَثَلِ ٱلْعَنكَبُوتِ
ٱتَّخَذَتْ بَيْتًاۖ وَإِنَّ أَوْهَنَ ٱلْبُيُوتِ لَبَيْتُ ٱلْعَنكَبُوتِۖ
لَوْ كَانُواْ يَعْلَمُونَ ﴿٤١﴾

> "The parable of those who take allies other than Allāh is like that of the spider who makes a home. And verily, the flimsiest of homes is the home of the spider, if they only knew" [Sūrah *al-ʿAnkabūt*; 41].

So committing *shirk* provides one with absolutely no protection and leaves its practitioner vulnerable to all types of punishment, just like the web of the spider provides no protection for the spider.

Yet another example that Allāh gives is that of a man's relationship with his own slaves:

ضَرَبَ لَكُم مَّثَلًا مِّنْ
أَنفُسِكُمْۖ هَل لَّكُم مِّن مَّا مَلَكَتْ أَيْمَٰنُكُم مِّن شُرَكَآءَ فِى
مَا رَزَقْنَٰكُمْ فَأَنتُمْ فِيهِ سَوَآءٌ تَخَافُونَهُمْ كَخِيفَتِكُمْ
أَنفُسَكُمْۚ كَذَٰلِكَ نُفَصِّلُ ٱلْءَايَٰتِ لِقَوْمٍ يَعْقِلُونَ ﴿٢٨﴾

> "He presents to you an example from yourselves. Do you have among those whom your right hands possess any partners in what We have provided for you, so that you are equal therein, and you fear them, as you would one another? Thus do we detail the verses for a people who use reason" [Sūrah *al-Rūm*; 28].

The argument that is being used in this verse is: if you yourselves do not consider your possessions and slaves as equal to you, then how can you make Allāh's creation equal to Allāh?

In another analogy, Allāh states:

وَمَن يُشْرِكْ بِٱللَّهِ فَكَأَنَّمَا خَرَّ مِنَ
ٱلسَّمَآءِ فَتَخْطَفُهُ ٱلطَّيْرُ أَوْ تَهْوِى بِهِ ٱلرِّيحُ فِى مَكَانٍ سَحِيقٍ

"And whoever commits *shirk* with Allāh, then it is as if he is falling from the skies, so the birds pluck [away his meat], or the winds blow him to a remote place" [Sūrah *al-Ḥajj*; 31].

Ibn al-Qayyim comments:

> So ponder over this example, and how precise it is in describing the state of he who commits *shirk* with Allāh, and places his hope with other than Him. In this example, it is as if He has drawn a comparison between the exaltedness, vastness and nobility of *tawḥīd* to that of the skies… And He has compared between he who leaves *tawḥīd* and *īmān* to one who falls from the skies to the lowest pits, where there is nothing but constriction and pain. And the birds that tear him to pieces and break his bones apart are the *Shayāṭīn*, which Allāh sent upon him to agitate him, and to take him to his place of destruction. So every single *Shayṭān* has a piece of his religion and heart, just like every bird has a piece of his bones and flesh. And the wind that blows him to a remote, desolate place, is his very desire, which is what carries him to throw himself to the lowest of all places, and fall from the skies.[26]

In yet another verse, Allāh states:

يَٰٓأَيُّهَا ٱلنَّاسُ ضُرِبَ مَثَلٌ فَٱسْتَمِعُوا۟ لَهُۥٓ ۚ إِنَّ ٱلَّذِينَ
تَدْعُونَ مِن دُونِ ٱللَّهِ لَن يَخْلُقُوا۟ ذُبَابًا وَلَوِ ٱجْتَمَعُوا۟ لَهُۥ ۖ
وَإِن يَسْلُبْهُمُ ٱلذُّبَابُ شَيْـًٔا لَّا يَسْتَنقِذُوهُ مِنْهُ ۚ ضَعُفَ
ٱلطَّالِبُ وَٱلْمَطْلُوبُ ﴿٧٣﴾

"O mankind! An analogy has been given, so pay heed to it. Those that you call out to besides Allāh will never be able to create a fly, even if they all combined (together) to achieve it. And if a fly were to snatch something from them, they would not be able to retrieve it. How weak is the seeker, and the one whose (help) is sought!" [Sūrah *al-Ḥajj*; 73].

Ibn al-Qayyim writes,

> It behooves every worshipper that he let his heart pay attention to this example, and ponder over it greatly, for it cuts off the very roots of *shirk* in his heart. This is because the least that an object of worship should be able to do is to create something that will benefit its worshipper, and to destroy something that causes it harm. However, these gods that the *mushriks* worship besides Allāh will not even be able to create a fly, even if they all combined their powers together to do so. So if they cannot even create a fly, how can they create something greater than a fly? And neither can they protect themselves against such a fly if it takes something from them, such as the perfume or

---

[26] Paraphrased from *I'lām al-Muwaqi'īn*, 1/196.

other materials which are put in front of it. So neither can they create a mere fly, which is of the smallest and weakest of animals, nor can they protect themselves from it, or retrieve what was taken from them by it. So there is no god weaker than these gods, or more incapable than them! If that is the case, then how can any intelligent man prefer to worship such an idol over Allāh? And this parable is of the most eloquent and powerful parables that Allāh has revealed to show the futility of *shirk* and the ignorance of those who fall into it. It proves how unintelligent the *mushriks* are, and shows that *Shayṭān* plays with their minds more than small children play with a ball. [27]

3. The Stories of the Qur'ān

Yet another manner in which the Qur'ān displays the futility of *shirk* is by mentioning the stories of previous nations. How many were the nations and empires destroyed due to their falling into *shirk*?

When the people of Nūḥ did not respond to his call, and continued to worship their idols, Allāh destroyed all of mankind, except for Nūḥ and his followers. Likewise, the people of Ād, Thamūd, and Midyan – the nations which the early prophets of Arabia were sent to – were all destroyed due to their *shirk*. Traces of their civilisation still remain, yet there is no trace of them. And how about the powerful Pharaohs of Egypt, whose tombs and pyramids remain a marvel to this day? Who destroyed them, and what was the cause of their destruction?

In fact, Allāh clearly mentions in the Qur'ān that the primary reason why nations of the past were destroyed was because of *shirk*:

قُلْ سِيرُوا۟ فِى ٱلْأَرْضِ فَٱنظُرُوا۟ كَيْفَ كَانَ عَـٰقِبَةُ ٱلَّذِينَ مِن قَبْلُ ۚ كَانَ أَكْثَرُهُم مُّشْرِكِينَ ﴿٤٢﴾

"Say: travel through the land, and see what was the result of those before (you). Most of them committed *shirk*" [Sūrah *Al-Rūm*; 42].

Evidences from the Sunnah

The Prophet (ﷺ) detailed the futility of *shirk* in many different *aḥādīth*. Perhaps the most explicit parable given in the Sunnah is the ḥadīth in which the Prophet (ﷺ) narrated a sermon that Yaḥyā (John), the cousin of 'Īsa, gave to the Children of Israel. Yaḥyā said, "The example of he who commits *shirk* with Allāh is like that of a person who purchased a slave from his most precious money, with gold or silver, then placed him in a house and said: 'Work, and give

[27] Ibid., 1/198.

me (some of your wages).' So the slave began to work, but gave the money to other than his master. So which one of you would be pleased that his slave act like that? Verily, Allāh created you, and gave you sustenance, so worship Him, and do not commit any *shirk* with Him."[28]

In this example, the Prophet (ﷺ) demonstrated the essence of *shirk*. Allāh is our Creator and Sustainer. He gives us all that we need. Then why is it that some amongst us refuse to worship Him, and instead worship a deity that has no relationship to us, nor does it have any favours over us?

Ibn al-Qayyim writes,

> So in this noble and great ḥadīth that every single Muslim should memorise and attach himself to, the Prophet (ﷺ) mentioned matters which save a person from *Shayṭān*, and cause him to achieve success in this world and the Hereafter. He mentioned a parable of the person upon *tawḥīd*, and the one upon *shirk*. The person upon *tawḥīd* is like one who works for his master in his house, and does the work his master laid out for him. And the one upon *shirk* is like the person who works in his master's house, but gives his income to other than his master. Such is the state of the *mushrik*, for he works for other than Allāh, while living in the land of Allāh. And he seeks to draw close to the enemy of Allāh by using the blessings of Allāh. And if a slave of any person were to be like this, then such a slave would be the most despised slave to his master, and he would be extremely angry with him, and seek to expel him [from his service]. Yet, such a slave is a created being, just like he is. Both of them are in need of external favours (i.e., help from Allāh). So how, then, will be the case with the Lord of the Worlds Who provides every single person with every single need of his? None does so except He, and none provides any good except He, and none repels an evil except He. To Him alone is attributed the creation of His servant, and the giving of blessings, and His protection, and sustenance, and forgiveness, and the caring of his needs. So how is it befitting, when this is the case, that a person equates another being as worthy of love, and fear, and hope...such that he loves this object just like he loves Allāh, or even more so, and he fears it and hopes from it, just like he does from Allāh, or even more so![29]

Evidences from Intellect

The human intellect, although not an independent source of belief, is always in agreement with Divine Law as long as it has not been corrupted by man. Thus, human intellect, or 'common sense', tells a person that *tawḥīd*

---

[28] Reported by al-Tirmidhī (# 2790), and authenticated by al-Albānī in *Ṣaḥīḥ al-Jāmi'* (# 1724).

[29] Paraphrased from *al-Wābil al-Sayyib*, pp. 41-42.

is inherently correct, and *shirk* inherently wrong and evil. If Allāh is the One Who created everything in perfection, then is not He, and only He, worthy of worship? And if He is the only One capable of responding to the plea of the worshipper, then why turn to powerless objects for help? How is any other object worthy of worship?

Allāh addresses this common sense in every man by asking a number of rhetorical questions in the Qur'ān:

أَفَمَن يَخْلُقُ كَمَن لَّا يَخْلُقُ أَفَلَا تَذَكَّرُونَ ﴿١٧﴾

"Is the One Who creates equivalent to the one who does not create? Do you not think?" [Sūrah *al-Naḥl*; 17]

أَيُشْرِكُونَ مَا لَا يَخْلُقُ شَيْئًا وَهُمْ يُخْلَقُونَ ﴿١٩١﴾

وَلَا يَسْتَطِيعُونَ لَهُمْ نَصْرًا وَلَا أَنفُسَهُمْ يَنصُرُونَ ﴿١٩٢﴾

"Do they commit *shirk* (with Allāh by worshipping) those (deities) which do not create anything while they themselves are created? And neither can they benefit them, nor can they benefit themselves" [Sūrah *al-A'rāf* 191-192].

So Allāh shows the foolishness of *shirk* by asking people of intelligence these simple questions.

Evidences from *Fiṭrah*

Even *fiṭrah*, human instinct, inherently abhors *shirk*. Since *fiṭrah* calls for *tawḥīd*, it is in constant opposition to *shirk*. That is why the *mushrik* will never be able to find peace while he is worshipping other than Allāh. It is only worship of Allāh that brings peace and contentment to the soul:

أَلَا بِذِكْرِ ٱللَّهِ تَطْمَئِنُّ ٱلْقُلُوبُ

"Verily, with the Remembrance of Allāh does the heart find tranquility" [Sūrah *al-Ra'd*; 28].

So, with worship of Allāh the soul finds its peace and tranquility. And with rejection of Allāh it finds constraints and hardships:

وَمَنْ أَعْرَضَ عَن ذِكْرِى فَإِنَّ لَهُۥ مَعِيشَةً ضَنكًا

"So whoever turns away from My Remembrance, will of a surety have a depressed (and difficult) life" [Sūrah *Ṭā Hā*; 124].

And one of the prophets stated,

وَمَا لِىَ لَآ أَعْبُدُ ٱلَّذِى فَطَرَنِى وَإِلَيْهِ تُرْجَعُونَ ﴿٢٢﴾

"And what is the matter with me, that I do not worship the One Who created me (*faṭaranī*) and to Him will I return?" [Sūrah *Yā Sīn*; 22].

So these evidences clearly prove that *shirk*, while being the greatest of all evils, is also the most futile of acts.

From these three examples, it is clear that *shirk* can occur in any of the three types of *tawḥīd*. The primary benefit of this scheme is that it helps a person understand the reality of *shirk*. Many people do not realise that it is *shirk* to, for example, claim that a certain *shaykh* or *Imām* is all-knowledgeable. Only when a person is shown that this is an attribute that is exclusive to Allāh will he realise that attributing it to other than Allāh is *shirk*. This scheme also helps a person understand the three types of *tawḥīd* in a fuller sense. As the saying in Arabic goes, 'By knowing the opposite, you will understand the matter.'

2. Major and Minor *Shirk*

Shirk can also be divided into two categories: major *shirk* (*shirk akbar*), and minor *shirk* (*shirk aṣghar*). This categorization is based on clear evidences from the Qur'ān and Sunnah.

When one examines the texts of the Qur'ān and Sunnah, it is apparent that *shirk* is not all of one level; rather, there is major *shirk*, and minor *shirk*. The Prophet (ﷺ) explicitly mentioned these two types of *shirk*. The Prophet (ﷺ) stated:

"The matter that I fear most for you is minor *shirk* – *riyā*."[34]

In this ḥadīth, the Prophet (ﷺ) explicitly mentioned minor *shirk*, thus differentiating it from major *shirk*. He also mentioned one of the most common types of minor *shirk*, which is showing off one's religious deeds for the sake of impressing others. Other *aḥādīth* also provide additional examples of minor *shirk*.

The question arises: what is the difference between these two types of *shirk* that are explicitly mentioned in the *aḥādīth*? Major *shirk* has already been defined above,[35] and that is the making of partners (*andād*) with Allāh. The discussions in this book are primarily centered around major *shirk*.

Minor *shirk*, on the other hand, has been defined as: every action or statement that the texts of the Qur'ān and Sunnah have called *shirk*, yet does not expel its practitioner from the fold of Islām.[36] Another definition is: equating other than

---

[34] Reported by Aḥmad in his *Musnad* (5/428), and others, and Ibn Ḥajr said that it is a *ḥasan* ḥadīth (*Bulūgh al-Marām*, p. 187). For a more detailed discussion of *riyā* and other forms of minor *shirk*, the reader is referred to *Riyā:Hidden Shirk*, by the author (Dār al-Fatāḥ, Sharjāh, 1996).

[35] The definition given above to major *shirk* also applies to minor *shirk*, for the one who commits minor *shirk* has also taken a *nidd*, or associate, along with Allāh, albeit not to the same level as one who commits major *shirk*. The discussion above concerns a more precise definition of minor *shirk* vis-à-vis major *shirk*.

[36] This is Ibn 'Uthaymīn's definition in his *Majmū' al-Fatāwā* (2/204).

Allāh with Allāh in a matter that is specific to Him, either by attributing it as a *means* or by way of *accident*.[37]

Alternately, it has also been defined as: every matter that the religion has prohibited and which is a means and channel to major *shirk*, and which Islamic Law has termed '*shirk*'.[38]

Examples of minor *shirk* include: *riyā* (showing off one's religious deeds), giving an oath by using a name other than Allāh's Names, and attributing occurrences to creation (for example, by saying: 'Were it not for the policeman, we would have been robbed'[39]).

---

[37] This definition was given to the author by a trustworthy student of knowledge, who stated that Sh. ʿAbd Al-Razzāq ʿAfifi approved of it. Additionally, Sh. Sāliḥ Āl al-Shaykh gives a similar definition in one of his lectures on *Kashf al-Shubuhāt*. This definition perhaps requires some explanation. Basically, it means giving an attribute or power of Allāh to any created object, either accidentally (i.e., without really intending to give powers of *Rubūbiyyah* to that object) or as a means (or channel), implying that that object had certain powers of its own. An example of the first type is when someone gives an oath using other than Allāh's Names (such as the phrase, 'By Jove', when it is uttered by one who does not believe in the divinity of Jove). Such an oath does not, in general, come from a conviction that the object that is being sworn upon is a god (otherwise this would be major *shirk*), but rather comes from an admiration of that object which only Allāh is worthy of. So to swear by one's parents, or one's honour, is minor *shirk* for the simple reason that it exalts an object that is not worthy of such exaltation. An example of the second type is to beautify one's prayer in order to gain the admiration of onlookers. Such a person does not direct his prayer to these onlookers (which would be major *shirk*), but rather seeks to gain their admiration of his worship. So he uses them as a *means* and *channel*, and not as the primary goal of his worship.

[38] This is the definition of the *al-Lajnat al-Dā'imah* in its *Fatāwa* (1/517). It should be noted that, in reality, these are not precise definitions, as they do not define the essence of minor *shirk*. Rather, they are 'circular' in nature. Therefore, the practice of some scholars, such as Ibn al-Qayyim and al-Ḥāfiẓ al-Ḥakamī, has been to merely mention examples of minor *shirk* without giving any definitions. It seems there is no precise definition that *describes* and *qualifies* minor *shirk* from major *shirk*, even though it is clear, because of the texts of the Qur'ān and Sunnah, which acts qualify as major *shirk* and which ones as minor (see: *Taysīr al-ʿAzīz al-Ḥamīd*, p. 45; *Maʿārij al-Qabūl*, pp. 489-499; *al-Da'wā al-Dawā*, pp. 314- 316).

[39] The proper way to phrase such comments is: "Were it not for the protection of Allāh, and then the efforts of this policeman, we would have been robbed;" and, "Were it not for the Mercy of Allāh, and then the bravery of the army, we would have been defeated," etc. Thus, all such occurrences should be mentioned with Allāh's Name first, and then the name of others.

The primary differences between major and minor *shirk* are:

1. Major *shirk* expels a person from Islām, whereas minor *shirk* does not.

2. Major *shirk* necessitates a person's eternal punishment in the Fire of Hell (unless its practitioner repents before he dies), whereas minor *shirk* does not entail eternal punishment. Even if a person is punished for minor *shirk* in the Fire of Hell, such punishment will only be temporary, and he will eventually be freed after atoning for his sins.

3. Major *shirk* nullifies *all* of a person's good deeds, whereas minor *shirk* only nullifies the deed that is related to it.

4. Major *shirk* makes it permissible for a Muslim to take the life and property of its practitioner (if and only if there is a state of war between an official Muslim state and the country where this practitioner lives), whereas minor *shirk* does not make it permissible.

5. There is a difference of opinion about whether Allāh can forgive minor *shirk* without punishment. As for major *shirk*, Allāh has clearly stated that He will never forgive it (as in Sūrah *al-Nisā'*; 48), but does this verse apply to minor *shirk* as well? (The difference of opinion here revolves around a person who committed minor *shirk* and did not subsequently repent from it until he died: must he of a surety be punished for his minor *shirk* before he enters Paradise, or is there a possibility that Allāh might forgive him? As for the one who repents from minor (and major) *shirk*, then there is no difference of opinion amongst scholars that Allāh will forgive him).

   Scholars have different views on this issue,[40] but it seems – and Allāh knows best – that minor *shirk* falls under the category of sins that Allāh can forgive without any punishment if He so desires. This seems to be the stronger of the two opinions since, in general, the Qur'ānic references are to major *shirk* (unless the context shows otherwise); thus, when Allāh states that He will not forgive *shirk*, it appears that it is major *shirk* that is being referred to. And Allāh knows best.

It should be noted that major *shirk* and minor *shirk* only relate to *Ulūhiyyah*; as for *Rubūbiyyah* and *Asmā wa l-Ṣifāt*, then any *shirk* in these matters is major *shirk*.[41] Also, minor *shirk* is a stepping stone to major *shirk*; once a person habitually falls into it, he can be assured that this will lead him to major *shirk*.

Lastly, minor *shirk* does not mean that such *shirk* is trivial in the sight of Allāh! Rather, scholars have unanimously agreed that minor *shirk* constitutes

---

[40] Even Ibn Taymiyyah had two opposing views on this issue.

[41] *al-Da'wā al-Dawā* of Ibn al-Qayyim, p. 320.

one of the most major sins. It is termed 'minor', not because it is insignificant, but rather to prove that, relative to major *shirk*, it is not as severe.

3. Apparent and Hidden *Shirk*

Some scholars have also categorised *shirk* as apparent (*ẓāhir*) and hidden (*khafīy*).[42] This is based on the Prophet's (ﷺ) ḥadīth:

> "*Shirk* amongst you is more hidden than the crawling of an ant."[43]

Hidden *shirk* is that which occurs in a person's heart, and which other people cannot see or ascertain. For example, if one's heart calls out to other than Allāh at times of distress, this is an example of hidden *shirk*. Likewise, if a sick person puts his complete trust in a doctor to cure his disease (neglecting the fact that Allāh is the One Who cures), this too is a type of hidden *shirk*.

Apparent *shirk* is that type of *shirk* which is clear, and is related to a person's outward actions. For example, prostrating to an idol, or sacrificing an animal in the name of a spirit, is an act of apparent *shirk*.

This categorisation does not have as much practical value as the preceding two categorisations. Perhaps the main benefit of this categorisation is that, when a person realises that certain types of *shirk* are hidden, he will be more cautious of them. Shaykh al-Islām Ibn Taymiyyah noted that hidden *shirk* is related to a person's love, fear and hope when it is directed to other than Allāh. It results from a weakness in one's heart when one's heart is not attached to Allāh. Most of mankind is afflicted with this type of *shirk*, except for those few whom Allāh has saved from this disease.[44]

---

[42] It should be noted that some scholars have stated that *shirk* is of three types: major, minor, and hidden. Thus, they have combined these last two different categorisation schemes into one. However, it seems apparent – and Allāh knows best – that hidden *shirk* is not a third category *vis-à-vis* major and minor *shirk*, but rather is a separate category all-together from them. Thus, it is possible that major *shirk* can be hidden (for example, the manner in which Christians love Jesus Christ), and minor *shirk* can be hidden as well (for example, the act of beautifying one's *Ṣalāt* in order to impress onlookers). Likewise, it is possible that major *shirk* could be apparent (such as prostrating at grave), and minor *shirk* as well (such as giving an oath using a name other than Allāh's).

[43] Reported in *Musnad Abī Yaʿlā* (1/60) and others; al-Albānī declared it authentic in *Ṣaḥīḥ al-Targhīb wa l-Tarhīb* (1/91).

[44] See *Majmūʿ al-Fatāwa* 1/93 and 10/214.

In another ḥadīth, Ḥudayfah ibn al-Yamān asked the Prophet (ﷺ) about the future of the Muslims: would it be evil or good? After mentioning that there would be evil followed by good, the Prophet (ﷺ) was then asked by Ḥudayfah, "Will there be (yet another) evil after that good?" He responded, "Yes! Callers that are calling to the doors of Hell. Whoever responds to them will be thrown into it."[49] Once again, the Prophet (ﷺ) informed us of the existence of callers that, instead of calling people to *tawḥīd*, will in fact be calling to deviation and *shirk*, such that it is as if they are calling people to enter the Fire of Hell.

Following One's Ancestors and Culture

One of the primary causes of *shirk* is that many people never question the beliefs of their forefathers, or the religion of their society. Man has in him the inherent weakness of exalting his own ancestors and culture, such that he refuses to reject any evil elements that might be present therein.

Allāh frequently mentions that people reject the call of *tawḥīd* solely because their ancestors were not upon it.

وَإِذَا قِيلَ لَهُمُ ٱتَّبِعُوا۟ مَآ أَنزَلَ ٱللَّهُ قَالُوا۟ بَلْ نَتَّبِعُ مَآ أَلْفَيْنَا عَلَيْهِ
ءَابَآءَنَآ ۗ

"And when it is said to them: 'Follow what has been revealed by Allāh', they respond, 'Rather, we will follow what we found our forefathers upon'" [Sūrah *al-Baqarah*; 170].

The Qur'ān informs us that this excuse was the primary retort of those who rejected *tawḥīd*:

بَلْ قَالُوٓا۟
إِنَّا وَجَدْنَآ ءَابَآءَنَا عَلَىٰٓ أُمَّةٍ وَإِنَّا عَلَىٰٓ ءَاثَٰرِهِم مُّهْتَدُونَ ﴿٢٢﴾
وَكَذَٰلِكَ مَآ أَرْسَلْنَا مِن قَبْلِكَ فِى قَرْيَةٍ مِّن نَّذِيرٍ إِلَّا قَالَ مُتْرَفُوهَآ
إِنَّا وَجَدْنَآ ءَابَآءَنَا عَلَىٰٓ أُمَّةٍ وَإِنَّا عَلَىٰٓ ءَاثَٰرِهِم مُّقْتَدُونَ ﴿٢٣﴾
۞ قَٰلَ أَوَلَوْ جِئْتُكُم بِأَهْدَىٰ مِمَّا وَجَدتُّمْ عَلَيْهِ ءَابَآءَكُمْ ۖ قَالُوٓا۟
إِنَّا بِمَآ أُرْسِلْتُم بِهِۦ كَٰفِرُونَ ﴿٢٤﴾

"Rather, they say: 'Indeed, we found our forefathers upon a religion, and we will be guided (by following) their footsteps.' Similarly, We did not

[49] Part of a long ḥadīth narrated by Muslim (# 3606).

> send before you any warner into a city except that its affluent said, 'Indeed, we found our fathers upon a religion, and we are following them in their footsteps.' [Each warner] said: 'Even if I brought you better guidance than that [religion] of your forefathers?' They said, 'Indeed, we are disbelievers in what you have been sent with' [Sūrah *al-Zukhruf*; 22-24].

It is for this reason that the Prophet (ﷺ) stated,

> "Every child is born upon the *fiṭrah*, but then his parents make him a Jew or Christian."[50]

And it was this very reason that prevented Abū Ṭālib from accepting the religion of his nephew, for, when the Prophet (ﷺ) presented Islām to him at his deathbed, Abū Jahl asked incredulously, "Are you going to leave the religion of (your father) 'Abd al-Muṭṭalib?" So Abū Ṭālib preferred the religion of his forefathers over the worship of Allāh.

It is always the few and the courageous that are willing to take on the wrath of their community and family by rejecting the worship of false gods, in return for achieving Allāh's pleasure.

Shayṭān's Beautification of *Shirk* and Innovation

One of the ways that *Shayṭān* causes mankind to deviate is by beautifying sins, especially the sin of *shirk*. One needs only to look at the mental state of mind of those who practice *shirk* to see this reality. So one finds Christians lost in their 'love' of Jesus Christ, and the *Rāfiḍah* Shi'ite wandering aimlessly in 'protecting the rights' of the Prophet's (ﷺ) family, and the *Ṣūfīs* exalting the status of 'saints'. Each of these groups deceive themselves by merely camouflaging and disguising their acts of *shirk* behind seemingly beautiful concepts.

By distorting the reality of the acts of the *mushrikīn*, *Shayṭān* deceives them into believing that they are doing an act of good. Allāh describes such people in the Qur'ān:

قُلْ هَلْ نُنَبِّئُكُم بِالْأَخْسَرِينَ أَعْمَالًا ﴿١٠٣﴾ الَّذِينَ ضَلَّ سَعْيُهُمْ فِي الْحَيَاةِ
الدُّنْيَا وَهُمْ يَحْسَبُونَ أَنَّهُمْ يُحْسِنُونَ صُنْعًا ﴿١٠٤﴾

> "Say: Shall We inform you of the greatest losers as to [their] deeds? [They are] those whose effort is lost in this worldly life, while they think they are doing good deeds" [Sūrah *al-Kahf*; 103-104].

These people are those who spent their lives practicing *shirk*, believing that they would please Allāh by such *shirk*. So Allāh describes them as the greatest of

[50] Reported by al-Bukhārī (# 2758).

losers, since they have worked hard throughout their lives, yet will end up in the Fire of Hell as a consequence of their *shirk*.

The Prophet (ﷺ) referred to this reality and tactic of *Shayṭān* when he stated,

> "There will be a group of people in my nation who will try to make alcoholic beverages permissible, by calling it with other than its actual name."[51]

In this ḥadīth, one of the tactics of *Shayṭān* is exposed: that of calling evil matters by beautiful names. So if a person is asked why he is worshipping the Prophet (ﷺ), his immediate response is, "Do you dare to show disrespect to the Prophet (ﷺ)? What I am doing is in fact an indication of my extreme and sincere love for him, and if you had this love, you too would do what I do." He tries to hide this blatant *shirk* in the guise of 'loving' the Prophet (ﷺ), not realising that, in reality, directing acts of worship to the Prophet (ﷺ) is, in essence, rejecting his message and belying him.

Iblīs, the accursed leader of all *Shayāṭīn*, himself declared that he would try his best to beautify sins to mankind:

قَالَ رَبِّ بِمَآ
أَغْوَيْتَنِي لَأُزَيِّنَنَّ لَهُمْ فِي ٱلْأَرْضِ وَلَأُغْوِيَنَّهُمْ أَجْمَعِينَ ﴿٣٩﴾

> "He said, 'My Lord, since you have deceived me, I will indeed beautify for them (every evil) in this world, and will of a surety cause all of them to be misguided'" [Sūrah *al-Ḥijr*; 39].

And without a doubt, the greatest evil that he seeks to beautify is the evil of *shirk*, as the Prophet (ﷺ) stated that Allāh said,

> "I have created my servants, all of them, pure (and inclined towards my worship), but the *Shayāṭīn* came and diverted them from their religion. They prohibited them from matters that I allowed for them, and commanded them to associate partners with Me...."[52]

Incorrect Comparisons

One of the ways in which *shirk* occurs is when man makes an incorrect analogy or comparison. The first one to do so was Iblīs himself, when he felt that he was better than Adam, merely because he was created from fire, whereas Adam was created from clay. So Iblīs laid the foundation for all such incorrect analogies.

---

[51] Reported by al-Nasā'ī (# 5564), Abū Dāwūd (# 3688), and others, with an authentic chain.

[52] Reported by Muslim (# 2876).

Of these analogies is:

1- Comparing the created to the Creator. By giving any object of creation attributes that belong solely to Allāh, man falls into *shirk*. The claim of the Christians that Jesus is the one who grants salvation is a clear example of giving the rights of Allāh to the created. Likewise, the beliefs of the Shī'ites with regards to their *Imāms*, and the *Sūfīs* with regards to their Shaykhs, fall under this category.

2- Comparing the Creator to the created. An example of this is the comparison that extreme *Sūfī* groups give when justifying their *shirk*. They state, "Just like an average person cannot approach a mighty king except through a minister or person of power, so too it is not possible for a sinful person's *du'ā* to be answered until he goes through a prophet or saint." Thus, they compare Allāh to a king. Ibn Taymiyyah, in a lengthy discussion, shows the fallacy of this comparison by pointing out that such intermediaries between laymen and a king perform one of three functions. Firstly, they can act as informers, informing a just and pious king of the needs of the people, since such laymen would not typically have access to the king. And of course this function is not needed for Allāh, since He is aware of the most secret of secrets. Secondly, such intermediaries might act as helpers, for a king cannot personally take care of all the affairs of his people. So these ministers and intermediaries can be assistants in the execution of the king's affairs. Once again, this analogy does not apply to Allāh, since Allāh does not need any help, nor can any object 'help' Allāh in any matter. Thirdly, it is possible that a king will not fulfill a request except to please a particular person. Thus, if a person of no status were to ask such a king, he would not be responded to unless a person of status interceded on his behalf. And such a king, by all standards, is an unjust and tyrannical monarch, for he does not respond to requests except for personal benefit. Therefore, this too cannot be applied to Allāh, for He is the Most Merciful, and His Justness encompasses all matters. So Ibn Taymiyyah proves that, in reality, this analogy is a proof *against* those who seek to use it, even though at first glance it might seem to represent proof for them.[53]

3- Comparing pious people to prophets. The belief of the *Sūfīs* that 'saints' (or *'awliyā*) emit blessings (*baraka*) from their bodies and possessions is an example of this. It was only the persona of the Prophet (ﷺ) that Allāh blessed to such a degree, for his very body, and the objects that he touched, would become blessed objects. That is why the Companions would be eager to obtain the remnants of his *wuḍu*, or collect his hair and sweat, for they

---

[53] *Majmū' al-Fatāwa* 1/129-131.

they will fall into the Fire of Hell (in another narration: so every nation will follow that which it used to worship, so much so that those who worshipped the Sun will follow the Sun, and those who worshipped the moon will follow the moon, until they all fall over each other into the Fire of Hell). This will continue, until no (nation) will be left, except those who worshipped Allāh – the pious and impious amongst them (in another narration: the believers and the hypocrites amongst them)... Then, their Lord will come to them in a Shape (*Sūrah*) that they will not recognize, and He will ask them, 'What are you waiting for? For every nation must follow what it used to worship.' They will reply, 'We separated ourselves from mankind in the *dunyā*, even though we were in extreme need of them, yet we did not accompany them.[56] And we are waiting for our Lord that we used to worship.' So Allāh will say to them, 'I am your Lord...'"[57]

In other narrations of this ḥadīth, the Prophet (ﷺ) also described that the Christians and Jews will follow each other into the Fire of Hell – the Christians being led by a cross.

All objects that were worshipped besides Allāh and were content with this worship will lead the people that worshipped them into the Fire of Hell. The question arises, however, regarding those who were worshipped yet did not approve of such worship, such as Jesus, son of Mary. This same question was asked by the *mushrikūn* of old as well, in an attempt to discredit the Prophet (ﷺ).

Once, the Prophet (ﷺ) was calling the pagans of Makkah to *tawḥīd*. In the course of his preaching, he recited:

إِنَّكُمْ وَمَا تَعْبُدُونَ مِن دُونِ
ٱللَّهِ حَصَبُ جَهَنَّمَ أَنتُمْ لَهَا وَٰرِدُونَ ﴿٩٨﴾ لَوْ كَانَ
هَٰٓؤُلَآءِ ءَالِهَةً مَّا وَرَدُوهَا ۖ وَكُلٌّ فِيهَا خَٰلِدُونَ ﴿٩٩﴾

"You all that you worship besides Allāh will be fuel for the Fire of Hell – all of you will enter it. If these [that you worship] were gods, they would not have entered it – and all [of you] will be eternally damned [to it]" [Sūrah *al-Anbiyā'*; 98-99].

---

[56] The intent here is that the believers did not follow the ideologies and religions of their fellow men in this world, and thus did not accompany them. Therefore, if they did not accompany them in the *dunyā*, even though they were in need of them, then why should they accompany them in the Hereafter, when they are being led to the Fire of Hell?

[57] Part of a lengthy ḥadīth narrated by al-Bukhārī (# 4581 with this wording, and with other wordings in other places), Muslim (# 182), and others.

This argument – that if these idols were true gods, they would not enter the Fire of Hell – was too powerful to be refuted by them, so they left the Prophet (ﷺ). Discussing this argument in another gathering of theirs, one of them who had not been present earlier boasted, "If only I had been with you, I would have defeated Muḥammad in his argument!"

"How so?" they asked.

"Does he not presume," he replied, "that all that is worshipped besides Allāh will go into the Fire of Hell? Then what does he say about the angels that we worship? Or Jesus Christ whom the Christians worship? Will they too be thrown into Hell?" Impressed with this response, they returned to the Prophet (ﷺ) and presented it to him, presuming that they had won the argument. At this, Allāh revealed:

إِنَّ ٱلَّذِينَ
سَبَقَتۡ لَهُم مِّنَّا ٱلۡحُسۡنَىٰٓ أُوْلَٰٓئِكَ عَنۡهَا مُبۡعَدُونَ ﴿١٠١﴾
لَا يَسۡمَعُونَ حَسِيسَهَاۖ وَهُمۡ فِي مَا ٱشۡتَهَتۡ أَنفُسُهُمۡ
خَٰلِدُونَ ﴿١٠٢﴾

> "Verily, those for whom the good has preceded from Us will be far removed from it [Hell]. They shall not even hear its hissing, and they shall dwell in that which their selves desire" [Sūrah *al-Anbiyā'*; 101-102].

The Prophet (ﷺ) said, "Whoever is pleased that he be worshipped besides Allāh will be with those who worshipped him."

Allāh also revealed, concerning this incident, another verse:

وَلَمَّا ضُرِبَ ٱبۡنُ مَرۡيَمَ
مَثَلًا إِذَا قَوۡمُكَ مِنۡهُ يَصِدُّونَ ﴿٥٧﴾ وَقَالُوٓاْ ءَأَٰلِهَتُنَا
خَيۡرٌ أَمۡ هُوَۚ مَا ضَرَبُوهُ لَكَ إِلَّا جَدَلَۢاۚ بَلۡ هُمۡ قَوۡمٌ خَصِمُونَ ﴿٥٨﴾

> "And when [Jesus] son of Mary is given as an example, your people cry out loud [in ridicule]. And they say, 'Are our gods better, or he?' They only brought him as an example in order to argue [with you] – but they are a quarrelsome people" [Sūrah *al-Zukhruf* 57-58].

In other words, the *mushrikūn* do not believe in Jesus in the first place, and they only quoted him in order to fight with and prevail over you in this argument. What the Prophet (ﷺ) had initially told them was completely true in the context that he said, for he was referring to the idols that they worshipped. By taking his statement out of context, and then bringing forth an example with Jesus that they themselves did not believe in, they displayed their quarrelsome and argumentative nature, and proved that they were not searching for the truth.[58]

To conclude: all objects that are worshipped besides Allāh are either inanimate, or animate. If inanimate (such as the Sun, moon, al-Lāt, and any other idol), these exact objects will be shown to the people that worshipped them, and they will then be led into the Fire of Hell. If these objects were animate and approved of this worship that was directed to them, then they too will lead their followers and worshippers into the Fire (even if they professed Islam, for one who allows others to worship him is not a Muslim). However, if these beings did not approve of such worship (such as Jesus, and the angels), then Allāh will not cause them any harm; rather, on the Day of Judgement, they will dissociate themselves from those who used to worship them, and then Allāh will punish these worshippers by throwing them into the Fire of Hell. With regards to the Christians, they will be led to the Fire behind a cross, for they have exalted this icon to such an extent that they have taken it as an idol besides Allāh.

Those who direct their *duʿās* and place their love and fear in saints and graves need to ask themselves: are they willing to be left by Allāh on the Day of Judgement, and be entrusted to these 'saints' instead?

[58] For this story, see *Tafsīr Ibn Kathīr*, 2/219, and 3/139.

9. The Difference Between *Shirk* and *Kufr*

Many people confuse the terms *kufr* and *shirk*: are they synonymous, or different?

Shirk has already been defined. *Kufr*, on the other hand, linguistically implies '...covering up something to such an extent that it is destroyed.'[59] From an Islāmic perspective, *kufr* is the opposite of Islām. A person is either a Muslim (meaning that he has *īmān*), or not (meaning that he is a *kāfir*).

There are many different types of *kufr*. One type is the *kufr* of denial, in which a person denies the truthfulness of the Prophet (ﷺ) and the authenticity of the Qur'ān. Another type is the *kufr* of arrogance, in which a person realises the truth, but is too arrogant to follow it. Such is the *kufr* of Iblīs and the Pharaoh of Mūsa. Another type of *kufr* is the *kufr* of doubt, where a person is not sure of the Prophet's (ﷺ) truthfulness, or of the authenticity of the Qur'ān. This type of *kufr* can only exist in an ignorant non-Muslim, for any person who studies the life of the Prophet (ﷺ), or the Qur'ān, cannot have any doubts regarding them. Yet another type is the *kufr* of hypocrisy (*nifāq*), in which a person outwardly claims to be a Muslim but in his heart does not believe in Islām. *Shirk* is one type of *kufr*.

Ibn Taymiyyah writes: "Whoever does not submit to what the Prophet (ﷺ) came with is a *kāfir*. It is irrelevant whether he believes that the Prophet (ﷺ) is a liar, or was simply too arrogant to believe in him, or turned away from him wanting to follow his desires instead, or was in doubt as to (the authenticity) of what he came with. So whoever denies what he has come with is a *kāfir*. In fact, one might even be a *kāfir* even if one does not deny him, that is if one does not believe in him."[60] Thus, any person who rejects the total religion of the Prophet (ﷺ) is a *kāfir*. And one of the ways in which a person rejects the message of the Prophet (ﷺ) is by committing an act of *shirk*.

---

[59] *Lisān al-Arab*, 5/145.

[60] *Majmū' al-Fatāwā* 3/315.

Therefore, every single act of major *shirk* is a type of *kufr*, but not every single type of *kufr* involves *shirk*. Thus, *kufr* is the general name given to any act, statement or belief that might expel a person from the fold of Islām. *Shirk* is merely one type of *kufr*, albeit the most common and evil form. It is possible for a person to reject Islām without necessarily falling into *shirk*, as is the case with Iblīs, and some orthodox Jews (since they worship only Allāh, and follow the Torah, yet deny the prophethoods of Jesus and Muḥammad (ﷺ), which is *kufr*). It is also possible to reject Islām by falling into *shirk* and *kufr* simultaneously, such as the Christians (since they claim that Jesus Christ is the Son of God – which is *kufr*; and give him divine powers, and direct acts of worship to him – which is *shirk*).

Many acts have elements of both *kufr* and *shirk* in them, even though each act might be more representive of one of these two matters. For example, atheism (rejecting the existence of a god) is pure *kufr*, but can also be considered a type of *shirk* as well. And idolatry is pure *shirk*, but is also a manifestation of *kufr*.

So *kufr* is in fact more general than *shirk*. Every *shirk* is *kufr*, but not every *kufr* is *shirk*.

10. The Prophet's (ﷺ) Protection of *Tawḥīd*

Of the fundamentals of our faith is the certainty that the Prophet (ﷺ) gave the complete message to mankind, and explained in detail every knowledge that is needed to discern between truth and falsehood. It is only with such complete knowledge that it was possible to proclaim:

ٱلْيَوْمَ أَكْمَلْتُ لَكُمْ دِينَكُمْ وَأَتْمَمْتُ
عَلَيْكُمْ نِعْمَتِي وَرَضِيتُ لَكُمُ ٱلْإِسْلَٰمَ دِينًا

> "Today I have perfected your religion for you, and completed My favours upon you, and chosen for you Islām as your way of life." [Sūrah *al-Mā'idah*; 3].

The Prophet (ﷺ) stated:

> "Verily, I have left you upon the shining path, its night is like its day."

Abū al-Dardā, after narrating this ḥadīth, said, "He has indeed told the truth, for he has left us upon the shining path whose night is like its day."[61] And Abū Dharr al-Ghifāri could truthfully proclaim: "The Prophet (ﷺ) passed away, and there was not a single bird that flaps its wings in the skies except that he had left us with knowledge concerning it!"[62] The meaning of this profound narration is that the Prophet (ﷺ) had instructed his nation with every single piece of information they needed in order to live in this life and achieve success in the Hereafter.

If this is the case, then without a doubt the Prophet (ﷺ) must have strived his utmost to protect the sanctity of *tawḥīd* against the evil of *shirk*. And one of the ways in which he did this was by closing all paths and doors that led to this evil, even though the path itself might not be prohibited.[63]

---

[61] Narrated by Ibn Abī ʿĀṣim in his *al-Sunnah* (# 47), and authenticated by al-Albānī.

[62] Reported by al-Ṭabarānī in his *al-Kabīr* (# 1647) with an authentic chain.

[63] There is a chapter in the science of *Usūl al-fiqh* which deals with 'Preventive Measures' (*Sadd al-Dharāʿi'*). An act might be permissible, in and of itself, but be deemed impermissible if it leads to something which is impermissible. For example, selling grapes is permissible, but selling them to a wine-maker is impermissible, since they would be used for something impermissible.

With this in mind, it becomes clear after even a cursory examination of the texts of the Sunnah that the Prophet (ﷺ) protected the sanctity of *tawḥīd* by every preventive measure possible. Some examples of these are as follows:

1- The Prophet (ﷺ) prohibited building mosques over graves, as this is one of the primary methods through which *shirk* is sanctioned. Once, his wife Umm Salamah mentioned the beautiful churches she had seen while she was in Abyssinia. The Prophet (ﷺ) proclaimed,

> "Those people, whenever a pious person died amongst them, would build places of worship over their graves, and carve out images of them. Such people are the worst of mankind in the sight of Allāh."[64]

2- He (ﷺ) also forbade burying the dead inside mosques, for it too is one of the primary ways that leads to *shirk*. He prayed on his death bed:

> "O Allāh! Do not make my grave an idol that is worshipped."[65]

Both of these acts are primary factors which cause people to exaggerate the status of pious people and prophets. The construction of mosques over graves, and vice-versa, is one of the primary stepping-stones to major *shirk*.

3- He (ﷺ) also forbade worshipping Allāh at places where *shirk* occurs, or has occurred. If there is a certain monument or land which has become famous for acts of *shirk*, it is in fact prohibited for a Muslim to make a point of praying to Allāh at that place. Once, a Bedouin came to the Prophet (ﷺ) and asked, "I have undertaken a vow with Allāh that I will sacrifice a camel at (a place called) Bawwānah." So the Prophet (ﷺ) asked him,

> "Was there an idol that was worshipped at this place during the times of *Jāhilīyyah*? Or was that place a place of their religious celebrations?"

When the man replied in the negative, the Prophet (ﷺ) allowed him to fulfill his vow.[66]

4- The Prophet (ﷺ) even forbade worshipping Allāh at times when other deities were worshipped. ʿUqbah ibn ʿĀmir reported: "The Prophet (ﷺ) prohibited us from praying or burying our dead during three hours (of the day): while the sun is rising until it rises above the horizon, while the sun is at its zenith until it starts to descend, and while it sets."[67] These are the times when fire-worshippers worship the sun and prostrate to it. Thus, to

---

[64] Reported by al-Bukhārī (1/523) and Muslim (# 528).

[65] Reported by Mālik in his *al-Muwaṭṭa'* (# 261).

[66] Reported by Abū Dāwūd (# 3313) and authenticated by Shaykh al-Islām Ibn Taymiyyah in his *Iqtiḍā al-Ṣirāṭ al-Mustaqīm* (1/436).

[67] Reported by Muslim (# 532).

avoid resembling them, Muslims are prohibited from praying at these times as well.

5- The Prophet (ﷺ) also prohibited the Muslims from excessively praising him, as this too is one of the primary ways of *shirk*. One only needs to look at the Christians, and how their excessive praise of Jesus Christ led them to blasphemy, in order to realise the dangers of over-exalting the status of prophets. The Prophet (ﷺ) is the best of all mankind, and the most noble of all prophets, yet he was sent to preach the worship of Allāh, and not to be worshipped along with Allāh. He (ﷺ) said:

   "Do not excessively praise me, like the Christians did Jesus the son of Mary. Rather, I am only the slave of Allāh, and His Messenger."[68]

   In this ḥadīth, the Prophet (ﷺ) described his position as being Allāh's 'slave' and 'Messenger'. With these two titles, the Muslim avoids the two extremes of the Jews and Christians. The Jews neglected the legacy of the prophets, mocked their rulings, and even killed some of them. On the other hand, the Christians exalted their prophet to such a level that they deified him. So the Muslim avoids both of these extremes, and takes the middle path, by affirming the mortality of the Prophet (ﷺ), and believing that he was the best of all men since he was inspired by Allāh. Note that the Prophet (ﷺ) prohibited excessive praising, which implies that praising him within the bounds of the *Sharīʿah* is allowed. As long as the descriptions given to him are sanctioned by the Qur'ān and Sunnah, it is an act of worship to praise the Prophet (ﷺ), and defend and honour him.

6- The Prophet (ﷺ) even forbade the Companions to stand up in his presence, fearing that such an act would lead to over-exaltation. Once, when he was forced to pray sitting down, the Companions prayed standing up behind him. He stated after the prayer:

   "You were about to imitate the practices of the Persians and Romans, for they stand up in the presence of their kings while (the kings) sit. Do not do that."[69]

7- The Prophet (ﷺ) also forbade image-making. *Shirk* began when people starting making images of creation, and to this day *shirk* hardly occurs except in the presence of images and icons. Thus, by prohibiting the making of images, the Prophet (ﷺ) stopped one of the greatest paths to *shirk*. He (ﷺ) stated:

---

[68] Reported by al-Bukhārī (# 3445) and Muslim (# 1691).

[69] Reported by Muslim (# 1341).

12. A Short Biography of Muḥammad ibn ʿAbd al-Wahhāb

The author of this work was Abū al-Ḥusayn Muḥammad ibn ʿAbd al-Wahhāb ibn Sulaymān ibn ʿAlī ibn Musharrif al-Wuhaybee, from the tribe of Tamīm.[76] He was born in the city of ʿUyaynah, which is in the middle of the Arabian Peninsula, in the year 1115 A.H. (1704 C.E.). He came from a family of scholars and learned men, for his father, ʿAbd al-Wahhāb ibn Sulaymān (d. 1153 A.H.) was one of the famous scholars of Najd, and the *Qaḍī* (religious judge) of ʿUyaynah. His grandfather, Sulaymān ibn ʿAlī (d. 1079 A.H.) was also well-known for his knowledge, as was his uncle Ibrāhīm ibn Sulaymān.

He memorised the Qur'ān before he was ten years old, and learnt from many scholars in his area, including his father and uncle. He also travelled to Madīnah and Iraq to study with its scholars. In Madīnah, he met and studied with the famous Indian scholar Muḥammad Ḥayat al-Sindī (d. 1165 A.H.), and was greatly impressed with him, as was the teacher with his student. He also studied with the ḥadīth scholar ʿAbdullāh ibn Sālim al-Baṣrī (d. 1134 A.H.), and the famous scholar ʿAbdullāh ibn Sayf.

As for his students, they are too many to be numbered. Foremost amongst them were his sons, Ḥusayn, ʿAlī, ʿAbdullāh and Ibrāhīm, and his grandson ʿAbd Al-Raḥmān ibn Ḥasan, who authored the famous *Fatḥ al-Majīd Sharḥ Kitāb al-Tawḥīd*. Also amongst his students were: ʿAbd al-ʿAzīz ibn Muḥammad ibn Saʿūd (d. 1218 A.H.), Ḥamad ibn Nāṣir ibn Mu'ammar (d. 1225 A.H.), and ʿAbd al-ʿAzīz ibn ʿAbdullāh ibn Ḥussayīn (d. 1237 A.H.).

The environment in which he found himself was indeed a very alien one. Grave-worship was rampant, as were many other innovations. There were a number of structures, trees, and mausoleums which were openly worshipped, and *tawāf* made around. Additionally, there were numerous 'cults' which worshipped various saints, living and dead, and sacrificed to them. The more

---

[76] Most of this biography is taken from the introduction to *Fatḥ al-Majīd*, pps. 14-20.

the Shaykh studied Islām, the clearer it became to him that these acts were acts that contradicted the pristine message of *tawḥīd* which the Prophet (ﷺ) came with. As a young man, he began speaking out against these evil practices, but was rejected, and expelled from various cities. During this time, he wrote his most famous work, *Kitāb al-Tawḥīd*, which was the spearhead of his *daʿwah*.

His pure and simple message of worshiping Allāh alone stirred the heart of Muḥammad ibn Saʿūd (1179 A.H.), one of the leaders of the province of Dir'iyyah (outside of modern-day Riyādh). Ibn Saʿūd invited him to his city, and in 1157 A.H formed an agreement with him that was to forever change the face of Arabia. Ibn Saʿūd promised to allow him to spread his *daʿwah* in return for religious guidance and support.

Muḥammad ibn ʿAbd al-Wahhāb took this opportunity to eradicate *shirk* from the Prophet's (ﷺ) land, which he was successful in doing. After conquering an enemy territory, he would destroy any mausoleums and other icons that were worshipped. This, obviously, bred forth many enemies towards the Shaykh, particularly 'scholars' that earned their livelihood promoting such *shirk*.

False propaganda against him and his teachings spread like wild-fire. The name 'Wahhābī' was concocted as a derogatory term for those who followed him, and to this day is applied as if it is a new sect of Islām, even though he himself did not introduce anything new into the religion, nor does 'Wahhabiyah' involve anything other than the pure teaching of the Qur'ān and Sunnah.[77]

So it was that false charges and accusations were levelled against him. He was even accused, without the slightest shred of evidence, of making himself a prophet!

Another accusation was that he considered all those who opposed him to be disbelievers (*kāfir*). This fabrication then led to the charge of him being amongst the Khawārij, the first splinter-group of Islām who were notorious for claiming everyone that opposed them to be disbelievers.

These accusations against the author were simply not true. In one of his works, he writes, "As for the charge that my enemies have accused me of: that I perform *takfīr*[78] merely by association, or that I perform *takfīr* on an ignorant

[77] It is amazing to note that many of the descriptions given to the 'Wahhābīs' by non-Muslims actually proves this point. It is all too common to see 'Wahhābīs' described as 'puritanical', 'ultra-orthodox', 'conservative', 'fundamentalists' or other such terms which, although intended to be disparaging, actually serve to show that the teachings of this personality did not innovate new doctrines into Islām. Also, it should be mentioned that no Muslim calls himself 'Wahhābī'; rather, those who follow the Qur'ān and Sunnah, and the major scholars of Islām (including this imām), do not base allegiance to any one individual or ascribe themselves to anyone except for the Prophet (ﷺ).

[78] *Takfīr*: the act of pronouncing another Muslim to be a disbeliever (*kāfir*).

person who has not had the evidences presented to him, then verily this is a fabricated slander."[79] He also wrote, "As for the lies that are spread against us, in order to cover the truth, and to confuse people, that we consider all Muslims to be disbelievers, the people of our times, and all the people for the last six centuries, except for those who follow us, and the lie based upon this lie, that we do not accept anyone's allegiance until he testifies that he was a pagan before joining us, and that both his parents were pagans (*mushriks*)...[80] then all of these slanders have absolutely no basis whatsoever. Every time we heard something of these lies, we replied, '*Subḥanak!* This is indeed a grave slander (and lie)' So whoever narrated this from me, or accuses me of these matters, then he has indeed lied and slandered me. And whoever has witnessed my situation, and attended my gatherings, and verified what (knowledge) is with me, knows of a certainty that all of these charges have been fabricated against me by the enemies of the religions and the brothers of *Shayṭān*! They only do this so as to repel people from submitting to Allāh alone with *tawḥīd* and worship, by leaving all forms of *shirk*. For verily Allāh has clearly stated that He will not forgive *shirk*, but will forgive anything less than that. So I firmly believe that whoever does any of the major sins, such as murdering another Muslim without any reason, or fornicating, or taking interest, or habitually drinking intoxicants, that such a person does not leave the fold of Islām, nor will he permanently be assigned to the Fire of Hell, as long as he died upon *tawḥīd*."[81]

And he also stated: "As for ruling someone to be a *kāfir*, then I consider a *kāfir* to be the person who knows the religion of the Prophet (ﷺ), then, after such knowledge, curses it, and prevents people from following it, and shows enmity to whoever follows it. So this is the one whom I consider to be a *kāfir*. And the majority of this nation – by Allāh's blessings – are not like this!"[82]

These beliefs that he expressed are the beliefs of all scholars of Islām. No where did he claim, or even hint, that any group that opposed him (especially those who only opposed the political expansion of Ibn Saʿūd), or those who did not migrate to his territory, or fight with him, were outside the fold of Islām. Such a charge, which is still spread by Orientalists and ignorant Muslims to this day, is simply baseless. The author states: "And if we do not pronounce as *kāfirs* those who worship idols (i.e., mausoleums) that are present upon the graves of

---

[79] *Mu'alafāt al-Shaykh* (3/10).

[80] These and other lies were spread during his life, and exist to this day. For example, the book *The Doctrine of Ahl al-Sunnah Versus the 'Salafī' Movement* (Al-Sunna Foundation, 1996), which is a translation of Jamal Effendi's work against the author, clearly mentions these lies as well (pp. 23- 27).

[81] *Al-Hadiyyah al-Suniyyah*, p. 40.

[82] *Al-Durrar al-Saniyyah* (1/73).

ʿAbd al-Qādir (al-Jīlani) and Aḥmad al-Badawī, due to their ignorance, and because they do not have people that explain their *shirk* to them, then how can we consider as *kāfirs* those who do not migrate to us, or one who does not consider everyone besides us to be a *kāfir*, or one who does not fight with us? Glorified be Allāh, verily this is an evil slander!"[83]

It must be pointed out that the majority of Orientalists eagerly proliferate such misconceptions about the 'Wahhābī sect', to such an extent that many people consider these charges to be undisputable facts. This is one of the reasons why it is necessary to translate and spread the works of this author, so that readers may see for themselves that he did not deliver anything new, nor did he found any 'sect'. Rather, he simply revived the pure and pristine teachings of the Prophet (ﷺ), like so many scholars did before him.

He wrote in one of his letters, when he was asked what he calls to: "And I am not, *alḥamdulillāh*, one of those who calls to the belief of the *Sūfīs*, or (the blind following) of a *faqīh*,[84] or one of the philosophical groups,[85] or even to one of the scholars that I myself respect, such as Ibn al-Qayyim, al-Dhahabī, Ibn Kathīr, and others. Rather, I call to Allāh alone, for He is One, having no partners, and I call to the Sunnah of the Prophet (ﷺ). And this is what he (ﷺ) commanded the first of his nation, and the last of them to. And I hope that I will not reject any truth if it comes to me. Rather, I call Allāh, and His angels, and the entire creation to witness, that if a word comes from you that is true, then of a surety I will accept it with all respect, and I will throw against the wall everything that goes against it, from the statements of all the scholars that I respect, except for the Prophet (ﷺ), for he is the only one that speaks nothing but the truth."[86]

In another letter, in response to a query posed by one of the scholars of Iraq, he wrote: "I wish to inform you that I am – by the blessings of Almighty Allāh – a follower (of the scholars of the past), and not an innovator. My belief and my religion that I consider to be correct in the sight of Allāh is the belief of *Ahl al-Sunnah wa l-Jamāʿah*, and this is what the scholars of the Muslims are upon, such as the four great *Imāms* (i.e., Abū Ḥanīfah, Mālik, al-Shāfiʿī, and Aḥmad ibn Ḥanbal), and those that truly follow them until the Day of Judgement. However, (all I have done is that) I have explained to people the importance of sincerity in worshipping Allāh, and I have warned them against making

---

[83] *Ibid.* (1/66).

[84] A scholar of jurisprudence. He is pointing out that he is not of those that call to the obligation of blindly following a particular religious scholar, or *madh-hab*.

[85] Referring to those Islamic sects that were based on or influenced by Greek philosophy, such as the *Muʿtazilah*, the *Ashʿarīs*, and the *Māturidis*.

[86] *Majmūʿ Mu'alafāt*, 5/252.

du'ā to the living or dead of the saints and others besides them. I have warned them against associating partners with Allāh and directing acts of worship that are specific for Allāh (to others). (Examples of such acts are) sacrificing, and vowing, and *tawakkul* (depending upon someone), and prostrating, and other acts that are rights only due to Allāh. No one deserves to be associated along with Allāh in these acts, neither a close angel, nor a sent prophet. And this message is what all the prophets called people to, from the first of them to the last of them, and this is what the *Ahl al-Sunnah wa l-Jamā'ah* are upon."[87]

Muḥammad ibn 'Abd al-Wahhāb wrote many works, in ḥadīth, *Tafsīr*, *fiqh*, and general topics. However, his primary focus was *tawḥīd*. The following is a list of his more famous works:

1. *Kitāb al-Tawḥīd* – his most popular and famous work.[88]
2. *Uṣūl al-Thalāthah*. A basic introductory level text concerning the fundamentals of Islām.[89]
3. *Al-Qawā'id al-Arba'ah*. In four basic principles, the author deals with explaining the fundamentals of *shirk*.[90]
4. *Kashf al-Shubuhāt*. The present work, which is a refutation of the most common arguments that are used by those who commit *shirk* to justify their actions.
5. *Mukhtaṣar al-Sīrah*.
6. *Mukhtaṣar Fatḥ al-Barī*.
7. *Mukhtaṣar Zād al-Ma'ād*.
8. *Masā'il al-Jāhilīyyah*. This work lists almost a hundred different matters that the Prophet (ﷺ) opposed and changed from the ways of the Arabs of *Jāhilīyyah*.
9. *Adab al-Mashy ilā l-Ṣalāt*.

---

[87] *Ibid.*, 5/36.

[88] Although the work has been translated a number of times, none of these translations explains the work in a detailed manner. Perhaps one of the more useful translations is that by Sameh Strauch (International Islamic Publishing House, Riyādh, 1998 A.H.), entitled *The Book of Tawḥīd*.

[89] The explanation of *Uṣūl al-Thalāthah* by Shaykh Muḥammad ibn Ṣāliḥ al-'Uthaymīn was translated by Dāwūd Burbank, and published by al-Hidaayah Publishing & Distribution, (Birmingham, 1998).

[90] This work has already been translated by the author, as *An Explanation of the Four Fundamentals of Shirk*, (al-Hidaayah Publishing & Distribution, Birmingham, 2002 CE).

10. Tafsīr Sūrat al-Ikhlāṣ.

And many other works and letters besides these. Most of his works were compiled and printed under the title *Majmūʿah Muʾalafāt al-Shaykh Muḥammad ibn ʿAbd al-Wahhāb.*[91]

The author was blessed with a sharp memory, and a strong intellect. His small booklets testify to his knowledge, for even though the words are brief, the benefit and understanding found in them is great. His tongue was continually busy with the remembrance of Allāh. He died in 1206 A.H. (1792 C.E.), at the ripe age of 91. Many of the famous scholars of his time praised him highly, such as al-Sanaʿānī (d. 1182 A.H.), and al-Shawkānī (d. 1255 A.H.).

May Allāh reward the Shaykh, and grant him the highest of Paradise!

[91] Printed in Riyādh, 1398 A.H., under the supervision of Imām Muḥammad ibn Saʿūd Islamic University.

13. An Explanation of *Kashf al-Shubuhāt*

The Clearing of Doubts

TEXT

بسم الله الرحمن الرحيم

اعلم رحمك الله أن التوحيد هو إفراد الله–سبحانه–بالعبادة وهو دين الرسل الذي أرسلهم الله به إلى عباده

Know – may Allāh have mercy on you – that *tawḥīd* is to single out Allāh in worship. And this is the religion of all the messengers whom Allāh sent to His servants.

EXPL.

Tawḥīd linguistically implies: 'The act of making something one.' When used in an Islāmic sense, the author defined it as: 'Singling out Allāh in worship.' This automatically necessitates believing in the Lordship of Allāh, and His Perfect Names and Attributes. Only when a person truly believes in Allāh's Perfect Nature will he or she direct all acts of worship to Him. Thus, a more comprehensive definition of *tawḥīd* is: 'To affirm Allāh's unique and perfect nature, by affirming His Lordship and His Names and Attributes, and to single Him out in worship.'

The word '*tawḥīd*' is mentioned in the Prophet's (ﷺ) Sunnah, and its usage is thus accepted by the early scholars of Islām. For instance, when the Prophet (ﷺ) sent the famous Companion Mu'ādh ibn Jabal to Yemen, he said to him,

> "Let the first matter that you call them to be that they single out Allāh the Exalted (Arabic: *yuwahhidu*)."*

* Reported by al-Bukhari (# 7372) and others.

In another ḥadīth, Jābir ibn ʿAbdillāh narrates that the Prophet (ﷺ), when he set out for Ḥajj, '...cried out with *tawḥīd*,' meaning that he (ﷺ) said *Lā ilāha illa Allāh*.

Early scholars of Islām also used this phrase frequently. Thus, for example, Imām al-Bukhārī (d. 256 A.H.) devoted an entire section of his *Ṣaḥīḥ* to this concept and named it *Kitāb al-Tawḥīd*. Another scholar, Abū Bakr Muḥammad ibn Khuzaymah (d. 311 A.H.) also wrote a book about the Allāh's Names and Attributes, which he titled: *Kitāb al-Tawḥīd*.[92] Muḥammad ibn Isḥāq ibn Mandah (d. 395 A.H.) also wrote a book on a similar topic which he too titled *Kitāb al-Tawḥīd*.[93] Therefore, the claim by certain later authors that this phrase has no basis is clearly false, as there are explicit references to it in the Sunnah of the Prophet (ﷺ), and by early scholars of Islām.

The author states that *tawḥīd* was the religion of all the prophets of Allāh. Proof of this is the verse:

وَلَقَدْ بَعَثْنَا فِي كُلِّ أُمَّةٍ رَّسُولًا أَنِ اعْبُدُوا اللَّهَ وَاجْتَنِبُوا الطَّاغُوتَ

"And We have indeed sent to every nation a prophet (saying:) 'Worship Allāh, and avoid false deities'" [Sūrah *al-Naḥl*; 36].

In another verse,

وَمَا أَرْسَلْنَا مِن قَبْلِكَ مِن رَّسُولٍ إِلَّا نُوحِي إِلَيْهِ أَنَّهُ لَا إِلَٰهَ إِلَّا أَنَا فَاعْبُدُونِ ﴿٢٥﴾

"And We have not sent before you any prophet except that We have inspired him that there is no deity worthy of worship except Me, so worship Me (alone)" [Sūrah *al-Anbiyā'*; 25].

TEXT

فأولهم نوح عليه السلام أرسله الله إلى قومه لما غلوا في الصالحين : ودا، وسواعاً، ويغوث، ويعوق ،ونسرا وآخر الرسل محمد ، صلى الله عليه وسلم، وهو الذي كسر صور هؤلاء الصالحين

The first of these messengers was Nūḥ, whom Allāh sent to his people after they exaggerated the status of righteous people, such as Wadd, and Suwāʿ,

---

[92] Printed in two volumes by *Maktabah Al-Rushd* (Riyādh, 1994), ed. by Dr. ʿAbd al-ʿAzīz ibn Aḥmad al-Shahwān.

[93] Available in two volumes, printed by *Maktabah al-Ghurabā al-Athariyyah* (Madīnah, 1994), ed. by Dr. ʿAlī Nāṣir al-Faqīhī.

and Yaghūth, and Ya'ūq, and Nasr. And the last of these messengers was Muḥammad (ﷺ), and he was the one who broke the images of these pious people.

The first messenger (*rasūl*) to be sent to mankind was Nūḥ. The first prophet (*nabī*) was Adam, the father of mankind. The difference between a messenger and a prophet is that a *rasūl* is one who is sent to a nation that does not believe in him, whereas a *nabī* is sent to a nation that does believe in him. In general, a prophet upholds the religious law (*Sharī'ah*) of the messenger before him, but there are some exceptions to this (such as Adam – since he was the first man and prophet). Proofs that Nūḥ was the first messenger are numerous. In one ḥadīth, the Prophet (ﷺ) described the Day of Judgement, and stated that all of mankind would seek intercession from the messengers in order that Judgement commence. So they went to Nūḥ, and said: EXPL.

"O Nūḥ! You are the first messenger sent to the people of the earth."[94]

The people of Nūḥ were the first generation that fell into the evil of *shirk*. Evidence of this has been given in the introductory chapters. Allāh mentions the idols that the people of Nūḥ used to worship:

وَقَالُوا۟ لَا تَذَرُنَّ ءَالِهَتَكُمْ وَلَا تَذَرُنَّ وَدًّا وَلَا
سُوَاعًا وَلَا يَغُوثَ وَيَعُوقَ وَنَسْرًا ﴿٢٣﴾

"And they said: Do not abandon your idols! And do not abandon Wadd, or Suwā', or Yaghūth, Ya'ūq, and Nasr" [Sūrah *Nūḥ*; 23].

Ibn 'Abbās stated, with regards to the origin of these idols, "These are the names of five pious men that lived at the time of Nūḥ. When they died, *Shayṭān* inspired their people to carve out images of them, which they placed in their places of gathering. They were not worshipped until that generation had died, and knowledge was lost. When that occurred, these structures were then worshipped (as gods)."[95]

These same idols were passed down from generation to generation, and existed at the time of the Prophet (ﷺ) amongst the *Jāhilīyyah* Arabs. Ibn 'Abbās stated: "The idols that were worshipped by the people of Nūḥ were passed down to the Arabs. As for Wadd, it belonged to the tribe of Kalb, at Dawmat al-Jandal. And Suwā' was for the tribe of Hudhayl, and Yaghūth for the tribe of Murad, and then to the tribe of Banī Ghateef at Jurf, the (city) of Saba'. And Ya'ūq was for the tribe of Ḥamadān. And Nasr belonged to the tribe of Himyar, of the family of al-Kilā'."[96]

---

[94] Reported by al-Bukhārī (# 3340) and others.

[95] Paraphrased from al-Bukhārī.

[96] Reported by al-Bukhārī (# 4920).

Thus, the Prophet (ﷺ), the last messenger to be sent by Allāh, was the one who finally destroyed the images of these idols. This was done during and after his conquest of Makkah, in the year 8 AH. The Prophet (ﷺ) destroyed all of the idols around the Kaʿbah, which totalled three hundred and sixty. He personally went around the Kaʿbah, and, with a stick in his hand, pushed each idol, and recited:

> "The truth has come, and falsehood destroyed; the truth has come and falsehood will not appear nor recur."[97]

He also ordered the Companions to destroy the idols in neighbouring cities.

TEXT

أرسله الله إلى أناس يتعبدون ويحجون ويتصدقون ويذكرون الله كثيراً ولكنهم يجعلون بعض المخلوقات وسائط بينهم وبين الله عز وجل

Allāh sent the Prophet (ﷺ) to a group of people who used to worship Him, and perform Ḥajj, and give charity, and remember Allāh. However, they would also make certain created objects intermediaries between them and Allāh.

EXPL.

The Arabs to whom the Prophet (ﷺ) was sent believed in and worshipped Allāh. They had inherited some of the acts of worship from the remnants of the religion of Ibrāhīm. Ḥajj was of these acts. The Qur'ān mentions the fact that the *mushrikūn* would perform *tawāf* around the Kaʿbah, and during the days of Ḥajj, would go to the holy sites of Muzdalifah, Mina, and Arafāt. Likewise, they would remember Allāh, especially during times of distress, and call out to Him for their dire needs. They also practiced other acts of worship as well, for they would be generous to guests, and care for relatives, and speak the truth.

However, along with these acts of worship which were directed to Allāh, they would also worship other than Allāh. They believed that Allāh was too sacred and holy for them to approach directly at all times, thus they invented intermediaries that they would worship besides Him. These intermediaries, according to the *Jāhilīyyah* Arabs, were not independent, all-powerful creators besides Allāh, but were rather holy people, angels, saints and other objects which were believed to enjoy special status with Allāh. They would openly admit, when asked, that they wanted to worship Allāh, and had a ready excuse for this worship of other objects.

TEXT

يقولون نريد منهم التقرب إلى الله تعالى ونريد شفاعتهم عنده

They would say as an excuse for this act, "We only desire to come closer to

---

[97] Reported by al-Bukhārī (# 4278).

Allāh through them, and we wish that they intercede for us with Him."

EXPL. So the ultimate goal in this worship was Allāh. However, they felt that these objects occupied a high status, and that, if they were to intercede with Allāh, their intercession would be accepted. They felt that if these intermediaries were pleased, they would, in turn, make sure that Allāh was pleased with them as well. So these Arabs did not believe that the gods that they worshipped were supreme beings besides Allāh. Rather, they felt that these beings – for various reasons – had reached a state where they were beloved by Allāh. Thus, they felt that by pleasing these gods and asking for their intercession, Allāh would in turn be pleased with them, and accept such intercession.

The Qur'ān mentions this fact in many verses. Allāh states:

وَيَعْبُدُونَ مِن دُونِ ٱللَّهِ
مَا لَا يَضُرُّهُمْ وَلَا يَنفَعُهُمْ وَيَقُولُونَ هَٰٓؤُلَآءِ شُفَعَٰٓؤُنَا
عِندَ ٱللَّهِ

"And they worship besides Allāh that which neither harms them nor benefits them, and they say, 'These are our intercessors with Allāh'" [Sūrah *Yūnus*; 18].

Allāh also quotes the *mushrikūn* as saying,

مَا نَعْبُدُهُمْ إِلَّا لِيُقَرِّبُونَآ إِلَى ٱللَّهِ زُلْفَىٰٓ

"We only worship them in order that they bring us closer to Allāh in ranks" [Sūrah *al-Zumar*; 3].

TEXT مثل الملائكة وعيسى ومريم وأناس غيرهم من الصالحين

So they would go through the likes of angels, and Jesus, and Mary, and others besides them, righteous people.

EXPL. These gods that they worshipped were not all the same. Some of them would worship angels, and claim that they were Allāh's daughters. Yet others, the Christians, would worship Jesus, and claim that he was Allāh's son. They would also worship Mary as the 'mother' of God. They also worshipped pious people. They would venerate graves, and build structures over the places that these holy men had lived and were buried in. These structures in turn became idols that were worshipped besides Allāh.

TEXT فبعث الله تعالى محمداً صلى الله عليه وسلم يجدد لهم دين أبيهم إبراهيم ويخبرهم

أن هذا التقرب والاعتقاد محض حق الله تعالى - لا يصلح منه شيء لغير الله ، لا لملك مقربٍ ولا نبي مرسلٍ فضلاً عن غيرهما

> Allāh therefore sent Prophet Muḥammad (ﷺ), to revive their old religion – the religion of their father Ibrāhīm – and to inform them that this act of trying to come closer to Allāh, and this belief (that they needed an intermediary to approach Allāh) was a right that is due only to Allāh. It is not proper to direct any of these acts of worship to any other being, whether it be a noble angel, or a sent prophet, much less to anyone of lesser status than them.

EXPL. The *Jāhilīyyah* Arabs were the descendants of the prophets Ibrāhīm and Ismā'īl. Thus, they had inherited the beliefs and religious practices of their forefather Ibrāhīm; as Allāh states in the Qur'ān:

وَإِن مِّنْ أُمَّةٍ إِلَّا خَلَا فِيهَا نَذِيرٌ ﴿٢٤﴾

> "There is not a single nation except that a warner has been sent to it" [Sūrah *Fāṭir*; 24].

The prophet of the Arabs, before the advent of Muḥammad (ﷺ), was their father Ibrāhīm.

So the Arabs still possessed the basic beliefs of Ibrāhīm. The children of Ismā'īl were upon *tawḥīd* for many generations. The first person to introduce idolatry amongst the Arabs was 'Amr ibn Luhay al-Khuzā'ī. On one of his journeys, he travelled to Syria, where he saw an idolatrous nation worshipping their idols. He asked them to give him one of these idols to take back with him to Makkah, which they did. They gave him an idol by the name of Hubal, which was to become the main idol of the tribe of Quraysh. 'Amr ibn Luhay also introduced superstitious practices that were previously unknown to his people. These practices involved directing acts of worship to various idols. Hence, the Prophet (ﷺ) stated,

> "I saw 'Amr ibn Luhay dragging his intestines in the Fire of Hell."[98]

The practices that were introduced by 'Amr ibn Luḥay were eventually accepted by almost all the Arabs before the Prophet's (ﷺ) advent. However, the beliefs and practices of the true religion of Ibrāhīm were not lost.

Proof of this is the existence of a group of people who called themselves *ḥanīf* (plural: *ḥunafā*). This word implied that they were 'inclining' away from the practices of their people towards the pure worship of Allāh.

These people had abandoned the ways of the idolatrous society in which they lived. Instead, they claimed to be following the religion of Ibrāhīm. They

---

[98] See *Sīrah Ibn Hishām*, 1/76.

قُل لِّمَنِ ٱلْأَرْضُ وَمَن فِيهَآ إِن
كُنتُمْ تَعْلَمُونَ ﴿٨٤﴾ سَيَقُولُونَ لِلَّهِ ۚ قُلْ أَفَلَا تَذَكَّرُونَ
﴿٨٥﴾ قُلْ مَن رَّبُّ ٱلسَّمَٰوَٰتِ ٱلسَّبْعِ وَرَبُّ ٱلْعَرْشِ ٱلْعَظِيمِ
﴿٨٦﴾ سَيَقُولُونَ لِلَّهِ ۚ قُلْ أَفَلَا تَتَّقُونَ ﴿٨٧﴾ قُلْ مَنۢ بِيَدِهِۦ
مَلَكُوتُ كُلِّ شَىْءٍ وَهُوَ يُجِيرُ وَلَا يُجَارُ عَلَيْهِ إِن
كُنتُمْ تَعْلَمُونَ ﴿٨٨﴾ سَيَقُولُونَ لِلَّهِ ۚ قُلْ فَأَنَّىٰ تُسْحَرُونَ ﴿٨٩﴾

"Say: To whom belongs the earth and whoever is in it, if you really know? They will respond, 'To Allāh.' Say: 'Then will you not remember?' Say: 'Who is the Lord of the seven heavens, and Lord of the Great Throne?' They will respond, 'Allāh.' Say: 'Then will you not fear Him?' Say: 'In whose hand is the realm (or control) of all things, while He protects, and none can protect against Him, if you should know?' They will respond, 'Allāh.' So say: Then how are you deluded" [Sūrah *al-Mu'minūn*; 84-89].

So these verses are absolutely clear and explicit in the fact that the *Jāhilīyyah* Arabs believed in the existence and Lordship of Allāh, and that Allāh, and only Allāh, creates, and gives sustenance, and is All-Powerful.

2- Verses that show the *Jāhilīyyah* Arabs believed in Allāh yet committed *shirk*. Allāh states,

وَمَا يُؤْمِنُ أَكْثَرُهُم بِٱللَّهِ إِلَّا وَهُم مُّشْرِكُونَ ﴿١٠٦﴾

"And most of them do not believe (*yu'min*) in Allāh except that they commit *shirk*" [Sūrah *Yūsuf*; 106].

In this verse, Allāh affirms that the *mushrikūn* have *īmān* (belief), yet they also have *shirk* along with their *īmān*.[104] Ibn 'Abbās explained this verse, and elaborated on the type of *īmān* that they had, when he said, "Their belief (*īmān*) in Allāh is that, if you were to ask them who created the skies and the earth and the mountains, they would say: Allāh! Yet, they committed *shirk* with him." 'Ikrimah (d. 104 AH) stated, "If you were to ask them who created them, and who created the heavens and earth, they would respond: Allāh. That is their belief in Him, yet they worship other than Him." Mujāhid (d. 100 AH) stated, "Their belief in Him is that they say: 'Allāh created us, and gives us our sustenance, and causes us to die.' So this is their belief, yet they commit *shirk* in their worship, and worship other than

[104] Obviously, the *īmān* that they had was of no benefit to them, since *shirk* automatically nullifies the fruits of *īmān*.

Him." Qatādah (d. 110 AH) said, "You will not meet a single one of them except that he would inform you that Allāh is his Lord, and that He created him and gave him sustenance. Yet, despite that, he will commit *shirk* in his worship (of Allāh)."[105] So these are explicit interpretations from the early scholars of Islām in which they explained that the *Jāhilīyyah* Arabs believed in Allāh's Lordship, and that their *shirk* was in His worship.

3- The *Jāhilīyyah* Arab's claim that they only worshipped these idols to come closer to Allāh. This is clear proof that they believed in the Lordship of Allāh, and that they understood that only Allāh can grant their requests. Thus, they would turn to these intermediaries in order that these requests have a greater chance of being answered by Allāh.

وَيَعۡبُدُونَ مِن دُونِ ٱللَّهِ
مَا لَا يَضُرُّهُمۡ وَلَا يَنفَعُهُمۡ وَيَقُولُونَ هَٰٓؤُلَآءِ شُفَعَٰٓؤُنَا
عِندَ ٱللَّهِۚ

"And they worship besides Allāh that which neither harms them nor benefits them, and they say, 'These are our intercessors in front of Allāh'" [Sūrah *Yūnus*; 18].

Allāh also quotes the *mushrikūn* as saying,

مَا نَعۡبُدُهُمۡ إِلَّا لِيُقَرِّبُونَآ إِلَى ٱللَّهِ زُلۡفَىٰٓ

"We only worship them in order that they bring us closer to Allāh in ranks" [Sūrah *al-Zumar*; 3].

So the *Jāhilīyyah* Arabs did not claim that these idols are All-Powerful, or that they control creation. Rather, they merely used them to reach Allāh, thus showing that Allāh was the ultimate object of their worship.

4- The fact that Allāh uses their belief in His Lordship as proof against them in their acts of *shirk*. In one series of verses, Allāh mentions the *mushrikūn*'s belief in Him as proof against them in their worship of others:

قُلِ ٱلۡحَمۡدُ لِلَّهِ وَسَلَٰمٌ
عَلَىٰ عِبَادِهِ ٱلَّذِينَ ٱصۡطَفَىٰٓۗ ءَآللَّهُ خَيۡرٌ أَمَّا يُشۡرِكُونَ ﴿٥٩﴾

[105] For these quotes, see *Tafsīr al-Ṭabarī*, 16/285-287.

أَمَّنْ خَلَقَ ٱلسَّمَٰوَٰتِ وَٱلْأَرْضَ وَأَنزَلَ لَكُم مِّنَ ٱلسَّمَآءِ
مَآءً فَأَنۢبَتْنَا بِهِۦ حَدَآئِقَ ذَاتَ بَهْجَةٍ مَّا كَانَ لَكُمْ
أَن تُنۢبِتُوا۟ شَجَرَهَآ ۗ أَءِلَٰهٌ مَّعَ ٱللَّهِ ۚ بَلْ هُمْ قَوْمٌ يَعْدِلُونَ ﴿٦٠﴾
أَمَّن جَعَلَ ٱلْأَرْضَ قَرَارًا وَجَعَلَ خِلَٰلَهَآ أَنْهَٰرًا وَجَعَلَ لَهَا
رَوَٰسِىَ وَجَعَلَ بَيْنَ ٱلْبَحْرَيْنِ حَاجِزًا ۗ أَءِلَٰهٌ مَّعَ ٱللَّهِ ۚ بَلْ
أَكْثَرُهُمْ لَا يَعْلَمُونَ ﴿٦١﴾ أَمَّن يُجِيبُ ٱلْمُضْطَرَّ إِذَا دَعَاهُ
وَيَكْشِفُ ٱلسُّوٓءَ وَيَجْعَلُكُمْ خُلَفَآءَ ٱلْأَرْضِ ۗ أَءِلَٰهٌ
مَّعَ ٱللَّهِ ۚ قَلِيلًا مَّا تَذَكَّرُونَ ﴿٦٢﴾ أَمَّن يَهْدِيكُمْ فِى
ظُلُمَٰتِ ٱلْبَرِّ وَٱلْبَحْرِ وَمَن يُرْسِلُ ٱلرِّيَٰحَ بُشْرًۢا بَيْنَ يَدَىْ
رَحْمَتِهِۦٓ ۗ أَءِلَٰهٌ مَّعَ ٱللَّهِ ۚ تَعَٰلَى ٱللَّهُ عَمَّا يُشْرِكُونَ ﴿٦٣﴾
أَمَّن يَبْدَؤُا۟ ٱلْخَلْقَ ثُمَّ يُعِيدُهُۥ وَمَن يَرْزُقُكُم مِّنَ ٱلسَّمَآءِ وَٱلْأَرْضِ ۗ
أَءِلَٰهٌ مَّعَ ٱللَّهِ ۚ قُلْ هَاتُوا۟ بُرْهَٰنَكُمْ إِن كُنتُمْ صَٰدِقِينَ ﴿٦٤﴾

"Say: Praise be to Allāh, and peace be upon His servants whom He has chosen. Is Allāh better or what they associate with Him? Is the One Who created the heavens and the earth, and sent down for you rain from the sky, causing to grow thereby gardens of joyful beauty, which you could not (otherwise) have grown its trees [not best]? Is there any deity besides Allāh [who did this, and is thus worthy of worship?] Rather, they are a people who ascribe partners [to Him]. Is He [not best] Who made the earth a stable ground, and placed within it rivers and made for it firmly set mountains, and placed between the two seas a barrier? Rather, most of them do not know. Is He [not best] Who responds to the call of the one in distress, and removes evil and make you inheritors of the earth? Is there a deity with Allāh? Little do you remember. Is He [not best] Who guides you through the darknesses of the land and sea, and who sends the winds as good tidings before His mercy? Is there a deity besides Allāh? Exalted is Allāh over what they associate with Him. Is He [not best] Who begins the creation, and then repeats it, and who provides for you from the heavens and earth? Is there a deity besides Allāh? Say: Produce your truth if you are truthful" [Sūrah *al-Naml*; 59-64].

In these verses, Allāh mentions matters which the *mushrikūn* themselves admitted to, and then asks the rhetorical question, 'Is there any *ilāh* (deity worthy of worship) besides Allāh?' In other words, if you admit that Allāh, and only Allāh, is the One Who is capable of all this, then who else is there that is worthy of worship besides Him? Thus, Allāh uses their belief in His *Rubūbiyyah* as proof against them.

5- The fact that the *mushrikūn* would turn to Allāh sincerely at times of distress, realising that only He could save them. This concept is mentioned numerous times in the Qur'ān, as, for example in:

فَإِذَا رَكِبُوا فِي
الْفُلْكِ دَعَوُا اللَّهَ مُخْلِصِينَ لَهُ الدِّينَ فَلَمَّا نَجَّاهُمْ إِلَى الْبَرِّ إِذَا
هُمْ يُشْرِكُونَ ﴿٦٥﴾

"So when they board the ships, they call out to Allāh in all sincerity, and when He saves them to the land, they commit *shirk*" [Sūrah *al-'Ankabūt*; 65].

In a second verse, Allāh states:

وَإِذَا مَسَّكُمُ الضُّرُّ فِي الْبَحْرِ ضَلَّ مَن تَدْعُونَ إِلَّا إِيَّاهُ

"And when a problem falls upon you while you are at sea, all those whom you call upon leave you except He (Allāh)" [Sūrah *al-Isrā'*; 67].

Also,

قُلْ أَرَأَيْتَكُمْ إِنْ أَتَاكُمْ عَذَابُ اللَّهِ أَوْ أَتَتْكُمُ السَّاعَةُ أَغَيْرَ
اللَّهِ تَدْعُونَ إِن كُنتُمْ صَادِقِينَ ﴿٤٠﴾ بَلْ إِيَّاهُ تَدْعُونَ فَيَكْشِفُ
مَا تَدْعُونَ إِلَيْهِ إِن شَاءَ وَتَنسَوْنَ مَا تُشْرِكُونَ ﴿٤١﴾

"Ask them: If the punishment of Allāh were to come to you, or the Day of Judgement, would you call upon other than Allāh, if you are truthful? Rather, Him alone would you call, and He will remove what has afflicted you if He wills, and you will forget (those objects) whom you do *shirk* with" [Sūrah *al-An'ām*; 40-41].

And Allāh says,

وَإِذَا مَسَّ الْإِنسَانَ ضُرٌّ دَعَا رَبَّهُ مُنِيبًا إِلَيْهِ ثُمَّ إِذَا خَوَّلَهُ
نِعْمَةً مِّنْهُ نَسِيَ مَا كَانَ يَدْعُو إِلَيْهِ مِن قَبْلُ

"And when an affliction touches man, he calls out to his Lord, humbly, and when He exchanges it with a good situation, he forgets what he was calling for before" [Sūrah *al-Zumar*; 8].

And finally,

وَإِذَا غَشِيَهُم مَّوْجٌ كَالظُّلَلِ دَعَوُاْ ٱللَّهَ مُخْلِصِينَ لَهُ ٱلدِّينَ

"So when the waves come out to them, like dark clouds, they call out to Allāh, making the religion sincere to Him..." [Sūrah *Luqmān*; 32].

So all of these verses clearly prove that the *mushrikūn* of old realised and believed in Allāh's complete power over everything. They knew that their idols and other objects of worship could not save them, nor did they have the power to do so, and that is why they ignored them at times of distress and called out directly to Allāh.

6- The *mushrikūn's* rejection of the pure worship of Allāh (*Tawḥīd al-Ulūhiyyah*), and not the existence or Lordship of Allāh. The only reason that the *mushrikūn* rejected Islām was that they refused to worship Allāh directly at all times, and not that they refused to believe in Allāh. Allāh states:

إِنَّهُمْ كَانُوٓاْ إِذَا قِيلَ لَهُمْ لَآ إِلَٰهَ إِلَّا ٱللَّهُ يَسْتَكْبِرُونَ ﴿٣٥﴾

"Indeed, when it was said to them, 'There is no deity (worthy of worship) except Allāh', they would become arrogant" [Sūrah *al-Ṣāffāt*; 35].

Allāh describes them in another verse:

وَعَجِبُوٓاْ أَن جَآءَهُم مُّنذِرٌ مِّنْهُمْ ۖ وَقَالَ ٱلْكَٰفِرُونَ هَٰذَا سَٰحِرٌ كَذَّابٌ ﴿٤﴾ أَجَعَلَ ٱلْءَالِهَةَ إِلَٰهًا وَٰحِدًا ۖ إِنَّ هَٰذَا لَشَىْءٌ عُجَابٌ ﴿٥﴾

"And they are amazed that a warner has come to them from amongst themselves. And the disbelievers said: 'This is a magician and a liar. Has he made the objects of worship (*āliha*) [only] One? Indeed, this is something very strange" [Sūrah *Ṣād*; 4-5].

In yet a third verse, they are described as:

ذَٰلِكُم بِأَنَّهُۥٓ إِذَا دُعِىَ ٱللَّهُ وَحْدَهُۥ كَفَرْتُمْ ۖ وَإِن يُشْرَكْ بِهِۦ تُؤْمِنُواْ ۚ

"That is because, when Allāh is called upon alone (i.e., with *tawḥīd*), you disbelieved, but when others were associated with Him (i.e., in *shirk*), you believed" [Sūrah *Ghāfir*; 12].

So the *mushrikūn* did not reject Allāh; rather, they rejected singling out Allāh in worship.

7- The *Jāhilīyyah* Arabs cry during Ḥajj. Ibn ʿAbbās reported that the *mushrikūn* would say (during Ḥajj): 'I respond to your call, O Allāh, I respond to your call. There is no partner that you have...' at this, the Prophet (ﷺ) would interject and say, 'Woe to you! Stop (here), stop (here),' but they would proceed, '...except a partner that belongs to you. You control him, and all that he controls.' They would say this while performing *tawāf* around the Kaʿbah.[106] In this narration, Ibn ʿAbbās mentions the Prophet's (ﷺ) stance towards their acts of worship during the early days of Makkah. The *mushrikūn* would affirm that Allāh has no partners, and the Prophet (ﷺ) would try to stop them at this point. However, they would proceed with their cry, and affirm partners who were under the complete control of Allāh. So they would affirm the complete Lordship of Allāh, and claim that these partners were under Allāh's total control, yet direct acts of worship to these partners. This narration is also explicit in that they ascribed total *Rubūbiyyah* to Allāh, and believed that these idols did not have any power in and of themselves. Rather, any power that they had, according to them, was derived from Allāh's permission.

So these are some of the evidences that the *Jāhilīyyah* Arabs believed in Allāh's existence and Lordship. In reality, this simple fact – that the *mushrikūn* believed in *Tawḥīd al-Rubūbiyyah* – is the crux of this simple tract. Once a Muslim understands this, he or she will realise that the *shirk* that these *Jāhilīyyah* Arabs performed was by directing acts of worship, such as *duʿā* and prayer, to other than Allāh, and not by affirming creators and all-powerful lords besides Allāh.

The primary problem is that many people believe *shirk* can only occur in *Rubūbiyyah*; that is, by claiming that there is an all-powerful lord besides Allāh. However, this is only one form of *shirk*, and not a common form at that. Most of mankind, including the Christians and the *mushrikūn* of the Prophet's (ﷺ) time, did not claim this. This is because the majority of mankind affirms the belief of One Supreme Creator. Their *shirk* does not involve inventing all-powerful gods besides Allāh; it involves directing acts of worship to other than Allāh.

Ibn Taymiyyah writes:"So the belief of the *mushrikūn* that Allāh is the Lord of everything, and the Master, and Creator, is not sufficient to save him from Allāh's punishment if he does not testify to *Lā ilāha illa Allāh*, such that no one (in his eyes) is worthy of worship except Allāh...Allāh has informed us that the *mushrikūn* would take intermediaries between them and Allāh. They would call out to them, and use them as intercessors without any permission from Allāh."[107]

---

[106] Reported by Muslim (2/842).

[107] *Majmūʿ al-Fatāwa* 3/105.

> Since they rejected the concept of *ilāh*, the Prophet (ﷺ) was sent to them to call them to the testimony of *tawḥīd*, which is *Lā ilāha illa Allāh*.

The testimony of faith is the crux of the religion of Islām. This testimony is what separates a Muslim from a non-Muslim, but only if he truly believes in it and practices it. Therefore, it is essential to discuss the actual meaning of this phrase, and the implications of this statement. EXPL.

The phrase translates as: 'There is no *ilāh* except for Allāh.' The first part of the testimony is a negation of all *ilāhs*. The second part is an affirmation that there is only one, unique *ilāh*, and that is Allāh.

An understanding of the word *ilāh*, therefore, is crucial in order for this phrase to be properly understood.

Ibn 'Abbās stated that it means, '...one whom everything turns to, and whom everyone worships.'[113] The famous commentator on the words of the Qur'ān, al-Rāghib al-Asbahānī (d. 425) stated: '*Ilāh* is a name given to every object that is worshipped.'[114] The famous lexicographer of the Arabic language, Ibn Manẓūr (d. 711), defined it as, '...any object that is taken as an object of worship,'[115] and al-Fayrūzabādi said: 'Every object that is worshipped is an *ilāh* for the one that worships it.'[116] Ibn Taymiyyah (d. 728 A.H.)wrote: "The meaning of *ilāh* is not 'One who has the capability to create', as many philosophical groups presume. For they believe that godship (*ilāhiyyah*) is the ability to create, and that whoever affirms that Allāh is the One Who creates, without any other creator, has testified to *Lā ilāha illa Allāh*. But indeed, the *mushrikūn* used to testify to this as well, and they were still considered *mushrikūn*. So the true *ilāh* is the one that is worthy of worship...and *tawḥīd* implies worshipping Allāh alone, without any partners. And *shirk* is to make with Allāh other objects of worship."[117]

So we find that these scholars all defined *ilāh* as an object of worship, and none of them mentioned that an *ilāh* must be a creator, or an all-powerful entity. In fact, none of the scholars of *tawḥīd*, or of the Arabic language, ever stated that an *ilāh* was a lord or creator in the eyes of the one who believed in it.

The significance of this simple fact is indeed profound. When a Muslim negates the existence of an *ilāh* besides Allāh, he or she is actually negating that any other object will be worshipped besides Allāh. One who bears witness to the *shahādah* will negate that there is any other purpose in his or her life except

---

[113] *Tafsīr al-Ṭabarī*, 1/54.

[114] *Al-Mufradāt,* p. 21.

[115] *Lisān al-Arab* (1/188).

[116] *Al-Qāmūs*, p. 1603.

[117] *Majmū' al-Fatāwā* 3/101.

to achieve Allāh's pleasure. This implies that all desires that go against the commands of Allāh must be rejected.

It is, therefore, incorrect to translate this testimony as 'There is no Creator (or Lord) except for Allah.' Had this been the understanding, the *Jāhilīyyah* Arabs would have accepted it and followed the Prophet (ﷺ), for they too believed that there was no Lord and Supreme Master except Allāh. But they understood the precise meaning of *ilāh* as an object that is worshipped, and realised that, if they bore testimony to this phrase, they would have to give up their idolatry, and change their way of life. Due to this realisation, they rejected the Prophet's (ﷺ) message.

So the *shahādah* literally translates as: 'There is no object of worship except Allāh.' However, the negation *Lā*, as used in the *shahādah*, must have two phrases after it: a subject (known in Arabic as *ism*), and a description of that subject (called a *khabar*). This is a fact agreed upon by all grammarians and theological groups in Islām. As can be seen, though, the phrasing of the *shahādah* only has a subject (i.e., the word: *ilāh*), but no description of that subject. Thus, different sects of Islām differed in their understanding of this phrase.

Most philosophical groups[118] understand '*ilāh*' as meaning 'creator and all-powerful lord'. Since they misunderstood the meaning of *ilāh*, they then added

---

[118] In particular, the *Ash'arīyah* and *Māturidiyyah*. Some of their definitions for *shirk* have already been listed. Although the details of this subject are beyond the scope of this small work, it must be pointed out that most *shirk* that occurs amongst Muslims actually occurs amongst *Ash'arī* groups or groups influenced by them. This is due to a number of factors. Firstly, the *Ash'arīs*, in general, do not emphasize the concept of *Tawḥīd al-Ulūhiyyah*, for *tawḥīd* according to them is restricted to affirming the existence and divine nature of Allāh (which is *Tawḥīd al-Rubūbiyyah*). When one turns to their source books, one finds dozens of pages devoted to the proofs of Allāh's existence (which is a matter that most of mankind agree upon), yet there is no discussion whatsoever of the *rights* that Allāh has over creation (that He be worshipped alone). This laxity with regards to *tawḥīd al-Ulūhiyyah* caused them to ignore its importance altogether. Secondly, most of the *Ash'arīs* define an *ilāh* as: 'One who can create independently,' and others as: 'One who is all-powerful' (see, for example, Fakhr al-Dīn al-Rāzi's (d. 606 A.H.) definition in his *Sharḥ Asmā Allāh*, p. 124). This definition, of course, contradicts the understanding of *all* classical linguists, and early scholars of Islām. Thirdly, based on this incorrect definition of *ilāh*, they then stated that *shirk* can only occur when a person affirms the existence of another *creator* besides Allāh. Therefore, according to most of them, if a person directs an act of worship to other than Allāh, but believes that that object does not have the independent power to create anything, then such a person has not committed *shirk*. Fourthly, the *Ash'arīs* defined *īmān* (faith) to be a belief of the heart, and excluded actions from *īmān*. Therefore, according to them, the only way a person could renounce *īmān* is by a belief of the heart; an act of *shirk* will not affect his *īmān*. Thus, the net result of all of these matters is that *shirk* crept into their societies, and was accepted by their scholars, simply because they did not understand the proper definition of *tawḥīd*.

the phrase *fī al-wujūd* (in existence) as a description (*khabar*). So to them, the *shahādah* translated as: 'There is no Creator in existence except Allāh', thus falling into two errors. Firstly, as we have already explained, an *ilāh* is separate from a *rabb*, or Lord. Thus, to translate *ilāh* as Creator is simply incorrect. Secondly, the addition 'in existence' as a description (*khabar*) does not match with the first part of the *shahādah* if it is understood properly (i.e., if a differentiation is made between an *ilāh* and a *rabb*). In other words, since the word *ilāh* does not mean Creator, it is not proper to have the phrase 'in existence' as the *khabar*, since this phrase only fits with the incorrect meaning of *ilāh*. It can be seen here that these groups consider *shirk* to be affirming creators and all-powerful lords besides Allāh, since that is what contradicts their understanding of the *shahādah*. Their definitions of *shirk* have already been given, and here we see the reason behind those definitions.

Other groups[119] understood the meaning of *ilāh* properly, but added the exact same *khabar* (i.e., 'in existence') as the previous group did. Therefore they translated the *shahādah* as, 'There is no object that is worshipped in existence except Allāh.' However, this understanding is extremely incorrect, for without a doubt there are hundreds, if not thousands or millions, of objects that are actually worshipped besides Allāh. The groups that understood the *shahādah* in this manner believed that everything in existence is a manifestation of Allāh. Therefore, according to them, everything that is worshipped is in fact Allāh! So to these groups, there is no such thing as *shirk* in the first place, since according to them prostrating to an idol, or to the sun and moon, is in fact prostrating to Allāh.

The correct understanding of this phrase, and the understanding of *Ahl al-Sunnah*, is to add the description *bi ḥaqq* (with truth), thus translating the *shahādah*, after altering it to standard English, as: 'There is no *ilāh* worthy of being an *ilāh* except Allāh', or, more simply, 'There is no deity worthy of worship except Allāh.'

Part of the implications of this statement is that a Muslim must free himself (*barā'ah*) of all other false deities. It is not sufficient that only Allāh be worshipped; rather, a Muslim must disbelieve in all false deities. Therefore, if a person worships Allāh alone, without committing any *shirk*, and follows the pillars of Islām, yet believes that the Christians are correct in their worship of Jesus, or that Buddhists will also attain paradise because of their asceticism, then in reality he or she is not a Muslim. This is because such a person has *allowed* other deities to be worshipped besides Allāh, even though he himself might not

[119] Such as the extreme *Sūfis* who propogated the belief of *waḥdat al-wujūd*.

have done so. Thus, by this belief, he has in fact negated his testimony of faith, 'There is no deity worthy of worship except Allāh.'

Allāh says:

فَلَمَّا تَبَيَّنَ لَهُۥٓ أَنَّهُۥ عَدُوٌّ لِّلَّهِ تَبَرَّأَ مِنْهُ

"So when it became clear to (Ibrāhīm) that he (Ibrāhīm's father) was an enemy of Allāh, he freed himself from him" [Sūrah *al-Tawbah*; 114].

And He commands the Prophet (ﷺ):

قُلْ إِنَّمَا هُوَ إِلَٰهٌ وَٰحِدٌ وَإِنَّنِى بَرِىٓءٌ مِّمَّا تُشْرِكُونَ

"Say: Indeed, He is only one *ilāh*, and I am of a surety free (i.e., have nothing to do) with what you associate with Him" [Sūrah *al-An'ām*; 19].

And the Qur'ān clearly says,

قَدْ
كَانَتْ لَكُمْ أُسْوَةٌ حَسَنَةٌ فِىٓ إِبْرَٰهِيمَ وَٱلَّذِينَ مَعَهُۥٓ إِذْ قَالُوا۟ لِقَوْمِهِمْ
إِنَّا بُرَءَٰٓؤُا۟ مِنكُمْ وَمِمَّا تَعْبُدُونَ مِن دُونِ ٱللَّهِ كَفَرْنَا بِكُمْ وَبَدَا بَيْنَنَا
وَبَيْنَكُمُ ٱلْعَدَٰوَةُ وَٱلْبَغْضَآءُ أَبَدًا حَتَّىٰ تُؤْمِنُوا۟ بِٱللَّهِ وَحْدَهُۥٓ

"There is for you an excellent example in Ibrāhīm and those with him, when they said to their people, 'Indeed, we are disassociated from you and from whatever you worship other than Allāh. We have denied you, and there has appeared between us and you animosity and hatred forever until you believe in Allāh alone...'" [Sūrah *al-Mumtaḥinah*; 4].

The author also mentions that the *Jāhilīyyah* Arabs understood from this phrase what the Muslims of his time understand by the term *sayyid*. This term is still in use to this day, and is used to signify a great saint, or religious leader. Although there is nothing inherently incorrect about the term *sayyid*, over time it became a stepping-stone to *shirk*, as these *sayyids* eventually became objects of worship besides Allāh. Examples of such people are: Sayyid 'Abd al-Qādir al-Jīlani, Sayyid Mo'īn al-Dīn al-Chishti, Sayyid Aḥmad Badawī, Sayyid Rifā'aī, Sayyid Tījāni, and others. All of these *sayyids* have – in the eyes of their followers – founded specific *Sufi* cults (or *tariqahs*), and are the objects of worship of thousands of people. Those who worship them believe that they occupy a noble status with Allāh, and thus, by pleasing them and turning to them, one's needs will be responded to. And this is exactly the beliefs of the pagans of old, and the understanding that they had of the term *ilāh*.

So the author affirms that the meaning of *ilāh* according to the Arabs is the same meaning that is understood by these groups by the term *sayyid*, and that is one whom others turn to for supernatural help, and to intercede for them with

Allāh. By using the language and vernacular that the audience of his time was familiar with, the author brings home the exact meaning of this word.

Once again, it is important to note that the descriptions given by certain sects to their objects of worship, such as the words *Shaykh*, *Sayyid*, or *Walī*, are not inherently wrong or prohibited. If used properly and in the right context, then such words are a part of the vernacular of Muslims. However, the use of these words by certain groups, such as the extreme *Sūfīs*, has become a justification for *shirk*.

The author thus indicates that the ruling on an act depends on its reality, and not on the name given to it. Therefore, if a person directs an act of worship to a certain person on the pretext that he is a *sayyid* or *walī*, it does not change the reality that *shirk* has been committed. By directing such an act to a *sayyid*, a person has actually made this *sayyid* an *ilāh* along with Allāh.

To summarize this section, an *ilāh* is one whom others turn to for supernatural help, either to gain some benefit from or to avert some evil. If the heart is constantly attached to an object, turning to it in a state of love and fear, desiring some good from it, and fearing a rejection, then that object becomes an *ilāh*. It does not matter whether later people call such objects *Walīs* of Allāh, or *Sayyids* or *Pīrs* – the reality of the matter is that once these objects are turned to for help, they become *ilāhs*.

TEXT

والمراد من هذه الكلمة معناها لا مجرد لفظها والكفار الجهال يعلمون أن مراد النبي صلى الله عليه وسلم بهذه الكلمة هو إفراد الله تعالى بالتعلق به ، والكفر بما يعبد من دونه والبراءة منه فإنه لما قال لهم قولوا : «لا إله إلا الله» قالوا: ﴿أجعل الآلهة إلهاً واحداً إن هذا لشيء عجاب﴾ (سورة ص، الآية: ٥).

And what is required from this testimony is the actual meaning and beliefs in its implications, and not merely its verbalisation. So the ignorant disbelievers knew that what the Prophet (ﷺ) meant with this phrase was to single out Allāh in one's concerns of the heart, so that all acts of worship are directed to Him alone, and to reject all other deities that are worshipped besides Him, and to declare one's separation and animosity to these deities. That is why, when the Prophet (ﷺ) told them, 'Say: *Lā ilāha illa Allāh*,' They responded, "Has he made the objects of worship one? Indeed, this is something very strange!" [Sūrah *Ṣād*; 5]

EXPL.

The phrase *Lā ilāha illa Allāh* is meant to be understood, believed in, and practiced. It is not sufficient merely to verbalise it, without knowing its meanings or implementing its conditions. For example, if a non-Muslim were asked to repeat this phrase in Arabic, not knowing its meaning, he or she would not become a Muslim merely by parroting this phrase. Likewise, if an insane person were taught to repeat this phrase, then even if he were to repeat it a thousand times it would not cause him to enter into Islām.[120]

The *Jāhilīyyah* Arabs fully understood the implications and meanings of this phrase. That is why they arrogantly rejected and ridiculed it. When the Prophet (ﷺ) called them to this phrase, they were amazed, and responded,

أَجَعَلَ الْآلِهَةَ إِلَٰهًا وَاحِدًا ۖ إِنَّ هَٰذَا لَشَيْءٌ عُجَابٌ ﴿٥﴾ وَانطَلَقَ الْمَلَأُ مِنْهُمْ أَنِ امْشُوا وَاصْبِرُوا عَلَىٰ آلِهَتِكُمْ ۖ إِنَّ هَٰذَا لَشَيْءٌ يُرَادُ ﴿٦﴾

"Has he made all the objects of worship into one? Indeed this is something very strange! We have never heard this amongst our fathers of old, indeed this is something that has been invented" [Sūrah *Ṣād*; 5-6].

TEXT

فإذا عرفت أن جهال الكفار يعرفون ذلك فالعجب ممن يدعي الإسلام وهو لا يعرف من تفسير هذه الكلمة ما عرفه جهال الكفار. بل يظن أن ذلك هو التلفظ بحروفها من غير إعتقاد القلب لشيء من المعاني ، والحاذق منهم يظن أن معناها «لا يخلق ولا يرزق ولا يدبر الأمر إلا الله» فلا خير في رجل جهال الكفار أعلم منه بمعاني «لا إله إلا الله» .

So when you realise that these ignorant disbelievers knew the precise meaning of this phrase, then it is indeed amazing that there are those who claim to be followers of Islām in our times and yet do not understand from this phrase what the ignorant disbelievers understood! Rather, he presumes that he is only required to verbalise this phrase, without necessarily believing with his heart any particular meaning. And the intelligent one amongst them believes that it means that there is no Creator, or Sustainer, or Controller except Allāh, which was exactly the belief of the pagan Arabs. And indeed, there is no good in a person when the pagan Arabs are more knowledgeable of the meaning of the phrase *Lā ilāha illa Allāh* than he!

EXPL.

Here the author mentions the incorrect understanding prevalent in his time concerning the testimony of faith. Many Muslims merely believed that this testimony need only be verbalised, regardless of whether one understands it or not.

Others – more learned and intelligent than the previous category – interpret this phrase to mean: 'There is no Creator, or Sustainer, or Controller except Allāh.' In other words, to such a person, this phrase only affirms the complete Lordship of Allāh (*Tawḥīd al-Rubūbiyyah*), while neglecting His right to be

---

[120] A person who is insane will not be held accountable for his deeds in this life. He will be tested on the Day of Judgement, where his fate will be decided.

worshipped (*Tawḥīd al-Ulūhiyyah*). And it is this understanding that is prevalent amongst most philosophical groups extant today.

Once it is understood that these philosophical groups defined *tawḥīd* to be the Lordship (*Rubūbiyyah*) of Allāh, the reader will then understand why these groups restricted *shirk* to matters of Lordship only. In other words, by restricting *tawḥīd* to only one of its branches, these groups were then forced to restrict their understanding of *shirk* as well. Thus, *shirk* according to them occurs by claiming that there are other creators besides Allāh, or by claiming that an object in and of itself is all-powerful. Directing an act of worship to other than Allāh, according to these groups, would not qualify as *shirk*. It was this understanding of *tawḥīd* that caused these groups, over time, to fall into the grave sin of *shirk*.

The amazing matter is that even the *Jāhilīyyah* Arabs understood the meaning of this phrase, in contrast to these philosophical groups, and that is why they rejected it. So how pitiful is the state of a Muslim when his knowledge and understanding of *Lā ilāha illa Allāh* is less than the knowledge of the *Jāhilīyyah* Arabs whom the Prophet (ﷺ) fought?

إذا عرفت ما ذكرت لك معرفة قلب ، وعرفت الشرك بالله الذي قال الله فيه: ﴿إن الله لا يغفر أن يشرك به ويغفر ما دون ذلك لمن يشاء﴾ (سورة النساء، الآية: ٤٨) وعرفت دين الله الذي. بعث به الرسل من أولهم إلى آخرهم الذي لا يقبل الله من أحد ديناً سواه وعرفت ما أصبح غالب الناس فيه من الجهل بهذا . TEXT

أفادك فائدتين: الأولى الفرح بفضل الله ورحمته كما قال الله تعالى: ﴿قل بفضل الله وبرحمته فبذلك فليفرحوا هو خير مما يجمعون﴾ (سورة يونس، الآية : ٥٨) وأفادك أيضاً الخوف العظيم فإنك إذا عرفت أن الإنسان يكفر بكلمة يخرجها من لسانه وقد يقولها وهو جاهل فلا يعذر بالجهل وقد يقولها وهو يظن أنها تقربه إلى الله كما كان يظن المشركون

So when you know with a certain knowledge three matters:

Firstly: the precise meaning of *shirk*, concerning which Allāh states, "Verily, Allāh does not forgive that *shirk* be performed with Him," [Sūrah *al-Nisā'*; 48]; Secondly: the religion of all of the prophets whom Allāh sent, from the first of them to the last of them, which is the only religion that He will accept from His creation; Thirdly: the fact that most of mankind have become ignorant concerning these facts; then you will benefit in two matters: Firstly: the joy of Allāh's Mercy and His Blessings, as He has stated: "Say: By the

Bounties of Allāh, and His Mercy, then let them rejoice in that..." [Sūrah *Yūnus*; 58] Secondly: a great fear, since if you know that a person may disbelieve due to one statement that comes out of his tongue, and he might even say it while he is ignorant, and this ignorance might not be an excuse for him, or he might say it believing that it brings him closer to Allāh like the disbelievers presumed, then the fear of falling into such disbelief will be severe, and one's eagerness to save himself from it will be strong.

EXPL. Here the author summarises what has preceded in three points, and then reminds the reader that these three point should instill in him two emotions.

The three points are:

1. The precise meaning of *shirk*
2. The fact that all of the prophets, from Adam to Muḥammad, were sent to warn against *shirk*, and to call to *tawḥīd*
3. The reality that most of mankind is unaware of these matters.

As for the precise meaning of *shirk*, the author has proven that it involves giving the rights of Allāh to creation. The most common occurrence of *shirk* is that acts of worship, such as *duʿā* and sacrifice, are directed to created objects. *Shirk* has been in existence since the time of Nūḥ, and it was because of the existence of *shirk* that Allāh sent prophets and messengers, in order to guide mankind from the darkness of *shirk* to the light of *tawḥīd*. Yet, most of mankind was, and remains, heedless to this reality, preferring the temporal pleasures of this world over obedience to Allāh. Even some Muslims have become oblivious to the reality of *tawḥīd*, and have fallen into major acts of *shirk* due to their ignorance in this regard.

If a person realises these matters, he will feel great happiness that Allāh has guided him to this understanding, and preferred him over many others. Every blessing that Allāh bestows upon a person should cause him happiness, so what greater blessing is there than a person truly understanding the meaning of this phrase? It is in fact the realisation and implementation of this phrase which is the very purpose of his creation. Allāh Himself commands believers to rejoice at His Blessings and Mercy, and has mentioned that these blessings are far greater and more precious than all the wealth and material possessions that mankind amasses.

At the same time, this realisation should instill great fear in a person, since he will realise that many people are committing *shirk* without seeing that it is *shirk*. Even the great patriarch Ibrāhīm expressed his great fear of *shirk*, for he prayed to Allāh,

وَٱجْنُبْنِي وَبَنِيَّ أَن نَّعْبُدَ ٱلْأَصْنَامَ ﴿٣٥﴾

> "And save me and my progeny from worshipping idols" [Sūrah *Ibrāhīm*; 35].

One of the scholars of the past commented, "So who is there that can feel safe from (this) tribulation after Ibrāhīm?" In other words, if even the great prophet Ibrāhīm is seeking protection from the evil of *shirk*, then how can one trivialise this great matter? From this, one sees the mistake of many Muslims today who state, "*Tawḥīd* is an easy concept to understand. And *shirk* is not something that Muslims fall into, and I do not feel worried that I can ever commit *shirk*." Such a statement can only emanate from one who is ignorant of the reality and dangers of *shirk*, for even the great prophets feared it. The Qur'ān is replete with dire warnings against *shirk*, and even Allāh's prophets are given a severe warning about this evil:

وَلَقَدْ أُوحِيَ إِلَيْكَ وَإِلَى الَّذِينَ مِن قَبْلِكَ لَئِنْ أَشْرَكْتَ لَيَحْبَطَنَّ عَمَلُكَ وَلَتَكُونَنَّ مِنَ الْخَاسِرِينَ ﴿٦٥﴾

> "And We have indeed inspired you, and (the prophets) before you, that if you commit *shirk*, then all your (good) deeds will be in vain, and you will be amongst the losers" [Sūrah *al-Zumar*; 65].

This verse is addressed to the Prophet Muḥammad (ﷺ) himself – the person who most perfected *tawḥīd* out of all of the Children of Adam. Yet, Allāh warns him, as He warned all the prophets before him, that if he were to fall into *shirk*, then all his good deeds would be of no value, and he would be amongst the losers on the Day of Judgement.

One might well ask: if the Prophet (ﷺ) could never commit *shirk* (as Allāh protected him from all sins), why is the verse addressed to him? By way of answer, this verse is one of the most emphatic verses detailing the dangers and evils of *shirk*. The point of benefit here is for the Muslims to realise that *shirk* is so evil that even if the greatest and most pious man were to fall into it, all of his good deeds would be destroyed, and he would not be successful in the Hereafter. So if this is the case with the leader of the Children of Adam (ﷺ), then what about someone of lesser status?

Ruling Others to be Disbelievers

The last sentence in this paragraph may be problematic for those who are unaware of the author's stance on this issue. In fact, it has been misquoted by many of his opponents. His enemies claim that the author would unconditionally pronounce *takfīr*[121] upon all those who opposed him. They also claimed that he would rule others to be disbelievers even if the evidence had not been established

[121] *Takfīr:* The act of declaring a person to be a disbeliever (*kāfir*).

against them, and they were ignorant of the nature of the acts that they were doing. This, without a doubt, is a clear lie, and can be proven so historically, and from the author's direct writings.

Before discussing this point, the reader must understand the difference between calling a specific *act* an act of disbelief (*kufr*), and calling a specific *person* who performs that act a disbeliever (*kāfir*).

Describing a certain act as *kufr* can be done if the texts of the Qur'ān or Sunnah prove that this specific act is one that entails disbelief. Disbelief (*kufr*) can occur by certain beliefs, statements or actions. An example of a specific belief that necessitates *kufr* is the claim of certain religions that Allāh took a son. An example of a specific statement that entails *kufr* is the act of ridiculing Allāh or His messengers, or any matter of Islām. An example of a specific act that entails *kufr* is prostrating to an idol. These are just some examples of how *kufr* can occur; the point here is that there are many beliefs, statements, and actions that are considered to be *kufr*.

The general rule is that a person who commits an act of *kufr* is a *kāfir*. However, even though this might be the general rule, to apply it to a specific person or situation is not allowed until certain conditions are met and certain impediments removed. This is because it is possible that a person commits an act of kufr, without necessarily becoming a *kāfir*.

Thus, it is permissible to generalise this and claim: "Any person who (for example) prostrates to a grave has committed *kufr* and *shirk*." However, if one sees a specific person prostrating to a grave, it is not permissible to immediately pronounce him a *kāfir* or *mushrik*. In other words, not every act of *kufr* (or *shirk*) makes its performer a *kāfir* (or *mushrik*). There are certain conditions that must be met, and certain impediments removed, before such a ruling can be issued. Of these conditions is that the person be sane and of age, and that he or she realises that this particular act is an act of *kufr*. And of the impediments that must be removed is that he or she not be forced into this act against his or her will. Additionally, such a person must possess his or her full senses, for it is possible at times of extreme happiness, sadness, or anger that a person might do something without being conscious of it. Yet another impediment is that such a person not have some perverted evidence which makes him believe that the act he is doing is in fact a part of religion. [122]

---

[122] It should be noted that not all the conditions or impediments have been listed here. For further details, the reader may research this issue in the classical works of *'aqīdah*, such as *Sharḥ al-'Aqīdah al-Ṭaḥāwiyyah*, and also *Sharḥ Kashf al-Shubuhāt* of Ibn 'Uthaymīn, pps. 42-45.

Going back to our example, if a person is seen prostrating at a grave, it is not permissible for someone to proclaim him a *kāfir* until he questions the person: is he sane and of age? Did he know that he was prostrating at a grave, or was he unaware of its presence? Did he realise that this act is an act of *shirk* that might expel him from the fold of Islām, or was he unaware of it (perhaps because he was new to Islām)? Did anyone force him – through threat of serious physical harm either to himself or to his family – to perform this act? And so on...

The point is that there is a difference between generalising a statement to include a description of an act of *kufr*, and applying that general statement to a specific person. So, one is allowed to say: "Any person who makes a *du'ā* to other than Allāh is a *mushrik* since he has committed *shirk*." However, if one sees a particular person then making a *du'ā* to other than Allāh, it is not permissible for him to immediately pronounce a verdict on this person, until he ensures that the particular conditions have been met, and all impediments removed. Since this matter is one which requires a certain level of knowledge, in general it is not permissible for the lay-Muslim to pronounce *takfīr* on anyone once that person has claimed that he or she is a Muslim.[123] The pronouncing of *takfīr* has very dangerous and severe consequences, and thus should be left to scholars and students of knowledge specialised in those areas. The Prophet (ﷺ) said, "Whoever calls a person a disbeliever (*kāfir*), or claims that he is the enemy of Allāh while that is not the case, will have (his call) returned to him." In another narration, he (ﷺ) said, "If a person performs *takfīr* on his brother, then it will reach one of the two of them."[124] So in these two *aḥādīth*, there is severe warning against calling others *kāfir*.

With this prelude in mind, we return to the statement of the author.

As was mentioned earlier, one of the factors that prevents a person who commits *kufr* from becoming a *kāfir* is that he be ignorant that the act that was committed is an act of *kufr*. In other words, ignorance can be used as an excuse for certain acts.

However, if a person does not know the author's stance in this regard, it is possible to misquote this paragraph in order to falsely accuse him of not taking

[123] Obviously, a person who admits that he is a Christian or Jew (or a follower of any other religion) has himself admitted that he is a *kāfir*, so there is no danger here of claiming he is a *kāfir*. The danger only arises when a person proclaims the testimony of faith and claims that he is a Muslim. The only exception to this rule is when scholars have unanimously agreed that a certain sect is outside the fold of Islām (for example, the Qadianis); in this case, the average Muslim has a right to consider all followers of these sects to be non-Muslims.

[124] Both of these wording are reported by Muslim in his *Ṣaḥīḥ* (1/248).

this excuse into account. This is because the paragraph reads: '...a person may disbelieve due to one statement that comes out of his tongue, and he might even say it while he is ignorant, and this ignorance might not be an excuse for him.'

At first glance, it might appear that the author does not allow ignorance as an excuse. But if one reads the paragraph carefully, this is not the case. The author clearly states that ignorance *might not* be an excuse, and did not say that ignorance is *never* an excuse, and the difference between these two phrases is very clear.

When one researches the author's position in this regard, and reads his other works, it becomes clear that he does indeed take into account that a person might be ignorant of the nature of his deed, and thus be excused. The author – as is the opinion of most of the scholars of *Ahl al-Sunnah* – holds the opinion that those acts of *kufr* which might be widespread, and whose evil not well-known to the lay-Muslim, are matters in which ignorance can be used as an excuse. For example, a person accepts Islām in the land of non-Muslims, and he does not know the details of Islām. It is possible that he might reject something from the Qur'ān or Sunnah, not because he wishes to do so, but because he does not believe that this matter is found in the Qur'ān or Sunnah. For such a person, his ignorance of this matter is an excuse for him which prevents him from becoming a *kāfir*.

On the other hand, there are certain matters in which ignorance cannot be used as an excuse. There are certain actions which every single person knows are actions of *kufr*, and one does not need to know the detailed proofs for such matters in order to realises that they are actions of *kufr*. Examples of such actions are: cursing Allāh, or ridiculing the Messenger (ﷺ), or accusing him (ﷺ) of being a liar. These are actions which every sane person knows cannot be performed by a Muslim (unless he is forced to do so, while in his heart he firmly believes the opposite). In such matters, no one can claim that he or she was ignorant that these actions were actions of *kufr*.

Therefore, the point here is that the author differentiates between those actions which are confusing, and whose nature many people might be unaware of, and those actions which are well-known to everybody to represent *kufr*.

In one of his works, the author writes, "As for the charge that my enemies have accused me of: that I perform *takfīr* merely by association, or that I perform *takfīr* on an ignorant person who has not had the evidences presented to him, then verily this is a fabricated slander."[125] He also wrote, "When a particular person performs an actions which necessitates *kufr*, then he is not accused of

---

[125] *Mu'alafāt al-Shaykh* (3/10).

kufr until the evidence is established against him, such that a person (who rejects this evidence) can then be accused of disbelief. And this is the ruling with regards to matters which are not obvious, so some people might be unaware of the evidences of it (being *kufr*). As for what occurs from such people of action that are clear and apparent, or that which is well-established in religion, then one does not need to stop (to establish the evidences) against the one who does this act."[126]

In yet another work, the author explicitly writes that those Muslims who worship graves cannot be considered disbelievers until the evidence is established against them: "And if we do not pronounce as *kāfirs* those who worship the idols (i.e., the mausoleums) that are present upon the graves of ʿAbd al-Qādir (al-Jīlāni) and Aḥmad al-Badawī, due to their ignorance, and because they do not have people that explain their *shirk* to them, then how can we consider as *kāfirs* those who do not migrate to us, or one who does not consider everyone besides us to be a *kāfir*, or one who does not fight with us? Glorified be Allāh, verily this is an evil slander!"[127]

From these texts and others, it is clear that the author holds the opinion that ignorance can be used as an excuse in matters that lay-Muslims might not be aware of. Even the phrasing of this very paragraph indicates so, for it states, '... that a person *may* disbelieve...', which means that he may possibly disbelieve, and he may possibly not, depending on the specific situation that he is in.

To summarise this section, the author points out the dangers of *shirk*, and of them is that it is possible that a person might fall into *shirk* without even being aware of it. This makes it even more imperative that a person study the types of *shirk* and be able to recognise its various forms.

TEXT

خصوصاً إن ألهمك الله تعالى ما قص عن قوم موسى مع صلاحهم وعلمهم أنهم أتوه قائلين: ﴿اجعل لنا إلها كما لهم آلهة﴾ (سورة الأعراف، الآية : ١٣٨). فحينئذ يعظم خوفك وحرصك على ما يخلصك من هذا وأمثاله

And take heed from the story of the people of Mūsa – if Allāh inspires you to benefit from it – when they came to him, despite their piety and knowledge, and asked him to, "Make for us a god, just like they have a god" [Sūrah *al-Aʿrāf;* 138]. So upon realising this, a person's fear of *shirk* and eagerness to know how to rid himself of it will increase.

EXPL.

Here, the author emphasises the fear that should be in the heart of a Muslim with regard to *shirk*. He gives the example of the people of Mūsa, the Children

[126] *Al-Durrar al-Saniyyah* (8/244).

[127] *Al-Durrar al-Saniyyah* (1/66).

of Israel, whom Allāh blessed over all other nations of their time. Despite their knowledge and piety, they almost fell into the sin of *shirk*. The Qur'ān narrates that they once passed by a nation that was worshipping an idol, so they asked Mūsa: 'Make for us a god, just like they have a god.' So the Children of Israel asked the Prophet of Allāh, who was sent to warn against *shirk*, to make them an idol! And if this is the case with a group of people who accompanied one of Allāh's mighty prophets, then what will be the case of one who has never seen a prophet, much less accompanied one? Should not his fear of falling into *shirk* be far greater?

TEXT

واعلم أن الله سبحانه من حكمته لم يبعث نبياً بهذا التوحيد إلا جعل له أعداء كما قال الله تعالى : ﴿وكذلك جعلنا لكل نبي عدواً شياطين الإنس والجن يوحي بعضهم إلى بعضٍ زخرف القولِ غروراً﴾ (سورة الأنعام ، الآية : ١١٢) .

وقد يكون لأعداء التوحيد علوم كثيرة وكتب وحجج كما قال الله تعالى: ﴿فلما جاءتهم رسلهم بالبينات فرحوا بما عندهم من العلم﴾ (سورة غافر الآية:٨٣)

And realise that Allāh, in His Infinite Wisdom, did not send a prophet with this message of *tawḥīd* except that He made certain people to be enemies of this prophet, as He stated, "And thus We have made for every prophet an enemy – devils from mankind and *jinn*" [Sūrah *al-An'ām*; 112]. And it is possible that these enemies of *tawḥīd* have much knowledge, and evidences and proofs to justify their actions, as Allāh stated: "So when our prophets came to them with clear signs, they rejoiced with what knowledge they had" [Sūrah *Ghāfir*; 83].

EXPL.

It is of the Infinite Wisdom of Allāh that the battle between truth and falsehood continues until the Day of Judgement. And this battle, which will be fought between the people of *tawḥīd* and the people of *shirk*, has great benefits and lessons. Of these benefits is the fact that life in itself is a test for mankind. The whole purpose of this test would become meaningless if there were no falsehood that a person had to repel. In other words, the very existence of such evil and falsehood ensures the existence of righteous people who must battle and repel this evil. So in this battle, the pure and holy is separated from the filth and evil. Another benefit is that the truth becomes even more clear to the people that follow it, as they must defend it with knowledge and evidence, and refute the claims of the enemies of truth.

Shaykh al-Islām Ibn Taymiyyah states, "And of the greatest causes of the victory of *īmān* and the religion, and of the clarification of the reality of the message of the prophets, is the appearance of those who oppose them with clear lies. This is because when the truth is denied and refuted with (false) arguments, Allāh then establishes through it matters which will clarify the truth, and destroy falsehood. These clear signs will clarify the evidences of truth, and elucidate the clear proofs, and demonstrate the falsehood of the evidences that are used to oppose it."[128]

So there has never been a prophet except that he had enemies, from amongst the *jinn* and men. Allāh states in the Qur'ān,

وَكَذَٰلِكَ جَعَلْنَا لِكُلِّ نَبِيٍّ عَدُوًّا
شَيَٰطِينَ ٱلْإِنسِ وَٱلْجِنِّ يُوحِي بَعْضُهُمْ إِلَىٰ بَعْضٍ زُخْرُفَ
ٱلْقَوْلِ غُرُورًا ۚ وَلَوْ شَآءَ رَبُّكَ مَا فَعَلُوهُ ۖ فَذَرْهُمْ وَمَا يَفْتَرُونَ

"And thus We have made for every prophet an enemy – devils from mankind and *jinn*. They inspire one another with beautiful speech, deceiving (people). And if Allāh willed, they would not do it, so leave them and that which they invent" [Sūrah *al-An'ām*; 112].

So these enemies aid one another in concocting arguments, and beautifying their speech, in order to misguide and deceive others.

Waraqah ibn Nawfal, whose story has already been mentioned, also informed the Prophet (ﷺ) of this fact. When Khadījah first brought the Prophet (ﷺ) to him, he said, "O how I wish I were still a young man! How I wish I could be alive when your people expel you!" The Prophet (ﷺ) asked, "Are they going to expel me?" Waraqah replied, "Yes! Never has a man come with what you have come with except that he was shown enmity. And if I am alive when that day comes, I will indeed assist you with a mighty assistance." Waraqah, however, died shortly after this.[129]

These enemies of the truth are not ignorant charlatans. Rather, they are armed with false knowledge, and have concocted many deceitful traps and arguments in order to convince people of their falsehood. So they misinterpret evidences in order to justify their misguided ways, and they refute the truth when it comes to them with false arguments and concocted evidences. And in this process they become leaders to the ignorant masses, who follow every eloquent speaker and dynamic personality. Their situation is similar to the enemies of the prophets before, who, when their messengers came to them, rejoiced in what little knowledge they had, and rejected the pure knowledge of the prophets. Even

---

[128] *Al-Jawāb al-Ṣaḥīḥ* (1/85-86).

[129] *Ṣaḥīḥ al-Bukhārī*, 1/11.

though their knowledge was in reality misguidance, their arrogance made them refuse to recognise the knowledge that the prophets came with. Similarly, callers to falsehood refuse to acknowledge the clear texts of the Qur'ān and Sunnah, and instead search for distorted evidences and manufactured arguments to support their deviations.

Therefore, let no one assume that callers to falsehood from amongst the Muslims are unarmed with texts from the Qur'ān and Sunnah. Rather, as is the case with all enemies of *tawḥīd*, they will have many arguments and evidences that they can present for their beliefs. And it is possible that callers to such misguidance might in fact be considered great scholars, and be well-versed in many Islāmic sciences. Indeed, even those who opposed the mighty prophets have been described by Allāh as having knowledge, so what about those who verbally claim to be *following* the prophets?

So if this is the case, what is the solution?

TEXT

إذا عرفت ذلك ، وعرفت أن الطريق إلى الله لا بد له من أعداء قاعدين عليه، أهل فصاحة وعلم وحجج ، فالواجب عليك أن تتعلم من دين الله ما يصير سلاحاً تقاتل به هؤلاء الشياطين الذين قال إمامهم ومقدمهم لربك –عز وجل– ﴿لأقعدن لهم صراطك المستقيم ثم لآتينهم من بين أيديهم ومن خلفهم وعن أيمانهم وعن شمائلهم ولا تجد أكثرهم شاكرين﴾ (سورة الأعراف، الآيتان : ١٦، ١٧) ولكن إذا أقبلت على الله تعالى وأصغيت إلى حجج الله تعالى وبيناته فلا تخف ولا تحزن ﴿إن كيد الشيطان كان ضعيفاً﴾ (سورة النساء ، الآية : ٧٦) والعامي من الموحدين يغلب الألف من علماء هؤلاء المشركين كما قال تعالى: ﴿وإن جندنا لهم الغالبون﴾ (سورة الصافات، الآية: ١٧٣). فجند الله تعالى هم الغالبون بالحجة واللسان ، كما أنهم الغالبون بالسيف والسنان وإنما الخوف على الموحد الذي يسلك الطريق وليس معه سلاح.

If you realise this, and you realise that the path to the worship of Allāh will always have enemies that will be upon it, who might be people of eloquence, and knowledge, and evidences, then it becomes obligatory to learn enough of Allāh's religion so that this knowledge can become a weapon with which you can fight these *Shayāṭīn*, whose leader and chief (*Iblīs*) said to Allāh: "I will of a surety sit on your Straight Path (to misguide them)" [Sūrah *al-A'rāf*; 16]. But, if you turn with sincerity to Allāh, and apply yourself to learning Allāh's evidences and His explanations, then fear not, nor worry! "Verily, the plot of *Shayṭān* is indeed very weak" [Sūrah *al-Nisā'*; 76]. And indeed, the average unlearned person from the people of *tawḥīd* can overcome a thousand of the

Sunnah. Thus, I cannot accept your interpretation of these verses and *aḥādīth*, and must instead believe in the clear (*muhkam*) texts of the Qur'ān."

This general response is one that can be used to respond to any deviation or innovation that a person might try to prove. All that a Muslim needs to know is the fundamentals of his religion, after which, armed with this basic knowledge, he can refute any evidence or argument thrown at him.

So even an unlearned person, as long as he understands the fundamentals of *tawḥīd* and *shirk*, can easily refute the greatest of scholars of deviation with this simple argument. Whatever point that people of innovation try to prove with their perverted understanding of the Qur'ān and Sunnah, one can always take it back to clear, unequivocal beliefs in order to refute their understanding.

Of these fundamentals that the author has already mentioned are:

1. That the *Jāhilīyyah* Arabs believed in Allāh, and that He created everything, and gives life and death, yet this belief did not cause them to enter into Islām.

2. That the people whom the Prophet was sent to worshipped different objects. Some of them worshipped idols and stones, whereas others worshipped angels and prophets. Yet, the Prophet (ﷺ) did not distinguish between these people, and considered them to be equal in their disbelief.

3. The reason why these people worshiped other objects was that they desired these objects to intercede on their behalves before Allāh. They reasoned that these beings enjoyed a high status and were beloved by Allāh, thus, by pleasing them they would in turn please Allāh. So this was the essence of their *shirk* – that they directed acts of worship to others besides Allāh, in this way hoping to get closer to Allāh.

4. Another fundamental which the author hints at is the very simple fact that the Prophet (ﷺ) was sent to mankind in order that mankind worship Allāh alone. He was not sent so that *he* be worshipped besides Allāh, or that mankind turn to saints and graves in order that they be venerated and asked at times of need. And this simple fundamental refutes all the arguments that the adversaries of *tawḥīd* bring in order to justify saint and prophet-worship.

These matters have been discussed thoroughly, and proven from the texts of the Qur'ān, in the previous sections.

There is yet another general response that can be used in order to outwit those who justify *shirk*. When such an adversay brings any proof from the Qur'ān or authentic Sunnah in order to justify his deeds, one can always ask the simple question: "Was this the understanding of the Companions, and the pious generations after them? Did the great Imāms, Abū Ḥanīfah, Mālik, Shāfiʿī, and Aḥmad ibn Ḥanbal, understand these verses or *aḥādīth* the way that you understand them? If that is not the case, and none of the scholars of the earlier generations claimed what you claim, then how can you put forward something new into this religion that was unknown to the best generations of Islām?"

Thus, with these simple matters, all of which are fundamental to the religion of Islām, one can respond to even the greatest of challenges of those who justify *shirk*.

The author concludes this general response by stating that no one will benefit from it except one whom Allāh has guided. This is because admitting one's ignorance is a very difficult matter for most people. The general response, however, requires one to state: 'I do not know the correct understanding of this evidence that you present.' Therefore, this response requires patience and humility, and necessitates that one put oneself in the position that one deserves. And how few are the people that are blessed with such perfect manners! However, the intelligent person realises that the way to achieve honour and respect is to recognise one's faults and weaknesses and admit to them. It is only the foolish person who believes that he can always convince everyone that he is more knowledgeable than they.

TEXT وأما الجواب المفصل فإن أعداء الله لهم اعتراضات كثيرة على دين الرسل يصدون بها الناس عنه

As for the detailed response, then know that the enemies of Allāh have many criticisms and doubts against the religion of all the prophets, which they use to prevent people from following the Path of Allāh.

EXPL. From this point onwards, the author begins detailing the actual arguments that are used by those who justify acts of *shirk*. He starts by mentioning the three most common tactics that they use.

The author also hints at a very important matter, and that is that a person who wishes to debate with such people must be aware of their evidences and arguments before he enters into such a debate. As for the lay-person, then it is sufficient for him to give the general response above, and then leave off debate. But as for the student of knowledge and the scholar, then it is imperative that he go beyond this basic response, and study the proofs and evidences of his opponents so that he is better prepared to defend the religion of *tawḥīd*.

So the author begins by mentioning the general response (which every single person is qualified to give), and then works his way up by detailing and refuting the explicit evidences used by the adversary. This shows his wisdom and farsightedness, for if someone stopped reading this tract at this point in time, or did not understand any of its detailed responses, then the general response would be sufficient in his daily affairs.

The First Argument

منها: قولهم نحن لا نشرك بالله شيأ ، بل نشهد أنه لا يخلق ولا يرزق ولا ينفع ولا يضر إلا الله وحده لا شريك له ، وأن محمداً صلى الله عليه وسلم لا يملك لنفسه نفعاً ولا ضراً فضلاً عن عبد القادر أو غيره. TEXT

ولكن أنا مذنب ، والصالحون لهم جاه عند الله، وأطلب من الله بهم

> Of these doubts is their saying: "We don't commit *shirk* with Allāh! Rather, we testify that there is no deity or power that creates, or gives sustenance, or benefits anyone or harms anyone except Allāh; He is Alone, having no partners or equals. And we testify that Muḥammad (ﷺ) is not able by himself to cause any benefit or cause any harm, much less the saint ʿAbd al-Qādir, or anyone else besides him. But, even though I testify all this, I realise that I am sinful, and these righteous people have a great status in front of Allāh, so I ask Allāh through them."

This is the most common argument that is presented by those who justify *shirk*. They claim that they testify to the pure and complete Lordship of Allāh, and that only He controls creation. However, they believe that they are too sinful to approach Allāh directly, and therefore they must call out to the prophets and saints in order that their *duʿās* and other aspects of worship be accepted. EXPL.

The meaning of their saying, '...I ask Allāh through them,' is that they ask these objects directly, so that these objects in turn ask Allāh. Alternately, it could mean that they ask them directly without mentioning Allāh at all. An example of the first type is their saying, "O ʿAbd al-Qādir al-Jilani! Request Allāh that He saves me from the distress that I am in!" An example of the second type is their saying, "O Prophet Muḥammad (ﷺ)! Forgive my sins on the Day of Judgement."[133] And both of these examples are blatant types of *shirk*.

This argument can be broken down as follows:

1- Their saying: 'We don't commit *shirk*,' and then affirming *Tawḥīd al-*

---

[133] Asking Allāh by mentioning the status of such people is an evil innovation, and a clear road to *shirk*. This too is common amongst such people, for they state, "O Allāh! I ask you by the status (or the rights) of Muḥammad." Although this type of *duʿā* is not *shirk* in and of itself, it is a stepping-stone to it, and an act that was not practiced by the early generations of Muslims.

Rubūbiyyah. Thus, this shows that their understanding of *tawḥīd* and *shirk* is flawed, for *tawḥīd* is more than just what they have affirmed.

2- Additionally, by negating a matter which they fall into, they prove their own ignorance of what *shirk* actually is. In reality, no Muslim would ever admit that he is falling into *shirk*, so what needs to be examined are a person's actions and beliefs, and not any verbal denial of *shirk*.

3- Their claim that these objects enjoy a high status in the sight of Allāh, which means that any request that they ask of Allāh will of a surety be granted to them.

The author then goes on to refute these points.

TEXT

فجاوبه بما تقدم وهو : أن الذين قاتلهم رسول الله صلى الله عليه وسلم مقرون بما ذكرت لي ، ومقرون أن أوثانهم لا تدبر شيئاً، وإنما أرادوا الجاه والشفاعة واقرأ عليه ما ذكر الله في كتابه ووضحه

So, when he presents this argument to you, respond to him with what has gone before in this tract, and that is that the same people that the Prophet (ﷺ) fought used to acknowledge all that you have mentioned, O negator of truth! And they openly admitted that their idols did not control anything. Rather, they desired from these objects their status in front of Allāh, and their intercession to Allāh on their behalf. And recite to him the verses that Allāh has mentioned in His Book, and explain these verses to him.

EXPL. The detailed response to this has already been given, and that is that the *Jāhilīyyah* Arabs were guilty of the exact same crime as these people are. They too believed in Allāh, and admitted that only He can respond to their *du'ās*. As Allāh states:

قُلْ أَرَءَيْتَكُمْ إِنْ أَتَىٰكُمْ عَذَابُ ٱللَّهِ أَوْ أَتَتْكُمُ ٱلسَّاعَةُ أَغَيْرَ ٱللَّهِ تَدْعُونَ إِن كُنتُمْ صَٰدِقِينَ ﴿٤٠﴾ بَلْ إِيَّاهُ تَدْعُونَ فَيَكْشِفُ مَا تَدْعُونَ إِلَيْهِ إِن شَآءَ وَتَنسَوْنَ مَا تُشْرِكُونَ ﴿٤١﴾

"Say: Tell me, if the punishment of Allāh, or the Day of Judgement, were to come, would you call out to other than Allāh, if you are truthful (in your response)? Nay, rather you would call Him alone, and He would respond to your request if He desires, and (at that point) you will forget those whom you associate with Him" [Sūrah *al-An'ām*; 40-41].

They too admitted that it was Allāh Who created them, and gave them sustenance:

وَلَئِن سَأَلْتَهُم مَّنْ خَلَقَ ٱلسَّمَٰوَٰتِ وَٱلْأَرْضَ وَسَخَّرَ ٱلشَّمْسَ
وَٱلْقَمَرَ لَيَقُولُنَّ ٱللَّهُ ۖ فَأَنَّىٰ يُؤْفَكُونَ ﴿٦١﴾ وَلَئِن سَأَلْتَهُم
مَّن نَّزَّلَ مِنَ ٱلسَّمَآءِ مَآءً فَأَحْيَا بِهِ ٱلْأَرْضَ مِنۢ بَعْدِ مَوْتِهَا
لَيَقُولُنَّ ٱللَّهُ ۚ قُلِ ٱلْحَمْدُ لِلَّهِ ۚ بَلْ أَكْثَرُهُمْ لَا يَعْقِلُونَ ﴿٦٣﴾

"And if you were to ask them: 'Who created the heavens and earth, and subjected the sun and moon?' They would surely respond, 'Allāh.' Then how are they deluded (into worshipping others)?...And if you were to ask them, 'Who sends down rain from the skies, and gives life thereby to the earth after its death?' they would surely respond, 'Allāh.' Say, 'All praise is due to Allāh!' But most of them do not reason" [Sūrah *al-ʿAnkabūt*; 61 and 63].

They too fully believed that their idols could not do anything of themselves, nor did they have any power to benefit or harm them unless Allāh willed:

قُل لِّمَنِ ٱلْأَرْضُ وَمَن فِيهَآ إِن
كُنتُمْ تَعْلَمُونَ ﴿٨٤﴾ سَيَقُولُونَ لِلَّهِ ۚ قُلْ أَفَلَا تَذَكَّرُونَ
﴿٨٥﴾ قُلْ مَن رَّبُّ ٱلسَّمَٰوَٰتِ ٱلسَّبْعِ وَرَبُّ ٱلْعَرْشِ ٱلْعَظِيمِ
﴿٨٦﴾ سَيَقُولُونَ لِلَّهِ ۚ قُلْ أَفَلَا تَتَّقُونَ ﴿٨٧﴾ قُلْ مَنۢ بِيَدِهِۦ
مَلَكُوتُ كُلِّ شَيْءٍ وَهُوَ يُجِيرُ وَلَا يُجَارُ عَلَيْهِ إِن
كُنتُمْ تَعْلَمُونَ ﴿٨٨﴾ سَيَقُولُونَ لِلَّهِ ۚ قُلْ فَأَنَّىٰ تُسْحَرُونَ ﴿٨٩﴾

"Say: To whom belongs the earth and whoever is in it, if you really know? They will respond, 'To Allāh.' Say: 'Then will you not remember?' Say: 'Who is the Lord of the seven heavens, and Lord of the Great Throne?' They will respond, 'Allāh.' Say: 'Then will you not fear Him?' Say: 'In whose hand is the realm (or control) of all things, while He protects, and none can protect against Him, if you should know?' They will respond, 'Allāh.' So say: Then how are you deluded?" [Sūrah *al-Mu'minūn*; 84-89].

Yet, despite all these professions, they were considered pagan idol-worshippers, for the simple reason that they would turn to other objects, and want these objects to intercede on their behalves with Allāh.

So if a person uses this argument, all one needs to do is prove that the *Jāhilīyyah* Arabs believed in Allāh just like this person does, yet they turned to other than Allāh, and thus were considered *mushrikūn*.

Ibn Taymiyyah explains: "Whoever affirms intermediaries between creation and Allāh, similar to the intermediaries that exist between kings and their peoples, is a *mushrik*. Rather, this is the essence of the religions of the pagans and the idol-worshippers. They would justify (their *shirk*) by saying: 'These are figures of prophets and pious people, and these are only *means* that we use to come closer to Allāh.' And this was the *shirk* that Allāh rejected from the Christians as well."[134]

The last point in the initial argument (that these objects enjoy high status with Allāh) is not explicity refuted by the author here. This argument can, however, be refuted in a number of ways:

1. This status does not give them the *right* that Allāh respond to their requests. No object, no matter how noble, has a right over the Creator in any regards. Such a right, if it existed, would contradict the total *Rubūbiyyah* of Allāh over the creation. How can someone whom Allāh created demand something, and expect a response, from Allāh Himself? In fact, even the Prophet (ﷺ), who by consensus is the most noble of all the creation, does not have this right over Allāh. In one ḥadīth, he (ﷺ) said:

    > "I asked my Lord for three things, but He gave me two of them, and prevented me from one. I asked my Lord that my nation not be destroyed by a drought, so He gave it to me. And I asked Him that my nation not perish by drowning, so He gave it to me. And I asked Him that fighting not occur between them, but He did not give it to me."[135]

    So if even the *du'ā* of the Prophet (ﷺ) does not carry this guarantee of an answer, then what is the status of the *du'ā* of someone less than he?

2. Even on the supposition that this right existed, the Qur'ān explicitly mentions that calling out to other than Allāh is *shirk*. Therefore, even if we hypothetically accepted the adversary's premise that these prophets and saints have a *right* over Allāh that their requests be answered, we can respond by stating that Allāh labelled asking these dead prophets and saints as a sin that He will not forgive.

3. Lastly, with regards to these 'saints' that they worship, then in reality there is nothing to prove that a particular person amongst them enjoys a high status in the sight of Allāh (except if the Prophet (ﷺ) himself mentions this, and such a case only occurs with the Companions). In other words, how can you prove that a particular person is in fact a *walī* of Allāh? This is a matter that only Allāh Himself knows.

---

[134] Paraphrased from *Majmū' al-Fatāwa*, 1/134.

[135] Reported by Muslim (# 2890) and others.

The author mentions ʿAbd al-Qādir as an example. His full name is ʿAbd al-Qādir ibn Abī Ṣāliḥ al-Jīlani. He was born in the year 470 AH, and lived most of his life in Baghdad. He was a famous ascetic, who authored a number of works. There are many miracles reported concerning him, although without a doubt most of them are fabrications. He died in 561 AH. Although his works are free from any type of *shirk*, and he himself never asked his followers to worship him, his grave to this day is one of the most famous icons of *shirk* in Islamic lands. He is, without exception, the most famous *Sūfī* 'saint', venerated by millions of Muslims world-wide. The irony of this is that he himself never asked nor called for such veneration; by all historical accounts, he was a pious man, engrossed in worship of Allāh, eager to call others to this worship. And this is how *shirk* typically starts: when people exaggerate the status of righteous people.

The Second Argument

TEXT

فإن قال : إن هؤلاء الآيات نزلت فيمن يعبد الأصنام ، كيف تجعلون الصالحين مثل الأصنام؟ أم كيف تجعلون الأنبياء أصناماً؟

Now, if he responds, "But these verses were revealed regarding people who used to worship idols! How can you compare the pious people that we turn to to idols? And how can you make prophets into idols?"

EXPL.

As soon as one proves the first point – that these people are guilty of what the *Jāhilīyyah* Arabs were guilty of – the immediate response is: "The people that you are talking about worshipped idols; structures made of wood and stone. How dare you compare the Prophet (ﷺ), or ʿAbd al-Qādir (or whoever else is being worshipped) to such filthy idols?"

In this response, the adversary presumes that *shirk* only occurs through idol-worship.

TEXT

فجاوبه بما تقدم.

فإنه إذا أقر أن الكفار يشهدون بالربوبية كلها لله ، وأنهم ما أرادوا ممن قصدوا إلا الشفاعة ، ولكن أراد أن يفرق بين فعلهم وفعله بما ذكر.

فاذكر له أن الكفار منهم من يدعو الأصنام ، ومنهم من يدعو الأولياء الذين قال الله فيهم ﴿ أولئك الذين يدعون يبتغون إلى ربهم الوسيلة أيهم أقرب﴾ (سورة الإسراء ، الآية : ٥٧) . ويدعون عيسى بن مريم وامه وقد قال الله تعالى : ﴿ما المسيح ابن مريم إلا رسول قد خلت من قبله الرسل وأمه صديقة كانا يأكلان الطعام انظر كيف نبين لهم الآيات ثم انظر أنى يؤفكون قل أتعبدون

من دون الله ما لا يملك لكم ضراً ولا نفعاً والله هو السميع العليم﴾ (سورة المائدة ، الآيتان- ٧٦-٧٥).

واذكر له قوله تعالى: ﴿ ويوم يحشرهم جميعاً ثم يقول للملائكة أهؤلاء إياكم كانوا يعبدون قالوا سبحانك أنت ولينا من دونهم بل كانوا يعبدون الجن أكثرهم بهم مؤمنون﴾ (سورة سبأ الآيتان: ٤٠: ٤١)

وقوله تعالى : ﴿وإذ قال الله يا عيسى ابن مريم أأنت قلت للناس اتخذوني وأمي إلهين من دون الله قال سبحانك ما يكون لي أن أقول ما ليس لي بحق إن كنت قلته فقد علمته تعلم ما في نفسي ولا أعلم ما في نفسك إنك أنت علام الغيوب﴾ (سورة المائدة ، الآية: ١١٦)

فقل له : عرفت أن الله كفر من قصد الأصنام ، وكفر أيضاً من قصد الصالحين وقاتلهم رسول الله صلى الله عليه وسلم ؟ .

Then once again respond to him with the knowledge that has already gone before in this tract. And that is because, if he admits that the pagans of old believed in the complete *Rubūbiyyah* of Allāh, and that they only desired by turning to their idols intercession on their behalf, and he desires to differentiate between what they used to do and what he is doing, then show him that amongst the disbelieving pagans were those that worshipped idols and stones, and also others that worshipped pious people. It is concerning these people that were worshipped besides Allāh that Allāh says, "These people are the ones calling out to their Lord, trying to find a means of nearness to Him, which of them will be closer (to Him)..." [Sūrah *al-Isrā'*; 57]. And some of these pagans would worship Jesus the son of Mary, and his mother, even though Allāh says: "Jesus the son of Mary is only a messenger; many are the messengers that have come before him. And his mother was a righteous woman" [Sūrah *al-Mā'idah*; 75]. And remind this person of the statement of Allāh, "And on the Day shall We resurrect them all, then He will say to the angels, 'Did these (people) used to worship you?' They will respond: 'Glory be to you...'" [Sūrah *Saba'*; 40-41]. And remind him also of Allāh's statement, "And when Allāh will ask, 'O Jesus the son of Mary, did you tell the people: take me and my mother as gods besides Allāh?'" [Sūrah *al-Mā'idah*; 116].

So after presenting all of these evidences tell him: "You now realise that Allāh pronounced disbelief upon those people who turned to idols, and He also pronounced disbelief upon those who turned to pious people. And the Prophet (ﷺ) fought all of these people and did not differentiate between them.

The response to this argument is in re-iterating the important concept that *shirk* is not dependant on *who* is worshipped besides Allāh, rather it is dependent on the fact that other than Allāh is being worshipped. So it does not matter whether one worships rocks or stones, or Jesus Christ or Muḥammad (ﷺ). The proofs for this have already been given, and are repeated here as well.

The author writes in his other work *al-Qawāʿid al-Arbaʿah*:

> The Third Principle: That the Prophet (ﷺ) came to a people who had different (objects) of worship: from them are the worshippers of the angels. And from them are the worshippers of the prophets and the pious. And from them are the worshippers of the trees and the stones. And from them are the worshippers of the sun and the moon. But the Messenger of Allāh (ﷺ) fought them all, and did not consider the differences between them.*

So the mere act of turning to other than Allāh entails *shirk*, regardless of the nature of the object. And this does not imply that the Prophet (ﷺ), or any pious person, is equivalent to a rock or a stone, for without a doubt the Prophet (ﷺ) is the most noble of Allāh's creation. The point is that such a comparison is irrelevant when it comes to *shirk* – even if the Prophet (ﷺ) is the best of creation, it does not change the fact that worshipping him is a clear and direct act of *shirk*. So relative comparisons are not given to the objects of worship besides Allāh, but rather to the fact that other than Allāh has been worshipped.

Imām al-San'ānī (d. 1182 A.H.) wrote, "If they ask: 'Are you going to equate those who believe in pious people and graves...to those who believed in idols?' Then I say: Yes! For the exact same acts that the (idol worshippers) were guilty of are also performed by these people, and they are equivalent in them. Rather, they have in fact surpassed them in their beliefs in the (powers) of these people, and their amount of worship that they do to them. So in reality there is no difference between them."[136] And al-Shawkānī (d. 1255 A.H.) wrote: "*Shirk* is to perform to other than Allāh an act than should only be performed to Him, regardless of whether that object is called by names the *Jāhilīyyah* Arabs used – such as idol or statue – or called by another name – such as *walī* or saint or mausoleum."[137]

---

* See: *An Explanation of the Four Principles of Shirk*, (p.25), by Abu Ammaar Yasir Qadhi (Al-Hidaayah Publishing & Distribution, 2002)

[136] Paraphrased from *Tathīr al-ʿItiqād*, p. 23.

[137] Paraphrased from *al-Durr al-Nadīd*, p. 18.

There is another point that must be countered in their argument, and that is their statement that these verses were revealed regarding the pagans of old. By this statement, they seek to imply that it is incorrect to use these verses upon Muslims of today. However, if their logic were taken to its extreme, the entire Qur'ān would then be null and void for our times. This is because the Qur'ān was revealed to a specific people, and catered to specific situations. To claim, then, that these verses should only apply to those situations and peoples nullifies the applicability of the Qur'ān! So a person can say, 'The verses pertaining to praying and fasting were revealed in reference to the Companions, and I do not have to abide by them." The danger of such thinking, then, is clearly manifest.

The point here is to remember that, although the Qur'ān might indeed have been revealed to cater for specific situations and peoples, this does not negate its applicability to other situations and times. The general rule with regards to *Tafsīr* that scholars have agreed upon is, "The ruling of a verse is taken from the generality of its wording, and not from the specificity of its revelation." Thus, although these verses might have been revealed with regards to the practice of the *Jāhilīyyah* Arabs, it is entirely valid to apply them to others who might be guilty of the same crime.

One of the author's descendants wrote in refutation of this concept, "And of the factors that prevent a person from understanding the Qur'ān is that it is presumed that the verses in which Allāh mentions the *mushrikūn*, and describes them and judges them, are specific to them. (So it is believed that these verses) are specific to a nation that has passed before them, eons before, and have disappeared without leaving any inheritors. And perhaps some of them might have read the books of *Tafsīr* stating that a certain verse was revealed regarding idol-worshippers, and another regarding Christians, so the ignoramus presumes that the verse is specific for them, and that the ruling does not apply to any other peoples. And without a doubt this is one of the greatest factors that comes between a person and a correct understanding of the Qur'ān and Sunnah."[138]

The verses that the author quotes revolve around the fact that the people of the Prophet's (ﷺ) time had different objects of worship, and that the Prophet (ﷺ) did not differentiate between these different objects. Whereas it is clearly established that they worshipped idols and statues, some of them used to worship pious people, such as al-Lāt, and others worshipped prophets, such as Jesus. Yet others worshipped angels. So even though all of these noble objects were worshipped at the time of the Prophet (ﷺ), the Prophet (ﷺ) did not exclude them from the ranks of the *mushrikūn*. All such people are guilty of *shirk*, just as those who worship idols and statues.

---

[138] Paraphrased from *Dalā'il al-Rusūkh*, p. 44.

The Qur'ān clearly points out that these objects of worship never called their peoples to worship them. The verse in Sūrah *al-Isrā'* that the author quotes describes the state of these people: "These people are the ones calling out to their Lord, trying to find a means of nearness to Him, which of them will be closer. They desire His Mercy, and fear His Punishment." So these servants of Allāh are constantly busy themselves in worshipping Him. They never asked their nations to exalt them to the status of gods, and on the Day of Judgement they will disown themselves from the very people that worship them. This verse also shows that, since they themselves are eager for the mercy of Allāh and fear His punishment, they are not worthy of being worshipped. They cannot even guarantee their own fate, so how can they help others?

More specifically, Allāh mentions that the angels, pious people and Jesus Christ will all free themselves of this worship that others did in their name.

وَيَوْمَ يَحْشُرُهُمْ جَمِيعًا ثُمَّ يَقُولُ لِلْمَلَٰٓئِكَةِ أَهَٰٓؤُلَآءِ إِيَّاكُمْ كَانُوا۟
يَعْبُدُونَ ﴿٤٠﴾ قَالُوا۟ سُبْحَٰنَكَ أَنتَ وَلِيُّنَا مِن دُونِهِم ۖ بَلْ كَانُوا۟
يَعْبُدُونَ ٱلْجِنَّ ۖ أَكْثَرُهُم بِهِم مُّؤْمِنُونَ ﴿٤١﴾

"And [mention] the Day when He will gather them all, and then say to the angels, 'Did these [people] used to worship you?' They will say, 'Exalted are you! [Rather], you are our Benefactor, not them. Rather, they used to worship the *jinn*; most of them were believers in them" [Sūrah *Saba'*; 40-41].

In this verse, Allāh mentions that He will question the angels on the Day of Judgement concerning those people that used to worship them. The angels will respond that they did not command these people to worship them, and that Allāh is their real protector. This verse also points out that most of the objects worshiped besides Allāh are occupied by evil *jinn* who deceive their worshippers.

In the other verses quoted by the author, Allāh mentions that Jesus Christ will free himself from those who worshipped him, for he will respond, after Allāh asks him,

سُبْحَٰنَكَ مَا يَكُونُ لِىٓ أَنْ
أَقُولَ مَا لَيْسَ لِى بِحَقٍّ ۚ إِن كُنتُ قُلْتُهُۥ فَقَدْ عَلِمْتَهُۥ ۚ تَعْلَمُ مَا فِى
نَفْسِى وَلَآ أَعْلَمُ مَا فِى نَفْسِكَ ۚ إِنَّكَ أَنتَ عَلَّٰمُ ٱلْغُيُوبِ ﴿١١٦﴾ مَا
قُلْتُ لَهُمْ إِلَّا مَآ أَمَرْتَنِى بِهِۦٓ أَنِ ٱعْبُدُوا۟ ٱللَّهَ رَبِّى وَرَبَّكُمْ ۚ وَكُنتُ
عَلَيْهِمْ شَهِيدًا مَّا دُمْتُ فِيهِمْ ۖ

> "Exalted are you! It was not [proper] for me to say something which I had no right to say. If I had said it, you would indeed have been aware of it; for you know what is in myself, and I do not know what is in yourself. You are the All-Knowledgeable, All-Wise. I only told them what You commanded me to tell them: 'Worship Allāh, my Lord and your Lord.' And I was a witness over them when I was present amongst them" [Sūrah *al-Mā'idah*; 116-117].

So even these objects of worship will, on the Day of Judgement, be enemies to the very people who worshipped them!

وَمَنْ أَضَلُّ مِمَّن يَدْعُوا مِن دُونِ اللَّهِ مَن
لَّا يَسْتَجِيبُ لَهُۥٓ إِلَىٰ يَوْمِ الْقِيَـٰمَةِ وَهُمْ عَن دُعَآئِهِمْ غَـٰفِلُونَ ﴿٥﴾
وَإِذَا حُشِرَ النَّاسُ كَانُوا لَهُمْ أَعْدَآءً وَكَانُوا بِعِبَادَتِهِمْ كَـٰفِرِينَ ﴿٦﴾

> "And who is more astray than he who invokes besides Allāh those who will not respond to him until the Day of Resurrection; and they are (even) unaware of their invocations. And when the people are gathered (on that Day), they will be enemies to them, and will disown their worship of them" [Sūrah *al-Aḥqāf*; 5-6].

Allāh describes that these objects of worship do not even hear the call of those who call out to them; and even if they could hear, they would not have the power to help them; and, finally, on the Day of Judgement, they will turn against their worshippers, and disown the worship that was directed to them.

In one of the most explicit verses in the Qur'ān which describes these beings that are worshipped besides Allāh, Allāh states,

وَالَّذِينَ
تَدْعُونَ مِن دُونِهِۦ مَا يَمْلِكُونَ مِن قِطْمِيرٍ ﴿١٣﴾ إِن
تَدْعُوهُمْ لَا يَسْمَعُوا دُعَآءَكُمْ وَلَوْ سَمِعُوا مَا اسْتَجَابُوا لَكُمْ ۖ
وَيَوْمَ الْقِيَـٰمَةِ يَكْفُرُونَ بِشِرْكِكُمْ ۚ وَلَا يُنَبِّئُكَ مِثْلُ خَبِيرٍ

> "Those whom you call out to besides Him do not (even) possess the membrane of a date-seed. If you call out to them, they do not hear your supplication; and if they (were to) hear, they would not respond to you; and, on the Day of Resurrection they will deny your *shirk* (to them); and no one can inform you [better] than the All-Knowledgeable" [Sūrah *Fāṭir*; 13].

The Third Argument

TEXT فإن قال: الكفار يريدون منهم وأنا أشهد أن الله هو النافع الضار المدبر لا أريد إلا منه ، والصالحون ليس لهم من الأمر شيء ولكن أقصدهم أرجو من الله شفاعتهم.

Now, it is possible that he will respond, "But the disbelievers actually intended from these objects benefit or help. As for me, then I testify that only Allāh is the One Who gives benefit and has the power to harm, the One Who controls all affairs. I only desire help from Him, and I fully realise that these pious people don't control anything. But I turn to them, hoping that their intercession will be accepted by Allāh."

EXPL. The essence of this argument is their claim that the pagan Arabs intended to worship these idols, believing that these idols could, in and of themselves, benefit them or save them from some harm. As for the act that they themselves do by turning to saints and prophets, they do not intend to *worship* them, for they realise that these saints and prophets do not have any independent power. Rather, they only desire that Allāh accept their *du'ā* through these pious saints, since these saints have a far higher status in the sight of Allāh than they themselves have.

TEXT فالجواب: أن هذا قول الكفار سواء بسواء وأقرأ عليه قوله تعالى: ﴿والذين اتخذوا من دونه أولياء ما نعبدهم إلا ليقربونا إلى الله زلفى﴾ (سورة الزمر ، الآية: ٣) وقوله تعالى : ﴿ويقولون هؤلاء شفعاؤنا عند الله﴾ (سورة يونس، الآية: ١٨).

So the response to this excuse is to say: This is exactly the excuse of the pagan Arabs of old – word for word. And the proof for this is when you recite to him the verse, "And those that have taken protectors besides Him (say): We only worship them to come closer to Allāh" [Sūrah *al-Zumar*; 3]. And recite to them also the verse, "And they say that these (idols) are our intercessors in front of Allāh." [Sūrah *Yūnus*; 18].

EXPL. In these two verses, Allāh mentions that the reason the pagan Arabs worshiped idols was so that these idols could act as intermediaries between them and Allāh. The *mushrikūn* of old felt themselves too sinful to approach Allāh directly, thus they would call out to other beings in the hope that these objects would then intercede with Allāh on their behalf. So the ultimate goal of the *Jāhilīyyah* Arabs was to please Allāh, and not to please their idols.

Similarly, the Muslims of our times who turn to saints and prophets have the exact same frame of mind as the *Jāhilīyyah* Arabs did. They do not intend to direct their worship to these saints and prophets, but rather to reach Allāh through them. And this is the exact excuse of the pagans of old. Both the pagans of old, and the *mushrikūn* of our own time, acknowledge that Allāh controls everything, and that these intermediaries do not of themselves have any power. Yet, both groups felt the need to reach Allāh through them, deeming themselves too sinful to approach Allāh directly.

It must also be pointed out that this excuse in reality does not hold any weight, for the simple reason that these intermediaries become gods (*ilāh*) besides Allāh. When a person turns to dead saints and prophets, his heart becomes attached to this created being; he desires to please him, and is fearful of his rejection. He hopes the best from such a person, and asks him for all his needs. So you find that, when he approaches such an object, his heart is full of humility, his bearing one of humbleness. And all of these matters proves beyond a shadow of doubt that he has in fact taken this saint or prophet as an *ilāh* (object of worship) besides Allah, for what else is worship than such veneration and humility?

TEXT واعلم : أن هذه الشبه الثلاث هي أكبر ما عندهم ، فإذا عرفت أن الله وضحها في كتابه وفهمتها فهماً جيداً فما بعدها أيسر منها.

And know that these three doubts and arguments that they have are the greatest evidences that they possess. So if you realise that Allāh has already made the futility of these doubts clear in His Book, and you have understood this well, then what follows is easier to understand and refute than what has preceded.

EXPL. So these three arguments are the crux of their evidences. This is well-known to all who have tried to convince such people of their actions. Once a person understands these points, and is able to explain them to his adversary with evidences from the Qur'ān, then the remaining points are easier.

The author now mentions other arguments, not as common as the three above, and goes on to detail their refutations as well.

The Fourth Argument

TEXT فإن قال: أنا لا أعبد إلا الله ، وهذا الإلتجاء إلى الصالحين ودعاؤهم ليس بعبادة.

فقل له: أنت تقر أن الله فرض عليك إخلاص العبادة وهو حقه عليك ، فإذا قال نعم فقل له: بين لي هذا الذي فرضه الله عليك وهو إخلاص العبادة لله وهو حقه عليك، فإنه لا يعرف العبادة ولا أنواعها.

> Now, if he says, "I only worship Allāh. But this turning that I do to these pious people and saints, and my calling upon them for my needs is not considered worship!" then respond to him as follows:
>
> "Do you agree that Allāh has made it obligatory for you to single Him out in worship (*Ikhlāṣ*), and that this worship is His sole right, and thus cannot be directed to any other object?"
>
> So when he responds, "Yes," then ask him: "Explain to me this concept that Allāh has made obligatory on you, meaning this sincerity that you must have to Him in your worship, and which is His sole right."
>
> Then you will see that he does not know the meaning of worship (*ʿibādah*) nor is he familiar with its categories.

This argument involves denial of worshipping other than Allāh. No Muslim, no matter how deviated in his ways, will admit that he worships other than Allāh. The fact that only Allāh deserves to be worshipped is an agreed upon principle by all Muslims. EXPL.

However, the fact of the matter is that many people are unaware of the meaning of the term worship, or *ʿibādah*. Because of this ignorance it is commonplace to see people committing *shirk* state, 'Turning to other objects, such as pious saints, and depending on them, and having one's heart attached to them, is not considered worship.'

In reality, what he has just described is the *essence* of worship! Ibn Kathīr defined worship, or *ʿibādah*, as: "... a state which combines the perfection of love, submission, and fear."[139] In other words, whenever a person feels in his heart the love of an object, combined with humbleness, humility, submission, and fear of rejection, and these feelings have been perfected (meaning that they exist in an intense and acute state), then in reality he worships that object.

One can also define *ʿibādah* from the perspective of what the worshipper must do. Ibn Taymiyyah defined *ʿibādah* to be: 'A comprehensive term, encompassing all apparent and hidden acts and statements that are beloved by Allāh.'[140]

In other words, *ʿibādah* can be defined as a *state* that the worshipper is expected to be in (and that is the definition given by Ibn Kathīr and others), and it can also be defined by the *actions* which are expected from him (and that is the definition given by Ibn Taymiyyah and others). This second definition is based on what the worshipper is expected to do. Thus, every single matter that Allāh loves can be considered an act of worship, for it brings a servant closer to Allāh.

---

[139] *Tafsīr Ibn Kathīr* 1/25.

[140] *Majmūʿ al-Fatāwa* 10/149.

The author now details certain types of worship in order to illustrate this point.

TEXT فبينها له بقولك قال الله تعالى: ﴿ادعوا ربكم تضرعاً وخفية ، إنه لا يحب المعتدين﴾ (سورة الأعراف، الآية: ٥٥) فإذا أعلمته بهذا ، فقل له: هل علمت هذا عبادة لله فلا بد أن يقول نعم ، والدعاء من العبادة .

فقل له إذا أقررت أنها عبادة ، ودعوت الله ليلاً ونهاراً ، خوفاً وطمعاً ، ثم دعوت في تلك الحاجة نبياً أو غيره هل أشركت في عبادة الله غيره؟ فلابد أن يقول: نعم

Now that he has shown his ignorance, you explain it to him by quoting the verse in which Allāh says, "Call upon your Lord in humility and fear" [Sūrah *al-A'rāf;* 55]. Once you have explained this verse to him, ask him, "Is this calling and *du'ā* a type of worship to Allāh?"

Then he must of a surety respond: "Yes! *Du'ā* is a type of worship."

So ask him, "If you admit that this *du'ā* is an act of worship, and you called upon Allāh, day and night, in fear of having your *du'ā* rejected and hopeful of a response from Him, but then at the same time called upon a prophet, or other than a prophet, to respond to the request that you made to Allah – did you by this action commit *shirk* with Allāh?"

Then he must of a surety respond, "Yes."

EXPL. *Du'ā* is one of the greatest and most noble acts of worship. Allāh says:

وَقَالَ رَبُّكُمُ ادْعُونِي أَسْتَجِبْ لَكُمْ ۚ إِنَّ الَّذِينَ يَسْتَكْبِرُونَ عَنْ عِبَادَتِي سَيَدْخُلُونَ جَهَنَّمَ دَاخِرِينَ ﴿٦٠﴾

"Verily, your Lord has said: 'Call upon Me, and I will answer you!' Those who are (too) arrogant to worship Allāh will enter Hell, humiliated!" [Sūrah *Ghāfir*; 60].

In this verse, Allāh has commanded us to ask Him and petition Him, and considered those who do not ask Him among those who are too arrogant to worship Allāh. From this, it is understood that *du'ā* is an act of worship, and this meaning has been explicitly stated by the Prophet (ﷺ). Nu'mān ibn Bashīr reports that the Prophet (ﷺ) said,

"*Du'ā* is worship."

He (ﷺ) then recited the verse,

> "Verily, your Lord has said: "Call upon me, and I will answer you!" Those who are (too) arrogant to worship Allāh will enter Hell, humiliated!"[141]

Therefore, *du'ā* is a type of worship; rather, it is among the greatest acts of worship, and one of the best ways to bring a worshipper closer to Allāh, all Glory and Praise be to Him. In this verse, Allāh equates *du'ā* with worship, for He commanded His servants to make *du'ā* to Him, and then stated that whoever is too arrogant to *worship* Him will enter the Fire of Hell. So from this it is understood that the worship referred to in this verse actually means *du'ā*.

In another verse, Allāh calls *du'ā* the *Dīn*, or the entire religion, for He says,

هُوَ ٱلْحَيُّ لَآ إِلَٰهَ إِلَّا هُوَ فَٱدْعُوهُ
مُخْلِصِينَ لَهُ ٱلدِّينَ ۗ ٱلْحَمْدُ لِلَّهِ رَبِّ ٱلْعَٰلَمِينَ ﴿٦٥﴾

> "He is the *Hayy* (Ever-Living), there is no deity except Him. So make *du'ā* to Him, to Him is the *Dīn* [Sūrah *Ghāfir*; 65]."

And there is no other act that has been equated or paralleled with the entire *Dīn*, or connected to the entire concept of worship (*'ibādah*).[142]

So once the author proves that *du'ā* is in fact a type of worship – in fact, the essence of worship – he then proceeds to prove that this automatically implies that making *du'ā* to other than Allāh would be *shirk*. Once a person understands that *du'ā* is an act of worship, a natural consequence of this understanding is the realisation that directing this act of worship to other than Allāh is an act of *shirk*.

Therefore, any person who calls out to an object, dead or alive, and makes *du'ā* directly to that object, has committed major *shirk* concerning which there is no difference of opinion amongst the scholars of *Ahl al-Sunnah*.[143]

---

[141] This ḥadīth is authentic, and is reported by Aḥmad and the four Sunans, and others, from Nu'mān ibn Bashīr, as reported in *Ṣaḥīḥ al-Jāmi'* # 3407.

[142] These paragraphs have been taken from the author's work *Du'ā: The Weapon of the Believer* (Al-Hidaayah Publishing & Distribution, Birmingham, 2001 CE). For more details on this topic, the reader is referred to this work.

[143] One must differentiate between making *du'ā to* an object (which is major *shirk* without any exceptions) and making *du'ā through* an object (which might be major *shirk* or might not be). Making *du'ā to* an object is done by asking that object directly for a matter that is clearly in Allāh's power . To ask a dead saint to bless one with a child, or to ask the Prophet (ﷺ) to forgive one's sins, are clear acts of major *shirk*. However, to make a *du'ā through* a person is of many different types and categories. Some of these categories are major *shirk* (such as asking a dead person who is buried in a distant place to pray to Allāh on one's behalf), and others are evil innovations, or *bid'ahs*, which might not be major *shirk* of themselves, but lead to major *shirk* (such as asking Allāh by the right of the Prophet (ﷺ), or by the blessings of the Prophet (ﷺ)).

The author mentions *du'ā* as an example since *du'ā* is the most common act that is diverted to other than Allāh.

A point of benefit here is that the wisdom of the author is shown in the manner through which he proves that *shirk* can occur in one's *du'ā*. By first proving that a person who makes *du'ā* to Allāh acknowledges that this *du'ā* is an act of worship, the author then forces this person to admit that directing this act of worship to other than Allāh must be *shirk*. Had he started off the argument by simply stating, "*Du'ā* to other beings is *shirk*," his adversary would have disagreed, and become argumentative.

TEXT فقل له : قال الله تعالى: ﴿فصل لربك وأنحر﴾ وأطعت الله ونحرت له ، هل هذا عبادة؟ فلابد أن يقول: نعم. فقل له إذا نحرت لمخلوق نبي أو جني أو غيرهما هل أشركت في هذه العبادة غير الله فلابد أن يقر ويقول : نعم

> Then move on to another example and quote him the verse, "So pray to your Lord, and sacrifice (only to Him)" [Sūrah *al-Kawthar*; 2].
>
> Now ask him "If you obey Allāh, and sacrifice an animal to Him using His name, is this an act of worship?"
>
> Then of a surety he must respond: "Yes!"
>
> So ask him, "Then if you sacrifice to a created object, whether a prophet or a *jinnī* or anything else, would you not have committed *shirk* in this act of worship, by directing it to other than Allāh?"
>
> Then of a surety he must respond, "Yes."

EXPL. Here the author mentions another of the most common acts of worship that is directed to other than Allāh, and that is the act of sacrificing animals.

Since Allāh is the Creator of all animals, it is necessary to mention Allāh's Name at the time of sacrificing any animal in order for that animal to be considered permissible food. If Allāh's Name is not mentioned, then the meat of such an animal is not considered lawful. Allāh states,

وَلَا تَأْكُلُوا مِمَّا لَمْ يُذْكَرِ اسْمُ اللَّهِ عَلَيْهِ وَإِنَّهُ لَفِسْقٌ

> "And do not eat of that upon which the name of Allāh has not been mentioned, for indeed, it is a grave disobedience" [Sūrah *al-An'ām*; 121].

Therefore, mentioning Allāh's name at the time of sacrifice is an act of worship. Any person who sacrifices an animal to Allāh must admit that the only reason he is doing so is to achieve Allāh's pleasure. Thus, by admitting that he seeks to please Allāh by this act, he must also admit that directing this act of worship to other than Allāh (by mentioning the name of a created object instead) is pure *shirk*. Yet, this too is a very common occurrence that is performed by some who profess Islām. At every mausoleum, it is common to see people sacrificing to the inhabitants of the grave, in the name of 'pious saints' or prophets. Such pagan practices are clear manifestations of *shirk*, and have nothing to do with the religion of the Prophet (ﷺ).

By proving that sacrifice is an act that is due to Allāh, the author proves that sacrificing to other than Allāh must be *shirk*.

TEXT

وقل له أيضا : المشركون الذين نزل فيهم القرآن ، هل كانوا يعبدون الملائكة والصالحين واللات وغير ذلك؟ فلا بد أن يقول : نعم ،

Now ask him, "The pagan Arabs that the Qur'ān refers to and the Prophet (ﷺ) was sent amongst, did they not worship angels, and pious people, and al-Lāt, and other objects?"

Then he must respond, "Yes."

EXPL.

After proving that *shirk* occurs by directing acts of worship, such as *du'ā* and sacrifice, to other than Allāh, the author then demonstrates that this was exactly the *shirk* of the *Jāhilīyyah* Arabs.

TEXT

فقل له : وهل كانت عبادتهم إياهم إلا في الدعاء والذبح والإلتجاء ونحو ذلك، وإلا فهم مقرون أنهم عبيده وتحت قهره ، وأن الله ، هو الذي يدبر الأمر، ولكن دعوهم والتجؤوا إليهم للجاه والشفاعة ، وهذا ظاهر جداً.

So ask him, "And what else was their worship of them except in their *du'ā*, and sacrifice, and turning towards them to seek help, and other such acts? For verily they used to admit that these objects of worship were servants of Allāh, and under His control, and that only Allāh controls all matters. So they would only turn to them and make *du'ā* to them due to their status in the sight of Allāh and to achieve their intercession. And all of this is very obvious to understand.

EXPL.

In other words, what was the *shirk* that the *Jāhilīyyah* Arabs were guilty of other than directing such acts of worship to saints and angels? And if this is the case, then what is the difference between you – O worshipper of saints and prophets – and the pagans of old? For both of you admit the complete Lordship of Allāh, and yet turn to intermediaries for your needs, justifying this by claiming that such intermediaries hold high positions in Allāh's sight.

Thus, the author methodically extracts the truth from his opponent, and shows his superior powers of reasoning. In this conversation, the adversary proves himself incorrect by his own testimonies.

So here the reader benefits, not only in the knowledge of the evidences of the Qur'ān and Sunnah, but also in the knowledge of reasoning with an adversary, and the methods of showing him to be incorrect. By acting like a wise teacher instead of a harsh enemy, the author shows that kindness and gentleness are essential requirements in order to win such arguments.

The Fifth Argument

TEXT

فإن قال: أتنكر شفاعة رسول الله صلى الله عليه وسلم وتبرأ منها؟ فقل: لا أنكرها ولا أتبرأ منها ، بل هو صلى الله عليه وسلم الشافع المشفع وأرجو شفاعته ، ولكن الشفاعة كلها لله ، كما قال الله تعالى: ﴿قل لله الشفاعة جميعاً﴾ (سورة الزمر، الآية: ٤٤).

ولا تكون إلا بعد إذن الله كما قال-تعالى-﴿من ذا الذي يشفع عنده إلا بإذنه﴾ (سورة البقرة، الآية : ٢٥٥) ولا يشفع في أحدٍ إلا بعد أن يأذن الله فيه كما قال-عز وجل- ﴿ولا يشفعون إلا لمن ارتضى﴾ (سورة الأنبياء ، الآية: ٢٨). وهو لا يرضى إلا التوحيد كما قال : ﴿ومن يبتغ غير الإسلام ديناً فلن يقبل منه﴾ (سورة آل عمران ، الآية ٨٥)

فإذا كانت الشفاعة كلها لله ، ولا تكون إلا بعد إذنه ، ولا يشفع النبي صلى الله عليه وسلم ولا غيره في أحد حتى يأذن الله فيه ، ولا يأذن إلا لأهل التوحيد تبين لك أن الشفاعة كلها لله فأطلبها منه، فأقول اللهم لا تحرمني شفاعته، اللهم شفعه في ، وأمثال هذا.

Now, if he argues with you and says, "Do you deny the intercession of the Prophet (ﷺ), and free yourself from it?" Then respond to him, "I do not deny it, nor free myself from it. Rather, he (ﷺ) is the intercessor, and the one whose intercession will be accepted. And I pray that I too will be able to attain his intercession. But the right of intercession belongs solely to Allāh, as He says: "Say: To Allāh belongs intercession, all of it" [Sūrah *al-Zumar*; 44]. And so it will not occur except after Allāh permits it to occur, as He states, "Who is there that can intercede, except with His permission?" [Sūrah *al-Baqarah*; 255]. And the Prophet (ﷺ) will not intercede on behalf of anyone until Allāh allows such intercession on his behalf, as He states, "And they will not intercede except on (behalf of those) whom He is pleased with" [Sūrah *al-Anbiyā'*; 28]. And Allāh will never be pleased except with a person upon *tawḥīd*, as He states, "So whoever desires as a religion other than Islām, it will never be accepted from him" [Sūrah *Āl-ʿImrān*; 85]. So if the right of intercession belongs only to Allāh, and will only take place after He allows it, and neither the Prophet (ﷺ) nor anyone else will intercede unless Allāh allows them to intercede on his behalf, and Allāh will not allow this intercession except for the people of *tawḥīd*, then it is clear that the whole concept of intercession belongs to Allāh. Therefore I will ask Him for it, so I say: 'O Allāh! Do not prohibit me from his (ﷺ) intercession. O Allāh! Cause him (ﷺ) to intercede for me.' And I make similar *du'ās*, in this fashion.

Here the adversary brings in another argument, and that is the concept of intercession, or *shafā'ah*. This is one of the most common arguments invoked by practitioners of *shirk*, for it was invoked by the *Jāhilīyyah* Arabs of old, and is invoked by the pagans of today. EXPL.

It therefore behooves the student of knowledge to understand the concept of intercession in Islām, so that he is aware of the correct understanding of this important chapter.

Intercession is the act of asking an intermediary to plead one's request in front of another person or diety. With regards to worldly intercession, its permissibility or impermissibility revolves around the matter concerning which intercession is sought. Thus, a person might go to an influential individual, and seek to redress some wrong done to him by asking him to take his petition to the ruler. Likewise, a person might desire a certain job which he is qualified for, and ask an influential person to intercede on his behalf with the employer. If the matter is good and noble, and the person befitting of such intercession, then the intercession will be rewarded by Allāh. On the other hand, if it is concerning a matter which is prohibited, or on behalf of one who is not worthy of such intercession, then such intercession is sinful. Intercession in matters of this world involves asking an intermediary to plead one's request in front of a third party.

Religious intercession, on the other hand, is a different matter. Religious intercession involves asking others for a matter which only Allāh has the right to be asked for. Thus, asking a dead saint, or a person not able to hear you, to ask Allāh to bless you with a child is an example of religious intercession.[144]

All such religious intercession is Allāh's sole right, as proven in the verse quoted by the author:

قُل لِّلَّهِ ٱلشَّفَٰعَةُ جَمِيعًا

"Say: To Allāh belongs intercession, all of it" [Sūrah *al-Zumar*; 44].

No one can intercede with Allāh unless and until Allāh gives him permission to do so. Additionally, even if Allāh allows a particular person or angel to

[144] It is permissible to ask a living person who is believed to be more pious to make a *du'ā* to Allāh on one's behalf, provided that one does not totally rely on that person's *du'ā*. For further details, see the relevant chapter in the author's work: *Du'ā: The Weapon of the Believer* (Al-Hidaayah Publishing & Distribution, 2001 CE).

intercede on another person's behalf, it is not obligatory upon Allāh to accept the intercession. Rather, Allāh will only accept intercession on a person's behalf if He is pleased with that person. These are the two conditions that are clearly mentioned in the Qur'ān in order for any intercession to be accepted by Allāh.

These two conditions are mentioned in a number of verses in the Qur'ān. In the Verse of the Throne, Allāh asks:

مَن ذَا ٱلَّذِى يَشْفَعُ عِندَهُۥٓ إِلَّا بِإِذْنِهِۦ

> "Who is there than can intercede in front of Him, except with His permission?" [Sūrah *al-Baqarah*; 255].

And Allāh also states,

يَوْمَئِذٍ لَّا تَنفَعُ ٱلشَّفَٰعَةُ إِلَّا مَنْ أَذِنَ لَهُ ٱلرَّحْمَٰنُ وَرَضِىَ لَهُۥ قَوْلًا

> "On that Day, no intercession will be of any benefit, except whom the Ever-Merciful has given permission, and has accepted his speech" [Sūrah *Ṭā Hā*; 109].

Thus, Allāh must give permission to anyone who intercedes in order for that intercession to be of any value. Additionally, even if Allāh gives such permission, it is not obligatory upon Allāh to accept such a person's intercession. Rather, Allāh will only accept intercession on behalf of one whom He is pleased with in the first place:

وَلَا يَشْفَعُونَ إِلَّا لِمَنِ ٱرْتَضَىٰ

> "And they cannot intercede except on behalf of one whom He approves" [Sūrah *al-Anbiyā'*; 28].

One verse which combines both of these conditions is:

وَكَم مِّن مَّلَكٍ فِى ٱلسَّمَٰوَٰتِ لَا تُغْنِى
شَفَٰعَتُهُمْ شَيْـًٔا إِلَّا مِنۢ بَعْدِ أَن يَأْذَنَ ٱللَّهُ لِمَن يَشَآءُ وَيَرْضَىٰٓ ﴿٢٦﴾

> "And there are many angels in the Heavens, whose intercession will be of no use whatsoever, except after Allāh grants permission to whomever He wills, and is pleased" [Sūrah *al-Najm*; 26].

So even the obedient, sinless angels in the Heavens cannot intercede unless Allāh grants them permission to do so, and even after this, their intercession will not be accepted, unless Allāh is pleased with the person on whose behalf intercession is sought.

One might ask: what is the point of intercession, when Allāh will decide who intercedes, and He must be pleased with the one on whose behalf intercession is sought? The response is that this fact shows Allāh's supreme power and control over His creation. It is not befitting that a created object have the *right* to intercede with Allāh, or to intercede on someone's behalf. Such a right – if it existed – would go against Allāh's authority and complete *Rubūbiyyah*.[145] Rather, *shafā' ah* is a means of honouring some people, by *allowing* them to intercede on behalf of others, and it is a means of showing mercy to others, by *allowing* certain people to intercede on their behalf.

Therefore, when one understands that the *shafā' ah* is totally dependent on Allāh, one sees the futility of asking someone else to intercede on his behalf in front of Allāh.

Without a doubt, the Prophet (ﷺ) has the greatest honour on the Day of Judgement with regards to *shafā' ah*. He will intercede on behalf of his entire nation on the Day of Judgement. But even this intercession is asked *from Allāh*, and not from the Prophet (ﷺ) himself! It is because of this that, after the call to prayer (*Adhān*), the Muslim makes a *du' ā* to Allāh, "O Allāh! The Lord of this Perfect Call, and the Established Prayer! Grant Muḥammad the *Waṣīlah* (a station in Paradise) and the Highest Rank of Paradise! And raise him to the Praised Station (*al-Maqām al-Maḥmūd* - i.e., the permission to intercede on the Day of Judgement) that You have promised him, for verily You do not break your promise." The Prophet (ﷺ) stated,

> "Whoever says, after the *adhān*, (...the above *du' ā*...), then my intercession will become obligatory for him on the Day of Judgement."[146]

So the Prophet (ﷺ) asked his *ummah* to pray to Allāh to grant him this Station, and whoever does so sincerely will be blest to attain this intercession.

The point that the author proves is that this *du' ā* is asked *of Allāh*, and not *of the Prophet* (ﷺ)! Likewise, the Companions, who were the most knowledgeable of this nation, never asked the Prophet (ﷺ) after his death to intercede for them, since they knew that after the Prophet's (ﷺ) death, it is not possible to request him to do anything. If this is the case with the Prophet (ﷺ), then what is the status of any pious saint in comparison?

The Prophet (ﷺ) himself pointed out the best way that a person can strive to ensure that he be granted his *shafā' ah* on the Day of Judgement. Abū Hurayrah asked him, "O Messenger of Allāh, who will have the greatest chance to gain your intercession on the Day of Judgement?" The Prophet (ﷺ) replied,

---

[145] Even the Prophet (ﷺ) could not intercede on behalf of his uncle Abū Ṭālib that Allāh save him from the Fire. Likewise, the Qur'ān mentions that the Prophet Nūḥ interceded on behalf of his son that Allāh save him from the flood, but Allāh did not accept this intercession, and reprimanded Nūḥ for asking, since his son was one whom Allāh was not pleased with (see Sūrah *Hūd*; 46-47).

[146] Reported by al-Bukhārī 1/152.

"The one who will have the greatest chance to be granted my *shafā'ah* is he who says: *Lā ilāha illa Allāh*, sincerely from his heart."[147]

In this ḥadīth, the Prophet (ﷺ) outlined, in clear and explicit terms, that the best way to gain his *shafā'ah* is by practicing *tawḥīd*, which entails leaving *shirk* in all its forms. For the one who states this *kalimah* sincerely from his heart must be practicing *tawḥīd* and avoiding *shirk*. The irony of all this is that those who commit these acts of *shirk* with pious saints and the Prophet (ﷺ) (by invoking upon them as intercessors) do it with the excuse that they want to gain the *shafā'ah* of the Prophet (ﷺ), and yet their action automatically disqualifies them from his *shafā'ah* because of their *shirk*. So the best way to gain this *shafā'ah* is by avoiding these same acts that are being performed by these people in the name of *shafā'ah*![148]

To summarise, the concept of *shafā'ah* is an integral part of the beliefs of Islām. However, all such intercession is the sole right of Allāh, and thus should be asked from Him. No object has the *right* to intercede with Allāh, or to have his intercession accepted by Allāh. Allāh states in the Qur'ān,

وَلَا يَمْلِكُ ٱلَّذِينَ يَدْعُونَ مِن دُونِهِ ٱلشَّفَٰعَةَ

"And those whom they call out to besides Him do not own (the right) of intercession" [Sūrah *al-Zukhruf*; 86].

In this verse, Allāh makes no exception; any object that is called out to besides Allāh does not control even the slightest part of intercession, for all such intercession belongs to Allāh alone.

Therefore, when one realises this, it becomes futile to ask others to intercede for you with Allāh. Rather, such requests lead to *shirk* since it assigns the rights of Allāh to other objects. Additionally, this was the exact same excuse that the pagans of old used in order to justify their *shirk*.

The Sixth Argument

TEXT

فإن قال النبي صلى الله عليه وسلم أعطي الشفاعة وأنا أطلبه مما أعطاه الله؟ فالجواب : أن الله أعطاه الشفاعة ونهاك عن هذا وقال ﴿فلا تدعو مع الله أحداً﴾ (سورة الجن ، الآية: ١٨) ، و طلبك من الله شفاعة نبيه عبادة ، والله نهاك أن تشرك في هذه العبادة أحدا ، فإذا كنت تدعو الله أن يشفعه فيك فأطعه في قوله: ﴿فلا تدعو مع الله أحداً﴾.

[147] Ibid., 1/33.

[148] The last few paragraphs have been taken from the author's An Explanation of *the Four Principles of Shirk* (Al-Hidaayah Publishing & Distribution, Birmingham, 2002 CE).

Now if he starts a new line of reasoning, and tries to justify his acts by saying, "The Prophet (ﷺ) has been given the right of intercession (*shafāʿah*) on the Day of Judgement, so I am asking him something that Allāh has given him," then the response to this is to say: "Indeed the Prophet (ﷺ) has been given the right of Intercession by Allāh, and at the same time Allāh has prohibited you from asking the Prophet (ﷺ) for it. Allāh states, "Then do not call anyone besides Allāh" [Sūrah *al-Jinn*; 18]. So the act of asking Allāh to bless you with the Intercession of the Prophet (ﷺ) is itself an act of worship. Thus, Allāh has prohibited you from committing *shirk* by directing this act of worship to other than Him. So if you wish to pray to Allāh to grant his (ﷺ) intercession for you, then obey Him when He says, "Then do not call anyone besides Allāh" [Sūrah *al-Jinn*; 18]."

EXPL. Here, the author proves that the fact that the Prophet (ﷺ) has been given the right of intercession does not justify asking this right of him. The very One that has given the Prophet (ﷺ) this right has also informed us that it is prohibited to call out to other than Him. The seeking of intercession for one's supernatural requests is an act of worship, and Allāh has clearly stated that, when such intercession is sought from other than Him, it is an act of *shirk*. Allāh states,

وَيَعۡبُدُونَ مِن دُونِ ٱللَّهِ
مَا لَا يَضُرُّهُمۡ وَلَا يَنفَعُهُمۡ وَيَقُولُونَ هَٰٓؤُلَآءِ شُفَعَٰٓؤُنَا
عِندَ ٱللَّهِۚ قُلۡ أَتُنَبِّـُٔونَ ٱللَّهَ بِمَا لَا يَعۡلَمُ فِي ٱلسَّمَٰوَٰتِ وَلَا
فِي ٱلۡأَرۡضِۚ سُبۡحَٰنَهُۥ وَتَعَٰلَىٰ عَمَّا يُشۡرِكُونَ ﴿١٨﴾

"And they worship besides Allāh that which will not harm them nor benefit them, and they say: 'These are our intercessors in front of Allāh.' Say: Are you going to inform Allāh of that which He does not know in the Heavens or the earth? Exalted is He, and far removed from that which they associate with Him" [Sūrah *Yūnus*; 18].

In this verse, Allāh states that taking intercessors between Himself and His creation is an act of worship, as the verse begins by stating, '...and they worship besides Allāh.' This 'worship' is then explained in the verse by the seeking of intercession from other objects. The verse concludes by stating that Allāh is exalted over the *shirk* that they do, thus equating this intercession with *shirk*.

It can also be stated as a refutation of this argument that there is not a shred of authentic evidence to suggest that intercession should be sought from the Prophet (ﷺ) after his death. The practice of the Companions and those after them in fact suggests the exact opposite. Even at times of extreme difficulty, the Companions never went to the grave of the Prophet (ﷺ), or sought his help after his death.

Once, during the time of 'Umar ibn al-Khaṭṭāb, there was a great drought that afflicted the people of Madīnah. Many people died, and everyone suffered severely. The Muslims, under the leadership of 'Umar, went outside the city to perform the prayer for rain (*Ṣalāt al-Istisqā*). After finishing the prayer, 'Umar said, "O Allāh! We used to perform *tawassul*[149] through the Prophet, (ﷺ), (while he was alive), and now we will perform *tawassul* through the uncle of the Prophet, (ﷺ), 'Abbās ibn 'Abd al-Muṭṭālib." So saying, he commanded 'Abbās to make a *du'ā* to Allāh for rain, and indeed, Allāh responded to his *du'ā*, and it rained in Madīnah.[150] In this incident, it is clearly proven that the Companions realised that the death of the Prophet (ﷺ) prohibited them from asking the Prophet (ﷺ) for any matter. At this particular instance, when the Muslims were in the most dire need for a response, none of the Companions thought of coming to the grave of the Prophet (ﷺ), or even of asking Allāh by the 'rights' of the Prophet (ﷺ). Rather, they realised that the Prophet (ﷺ) could not respond to them, and that it was not proper to ask *him* for anything. Therefore, they asked a living person, the uncle of the Prophet (ﷺ), to pray for them.

The author wrote in another work, "The person who states that intercession should be sought from him (ﷺ) after his death should prove his evidence for such a claim, from the Book of Allāh, or the Sunnah of the Prophet (ﷺ), or unanimous consensus. And the truth (wherever it is) is more deserving to be followed."[151]

Additionally, the true concept of intercession has been explained in the previous section. Once a person understands that every intercession is in fact a blessing from Allāh, it makes sense to ask Allāh directly for such intercession, and this is what the Prophet (ﷺ) told the Companions and the remaining Muslims after them to do.

TEXT

وأيضاً فإن الشفاعة أعطيها غير النبي صلى الله عليه وسلم ، فصح أن الملائكة يشفعون ، والأفراط يشفعون ، والأولياء يشفعون ، أتقول : إن الله أعطاهم الشفاعة فأطلبها منهم؟

فإن قلت هذا رجعت إلى عبادة الصالحين التي ذكرها الله في كتابه، وإن قلت : لا . بطل قولك «أعطاه الله الشفاعة وأنا أطلبه مما أعطاه الله».

Furthermore, another way to refute this line of reasoning is to realise that

[149] *Tawassul*: Seeking a means of nearness to Allāh. In this context, it refers to trying to increase the chances of a response to one's *du'ā*. See *Tawassul - Its Types & Its Rulings* by Shaikh Muhammad Naasiruddin al-Albaanee (Al-Hidaayah Publishing & Distribution, 1996, Birmingham, U.K).

[150] Reported by al-Bukhārī (4/209) and others.

[151] *Mu'alafāt al-Shaykh* (5/48).

the right to intercede has been given to other than the Prophet (ﷺ) as well. It has authentically been narrated that the angels intercede, and children who died before they reached the age of puberty will intercede on behalf of their parents, and the pious saints will intercede. Are you going to say that Allāh has given all of them the right to intercede, therefore I will ask it from them all? Because if you say this, then you have returned clearly to the saint-worship that Allāh has mentioned in His Book and which the pagan Arabs used to do. And if you say, "No, I will not ask intercession from all of them," then your own statement, "Allāh has given him (ﷺ) the right of intercession, therefore I will ask it of him," is refuted.

EXPL.

In this very clever response, Muḥammad ibn ʿAbd al-Wahhāb reminds the adversary, and the reader, that the right of intercession is not a specific right of the Prophet (ﷺ).[152] Rather, it has been authentically narrated that the angels, children, and pious people will all intercede on the Day of Judgement.

In one long narration describing the Day of Judgement, the Prophet (ﷺ) stated that Allāh will say, "The Angels have interceded, and the prophets have interceded, and the believers have interceded, and no one is left except the Most Merciful of all who have mercy (i.e., Allāh)." So saying, Allāh will take out from the Fire of Hell a group of people who have never performed any good.[153] In this ḥadīth, the fact that the angels, prophets and believers will all intercede is clearly shown.

Allāh also affirms that the angels will intercede in a number of verses in the Qur'ān, including:

وَكَم مِّن مَّلَكٍ فِي السَّمَاوَاتِ لَا تُغْنِي
شَفَاعَتُهُمْ شَيْئًا إِلَّا مِن بَعْدِ أَن يَأْذَنَ اللَّهُ لِمَن يَشَاءُ وَيَرْضَىٰ ﴿٢٦﴾

"And there are many angels in the Heavens, whose intercession will be of no use whatsoever, except after Allāh grants permission to whomever He wills, and is pleased" [Sūrah *al-Najm*; 26].

And the right of the believers to intercede has also been reported in numerous *aḥādīth*. In one of them, the Prophet (ﷺ) said,

---

[152] Intercession is of various types. The most common type is when Allāh allows someone to intercede on behalf of another person who has been destined to the fire of Hell that he be removed from Hell. This type of intercession is common to all prophets, angels, martyrs and pious people. Other types of intercession, such as the intercession to open the gates of Paradise, or to start the reckoning of the Day of Judgement (which is the *Maqām al-Maḥmūd*), is specific to the Prophet (ﷺ).

[153] Part of a ḥadīth narrated by al-Bukhārī (8/182) and Muslim (1/170).

> "A group of people larger than the (tribe) of Banī Tamīm will enter Paradise, due to the intercession of one person from my nation."

The Companions were surprised, and asked, "Someone besides you, O Messenger of Allāh (ﷺ)?" He said, "Someone besides me."[154] In another narration, the Prophet (ﷺ) affirmed that a Muslim child who died before reaching the age of puberty will intercede on behalf of his or her parents. He described them by saying,

> "...they will meet their parents, and hold on to their clothes, or their hands, just like I am holding on to the edge of your garment, and they will not stop, or he will not stop with them, until Allāh enters him and his parents into Paradise."[155]

From all the above, it is clear the right of intercession will be given to the angels, the believers, and children who died in their childhood.[156]

A person who asks the Prophet (ﷺ) for his intercession has one of two choices. He must either ask *all* of the above-mentioned categories for their intercession, in which case it is clear to even the most ignorant of Muslims that he would have fallen into obvious saint-worship; or he must differentiate between the Prophet (ﷺ) and others, and claim that he will only ask the Prophet (ﷺ). Now, even though the intercession of the Prophet (ﷺ) is greater than that of any other person, the fact of the matter is that these other categories have been given the right of intercession just as he has. So, on what basis will such a person not ask from other people, even though Allāh has clearly stated that the right of intercession has been given to them? Such a person has clearly contradicted himself, by claiming that the Prophet (ﷺ) has been given the right of intercession and therefore asking him, yet at the same time not asking others that have been given this right as well.

There is yet another way to respond to this argument, and it has already been given. We have already mentioned that the Prophet (ﷺ) will only intercede after Allāh allows him to intercede, and even then he will intercede on behalf of those whom Allāh is pleased with. Once a person understands that intercession is *purely* from Allāh, and that the Prophet (ﷺ) does not have a *right* over Allāh that He forgive someone, then the whole point of asking the Prophet (ﷺ) becomes pointless.

---

[154] Reported by al-Tirmidhī (4/626) who declared it *ḥasan Ṣaḥīḥ gharīb*, and al-Albānī stated that its chain was authentic (*Mishkāt al-Maṣābīh* 3/1558).

[155] Part of a longer ḥadīth reported by Muslim (3/2029) and others.

[156] It will also be given to other than these categories (such as the martyr); the author mentioned some of them as an example, and did not intend to imply that these were the only people who will intercede.

Lastly, another way to respond to this argument is by mentioning that the Prophet (ﷺ) has been given many matters, yet it is not permissible to ask these matters from him. It is well-known, for example, that the Prophet (ﷺ) has been given many blessings in Paradise. Is it permissible, therefore, to ask the Prophet (ﷺ) to be given of his blessings, merely because he has been granted them as well? Rather, it is Allāh Who should be asked, as He is the One Who grants the desires of His worshippers.

To summarize the response to this argument, it can be said:

1. Although Allāh has indeed given the Prophet (ﷺ) the right of intercession, at the same time He has prohibited you from asking this from him directly. Such a request falls under *du'ā*, and directing a *du'ā* to other than Allāh is *shirk*.
2. Allāh has given the right of intercession to other than the Prophet (ﷺ), so does this justify asking it of them? Will any of these people claim that it is permissible to go to the grave of a dead child and ask him to intercede with Allāh?
3. All intercession belongs to Allāh, even the Prophet's (ﷺ) intercession. Therefore, it should be asked from the One Who is in charge of it.
4. The Prophet (ﷺ) has been given many spiritual blessings, some of which will also be given, albeit to a lesser degree, to his followers. Does this justify asking him for these blessings as well?
5. There is not a shred of authentic evidence which sanctions asking the Prophet (ﷺ) directly for his intercession. None of the Companions, or the generations after them, ever did such a thing, nor was it even known during the first few centuries of Islām.

The Seventh Argument

فإن قال: أنا لا أشرك بالله شيئاً حاشا وكلا ، ولكن الإلتجاء إلى الصالحين ليس بشرك. TEXT

فقل له: إذا كنت تقر أن الله حرم الشرك أعظم من تحريم الزنا، وتقر أن الله لا يغفره ، فما هذا الأمر الذي حرمه الله وذكر أنه لا يغفره؟ فإنه لا يدري .

فقل له: كيف تبرئ نفسك من الشرك وأنت لا تعرفه؟ كيف يحرم الله عليك هذا ويذكر أنه لا يغفره ولا تسأل عنه ولا تعرفه ، أتظن أن الله عز وجل يحرمه ولا يبينه لنا؟

Now, if he says trying yet another argument, "I do not commit *shirk* with Allāh – it is not possible, and I would never do such a thing! But turning to pious people is not *shirk* in the first place."

Then ask him, "If you truly believe that Allāh has prohibited *shirk* more severely than He has prohibited illicit intercourse (*zinā*), and you admit that Allāh will not forgive it, then what is this grave matter that Allāh has prohibited, and stated that He will not forgive?"

Then you will see that in reality he will not know what *shirk* is.

So ask him, "How can you free yourself from *shirk*, and yet you don't even know what it is? Or how is it possible that Allāh has made this prohibited upon you, and has mentioned that He will not forgive it, and yet you do not ask about it, nor know it? Do you presume that Allāh prohibited it, yet did not explain it to us?"

EXPL. Here once again the author points out that those who worship saints and prophets in reality neither understand nor comprehend the meaning of *shirk*. It is not possible that *shirk* has been prohibited by Allāh so severely, yet not explained in His Book. So, if a person realises this, then why is it that he remains in ignorance about such a grave matter? If one does not know, then let him ask others who are more knowledgeable. For this reason, although ignorance might be an excuse for certain matters, it must also be kept in mind that ignorance cannot always be used as an excuse. A person who is ignorant has an obligation to learn certain matters, especially matters as important as *tawḥīd* and *shirk*.

In this paragraph, the author is gently reprimanding the adversary, and showing him that he has fallen short in his obligations and duties. For it is obvious that he has not taken the efforts and pains to study basic matters of his religion, yet he is arguing with others about these matters, trying his utmost to defend them and sanction them. And this is the case with most Muslims that fall into *shirk*. They will always be ignorant of their religion, having never studied the most fundamental of matters.

The one who believes that turning to saints is not *shirk* will obviously define *shirk* incorrectly, as the author goes on to illustrate.

TEXT فإن قال: الشرك عبادة الأصنام ونحن لا نعبد الأصنام ، فقل له : ما معنى عبادة الأصنام؟ أتظن أنهم يعتقدون أن تلك الأخشاب والأحجار تخلق ، وترزق ، وتدبر أمر من دعاها؟ فهذا يكذبه القرآن.

So if he says, "*Shirk* is the worship of idols, and we don't worship idols," then ask him, "What is the meaning of worshiping these idols? Do you think that the pagan Arabs used to believe that these rocks and stones actually create, and give sustenance, and control the affairs of those who beseech them? If you claim this then the Qur'ān itself refutes this idea."

EXPL. The point here is: whatever incorrect definition of *shirk* he gives can easily be refuted by clear texts of the Qur'ān. So, if he defines *shirk* to be the worship of idols, he must explain what he means by 'worship'. As has been repeatedly proven in previous sections, the *Jāhilīyyah* Arabs did not give supreme powers to these rocks and stones. Rather, they would use them to draw closer to Allāh. Therefore, it is simple to prove that placing intermediaries between creation and Allāh is the essence of *shirk*.

Thus, the adversary is forced either to admit, or be guided to, the correct definition of *shirk*.

TEXT فإن قال : إنهم يقصدون خشبة ، أو حجراً ، أو بنية على قبر أو غيره ، يدعون ذلك ويذبحون له ، ويقولون إنه يقربنا إلى الله زلفى ، ويدفع عنا الله ببركته أو يعطينا ببركته.

فقل : صدقت وهذا هو فعلكم عند الأحجار والبنايا التي على القبور وغيرها ، فهذا أقر أن فعلهم هذا هو عبادة الأصنام فهو المطلوب.

But if he responds, "They used to turn to these planks and stones, and mausoleums built over graves, and other icons, and would call out to them for their needs, and sacrifice to them, in order to come closer to Allāh, and so that Allāh would divert an evil afflicting them, or grant them their wishes due to their holiness and high status," then respond, "You have spoken the truth...and this is exactly what you people do in front of structures and edifices built on graves!"

So this person has finally admitted that these acts that they themselves do are in fact equivalent to idol worship, and this is the point that is meant to be understood.

EXPL. Once the adversary has properly defined *shirk*, or the correct definition is proven to him, he must admit and realise that he himself is guilty of *shirk* when he turns to pious saints for his needs, calling out to them, and sacrificing and directing other acts of worship to them.

TEXT ويقال له أيضاً : قولك الشرك عبادة الأصنام ، هل مرادك أن الشرك مخصوص بهذا وأن الإعتماد على الصالحين ودعاءهم لا يدخل في ذلك؟ فهذا يرده ما ذكر الله تعالى في كتابه من كفر من تعلق على الملائكة أو عيسى أو الصالحين. فلا بد أن يقر لك أن من أشرك في عبادة الله أحداً من الصالحين فهو الشرك المذكور في القرآن وهذا هو المطلوب.

> Also, as a clarification of your statement "*Shirk* is idol-worship,' do you mean to imply that *shirk* only occurs by this act? Do you presume that relying upon pious saints to answer you needs, and calling out to them does not come under *shirk*? If you believe so then the Qur'ān clearly refutes this misconception, as Allāh mentions the disbelief of those who attach themselves to the angels and direct acts of worship to them, and those who attach themselves to Jesus, or other pious people.
>
> Therefore, in summary he who is honest must admit that whoever does *shirk* in the worship of Allāh by directing an act of worship to pious people has indeed fallen into the exact same type of *shirk* that is mentioned in the Qur'ān, and this is the whole point that we wish to make them understand.

EXPL. In other words, it should be clear that *shirk* does not just occur with idols and statues. Unfortunately, most ignorant Muslims only think of this extreme form of *shirk* as *shirk*, and do not realise that *shirk* is of many types. The proper definitions of *shirk* have been given in the introductory chapters preceding the text. Ibn Taymiyyah aptly defined it as: "The reality of *shirk* is equating any created object with Allāh in some matters which only Allāh deserves; there is nobody that equates a creation of Allāh with Allāh in *all* matters. So whoever worships other than Him, or depends upon other than Him, has committed *shirk*."[157]

Ibn Taymiyyah points out a very important fact in this quotation, and that is that no religion or sect equates an object with the Supreme Lord in every single matter. Rather, every major world religion or movement singles out one supreme deity, and then places other objects in positions that only Allāh deserves, but they do so *in one or more respects*, and not in all matters. Thus, the Christians turn to Jesus Christ, beseeching him for salvation; yet, this is a right that only Allāh can grant, and only Allāh should be asked of. The Jews have allowed their rabbis to abrogate the law of the Torah, and have taken their rulings in the place of the actual Word of God. The majority of Jews do not obey the actual Law of the Torah; instead, they obey the opinions of men that clearly contradict the teachings of the Torah. Thus, they have taken these rabbis (as the Christians have taken their priests) as lords besides Allāh, for only Allāh has the right to legislate.

The point is that, when one examines the *shirk* that is present in other religions – even in extremely idolatrous religions such as Hinduism – one always finds the belief of one supreme being. *Shirk* occurs in these religions, not merely by giving powers of lordship (*Rubūbiyyah*) to others, but also by directing acts of worship to created objects.

---

[157] *Al-Istiqāmah,* 1/344.

So the refutation of this statement is by mentioning that the *mushrikūn* are not all idol-worshippers. Some of them worship Jesus Christ without making any idols or statues of him.[158] Others worship angels. Yet they are all guilty of *shirk*.

TEXT

وسر المسألة: أنه إذا قال أنا لا أشرك بالله.

فقل له: وما الشرك بالله؟ فسره لي؟

فإن قال : هو عبادة الأصنام.

فقل له: وما عبادة الأصنام؟ فسرها لي .

وإن قال: أنا لا أعبد إلا الله فقل: ما معنى عبادة الله فسرها لي؟ فإن فسرها بما بينه الله في القرآن فهو المطلوب، وإن لم يعرفه فكيف يدعي شيئاً وهو لا يعرفه؟

وإن فسره بغير معناه بينت له الآيات الواضحات في معنى الشرك بالله وعبادة الأوثان وأنه الذي يفعلونه في هذا الزمان بعينه.

وأن عبادة الله وحده لا شريك له هي التي ينكرون علينا ويصيحون منه كما صاح إخوانهم حيث قالوا: ﴿أجعل الآلهة إلهاً واحداً إن هذا لشيء عجاب﴾ (سورة ص، الآية: ٥).

The crux of the matter is that, if he tells you, "I don't commit *shirk* with Allāh," then ask him, "What is the meaning of committing *shirk* with Allāh? Explain it to me!"

And if he responds to that by saying, "It is the worshipping of idols," then ask him, "And what does it mean to 'worship' idols? Explain it to me!"

And if he responds by saying, "But I only worship Allāh!" then ask him, "And what does it mean to 'worship' Allāh? Explain it to me!"

Now, if he explains all of these terms according to the definitions that Allāh has clarified in the Qur'ān, then that is what is desired. And if he doesn't know the proper definitions, then how can he claim to be free of something while he is ignorant of its meaning? And if he explains these terms incorrectly, contradicting the proper definitions given in the Qur'ān, then you must

[158] In general, the Protestants and Russian Orthodox Christians dislike portraying Jesus Christ in statue form. However, Roman Catholics are much more lax in this regard, and find no qualms in displaying statues, not only of Jesus, but of Mary and any other 'saint' that they wish to worship.

explain to him with clear verses of the Qur'ān the precise meaning of *shirk*. You must prove to them that idol-worship is exactly what they themselves are doing in our times by worshipping these graves, and that they criticize us when we try to worship Allāh alone! So they cry out, just like their brethren of old did, and say, "Has he indeed made the objects of worship into one object? Verily this is a very strange thing!" [Sūrah *Ṣād*; 5].

EXPL. Here, the author summarises the preceding few arguments in this paragraph.

The definitions of these religious terms are of the utmost importance. It is no exaggeration to say that the correct understanding of these terms is a matter of life and death – rather, even more important than that! This is because an incorrect understanding of terms such as *tawḥīd*, *shirk*, or *'ibādah*, might easily lead a person to become a non-Muslim, thus ensuring his eternal punishment in Hell.

We have already defined, with evidences, the exact definitions of *shirk* and *'ibādah* more than once in the preceding pages. The problem, once again, is that most Muslims, when they hear these terms, only think of certain types of *shirk* or *'ibādah*, presuming that these types are the only examples of them. So, most Muslims only think of *'ibādah* as the daily *Ṣalāt*, or prostration, or other limited examples. They fail to realise that *'ibādah* is a comprehensive term that encompasses beliefs of the heart, statements of the tongue, and actions of the limbs. Any matter or act that is beloved by Allāh is an act of *'ibādah*; thus, whenever such an act is done with the intention of pleasing other than Allāh, it becomes an act of *shirk*. So *tawāf* is an act of worship, and that is why Muslims perform *tawāf* around the House of Allāh. Any time *tawāf* is performed around a grave or rock, it becomes an act of major *shirk*, since it is directed to other than Allāh. Likewise, *du'ā* is one of the most important and noble acts of *'ibādah*. Any time *du'ā* is performed to other than Allāh, it becomes an act of major *shirk*. And the examples are limitless.

The author points out an astounding phenomenon, and that is that these adversaries to *tawḥīd* actually object to the call of the pure worship of Allāh. By doing so, they have in fact fallen into the same league as the *mushrikūn* of old, who were amazed at the Prophet's (ﷺ) call to worship Allāh alone. There are literally dozens of works in print that seek to refute the author by proving the permissibility of calling out to dead saints, and seeking help from prophets, and other forms of clear *shirk*. Even the most ignorant Muslim realises that the Prophet (ﷺ) was sent so that only Allāh be worshipped, and not so that Muslims start worshipping graves and saints instead! This matter is so clear that it does not require any proof, as the Qur'ān and Sunnah is replete with proof to this effect.

The Eighth Argument

فإن قال: إنهم لم يكفروا بدعاء الملائكة، والأنبياء وإنما كفروا لما قالوا: الملائكة بنات الله. ونحن لم نقل: إن عبدالقادر، ولا غيره ابن الله. TEXT

Now, it is possible that he will start a totally different tactic to try to prove his beliefs, and he will say, "They, meaning the pagan Arabs, did not disbelieve because of their *du'ā* to the angels or prophets, or because they directed their acts of worship to other than Allāh! Rather, they disbelieved by claiming that the angels are daughters of Allāh. And we don't say that 'Abd al-Qādir, or these other saints are the sons of Allāh!"

The author now brings in a new argument that is used by the adversaries of *tawḥīd*. They claim that the reason the *Jāhilīyyah* Arabs were considered non-Muslims was because they attributed daughters to Allāh, and not that they directed acts of worship to the angels. Allāh mentions that the *Jāhilīyyah* Arabs used to believe that the angels were His daughters: EXPL.

أَلَآ إِنَّهُم مِّنْ إِفْكِهِمْ لَيَقُولُونَ ﴿١٥١﴾ وَلَدَ ٱللَّهُ وَإِنَّهُمْ لَكَٰذِبُونَ ﴿١٥٢﴾

"Verily, of their slanderous lies is their saying: 'Allāh has given birth.' And they are liars!" [Sūrah *al-Ṣaffāt*; 151 – 152].

And He says,

وَجَعَلُوا۟ لِلَّهِ شُرَكَآءَ ٱلْجِنَّ وَخَلَقَهُمْ ۖ وَخَرَقُوا۟ لَهُۥ بَنِينَ وَبَنَٰتٍۭ بِغَيْرِ عِلْمٍ ۚ سُبْحَٰنَهُۥ وَتَعَٰلَىٰ عَمَّا يَصِفُونَ ﴿١٠٠﴾ بَدِيعُ ٱلسَّمَٰوَٰتِ وَٱلْأَرْضِ ۖ أَنَّىٰ يَكُونُ لَهُۥ وَلَدٌ وَلَمْ تَكُن لَّهُۥ صَٰحِبَةٌ ۖ وَخَلَقَ كُلَّ شَىْءٍ ۖ

"And they made for Allāh partners from the *jinn*, while He has created them (the *jinn*). And they invented for Him sons and daughters, without any knowledge. Exalted is He and Glorified above what they describe. The Originator of the Heavens and earth – how can He have a child when He has no partner, and He has created everything else?" [Sūrah *al-An'ām*; 100-101].

And He states,

أَلَكُمُ ٱلذَّكَرُ وَلَهُ ٱلْأُنثَىٰ ﴿٢١﴾ تِلْكَ إِذًا قِسْمَةٌ ضِيزَىٰٓ ﴿٢٢﴾

"Do you have the male [children] while He has female [children]? Verily, that is an unjust division [Sūrah *al-Najm*; 21-22].

In other words, do you prefer male children for yourselves, while you claim that Allāh has daughters?

So the *Jāhilīyyah* Arabs did indeed claim that the angels were Allāh's daughters. This, claims our adversary, is the reason that the Prophet (ﷺ) fought them, and declared them to be disbelievers.

The author quotes four different responses in order to refute this claim, each one of them clearly proving the speciousness of this argument.

The First Response

TEXT

فالجواب: أن نسبة الولد إلى الله – تعالى – كفر مستقل، قال الله –تعالى– ﴿قُلْ هُوَ اللَّهُ أَحَدٌ . اللَّهُ الصَّمَدُ﴾ (الإخلاص: ١–٢) والأحد: الذي لا نظيرله. والصمد: المقصود في الحوائج. فمن جحد هذا فقد كفر – ولو لم يجحد آخر السورة. ثم قال تعالى – ﴿لَمْ يَلِدْ وَلَمْ يُولَدْ﴾ (الإخلاص: ٣) فمن جحد هذا فقد كفر – ولو لم يجحد أول السورة.

The response to this misconception is to say: "Claiming that Allāh has a child is a different type of disbelief, since Allāh says, 'Say: He is Allāh, the Unique (*al-Aḥad*). Allāh is the Eternally besought of all (*al-Ṣamad*)'" [Sūrah *al-Ikhlāṣ*; 1-2]. And the meaning of *al-Aḥad* is that there is nothing that is similar or equal to Him. And the meaning of *al-Ṣamad* is that all objects turn to Him for their every need. So whoever denies this has committed disbelief (*kufr*), even if he doesn't deny the last verse in the Sūrah. Allāh then says: "Neither does He beget, nor is He begotten" [Sūrah *al-Ikhlāṣ*; 3], so whoever denies this has committed disbelief, even if he doesn't deny the first part of the Sūrah.

EXPL.

Kufr is of many different types. It is sufficient for a person to be a *kāfir* by merely believing in or performing one act of *kufr*, as long as the other conditions for pronouncing someone to be a *kāfir* are met. Most world religions, and the *Jāhilīyyah* Arabs of old, commit *kufr* in numerous ways. Thus, the Christians believe that Allāh has a son, and this is *kufr*. They believe that there is a Holy Trinity, and this is a separate type of *kufr*. They believe that Jesus Christ deserves their prayer and *du'ā*, which is yet another type of *kufr*...and so on. If a person were only to believe in one of these matters, it would be sufficient for him to considered a *kāfir*.

Likewise, the *Jāhilīyyah* Arabs committed *kufr* in numerous ways. They used to believe that the angels were daughters of Allāh, and this is *kufr*. They also used to direct acts of worship to these angels, and this *is a separate type* of *kufr*.

The author quotes Sūrah *al-Ikhlāṣ* in its entirety, showing that Allāh is *al-Ṣamad*, meaning, 'One whom everything turns to for their needs.' Thus, a Muslim must turn to Allāh for the needs that he has. If a person rejects the Name *al-Ṣamad* by turning to other than Allāh, then he has fallen into a type of *kufr*.

The last verse of this Sūrah states, 'He does not beget, nor is He begotten.' If any person denies this, and claims that Allāh has a child, then he has committed *kufr* as well, even if he affirms that Allāh is *al-Ṣamad*.

The point here is that the belief that Allāh has a child is a type of *kufr*, and asking other than Allāh is another type of *kufr*.

The Second Response

TEXT

وقال الله تعالى -﴿مَا اتَّخَذَ اللَّهُ مِن وَلَدٍ وَمَا كَانَ مَعَهُ مِنْ إِلَهٍ إِذًا لَّذَهَبَ كُلُّ إِلَهٍ بِمَا خَلَقَ وَلَعَلَا بَعْضُهُمْ عَلَى بَعْضٍ سُبْحَانَ اللَّهِ عَمَّا يَصِفُونَ﴾ الآية (المؤمنون: ٩١)، ففرق بين النوعين، وجعل كلا منهما كفرا مستقلا.

وقال الله تعالى -﴿وَجَعَلُواْ لِلَّهِ شُرَكَاء الْجِنَّ وَخَلَقَهُمْ وَخَرَقُواْ لَهُ بَنِينَ وَبَنَاتٍ بِغَيْرِ عِلْمٍ سُبْحَانَهُ وَتَعَالَى عَمَّا يَصِفُونَ﴾ الآية (الأنعام: ١٠٠)، ففرق بين الكفرين.

And Allāh also said, "Allāh did not take any son, nor is there any other god besides Him" [Sūrah *al-Mu'minūn*; 19].

So Allāh differentiated between the two types of disbelief, and made every single type a separate category of disbelief. And Allāh said, "And they made partners besides Allāh (by worshipping) *jinns*" [Sūrah *al-An'ām*; 100], thus differentiating between the two types of disbelief.

EXPL.

The second response to their argument is that Allāh has clearly differentiated between these two types of *kufr* in many verses in the Qur'ān. The author quotes two of these verses in which both of these matters (ascribing children to Allāh, and ascribing partners to Allāh) are mentioned as *kufr*. Thus Allāh Himself, in these verses, differentiates between these two types of *kufr*, thus showing that they are not the same thing.

In the first verse quoted by the author, Allāh states,

مَا اتَّخَذَ اللَّهُ مِن وَلَدٍ وَمَا كَانَ مَعَهُ مِنْ إِلَٰهٍ

"Allāh did not take a son, nor is there an object of worship (*ilāh*) besides Him" [Sūrah *al-Mu'minūn*; 91].

Here Allāh differentiates between these two matters, and considers each one of them to be *kufr*.

In the second verse that he quotes, Allāh describes the *mushrikūn* by saying,

وَجَعَلُواْ لِلَّهِ شُرَكَآءَ ٱلْجِنَّ وَخَلَقَهُمْۖ وَخَرَقُواْ لَهُۥ بَنِينَ وَبَنَٰتِۭ بِغَيْرِ عِلْمٍۚ سُبْحَٰنَهُۥ وَتَعَٰلَىٰ عَمَّا يَصِفُونَ ﴿١٠٠﴾

"And they made partners besides Allāh, *jinns*, even though He created them; and they invented sons and daughter for Him! Exalted and Glorified is He above what they say" [Sūrah *al-An'ām*; 100].

Once again, Allāh clearly mentions that the *mushrikūn* are guilty of two separate matters: worshipping other than Him, and ascribing children to Him. So each one of these matters is sufficient for a person to be considered a non-Muslim.

The Third Response

TEXT

والدليل على هذا - أيضا- أن الذين كفروا بدعاء اللات - مع كونه رجلا صالحا - لم يجعلوه ابن الله. والذين كفروا بعبادة الجن لم يجعلوهم كذلك.

And yet another proof for this is that those who disbelieved by praying to al-Lāt did not consider him to be the son of Allāh, even though he was a pious man. Likewise, those that fell into disbelief by worshipping the *jinn* did not consider them to be children of Allāh.

EXPL.

The *Jāhilīyyah* Arabs, like most idolatrous religions, were not of one standard creed. Rather, there were numerous different and contradictory beliefs present amongst them, as is generally the case with purely idolatrous faiths. Of these beliefs was the worship of al-Lāt. Those who used to worship this idol did not believe that al-Lāt was a child of Allāh, yet that did not prevent the Prophet (ﷺ) from considering them to be disbelievers. Similarly, most of the objects of worship that the Arabs had, such as the *jinn*, were not considered to be Allāh's children.

Therefore, it is sufficient that a person directs an act of worship to a created object in order to be considered a *kāfir*, even if he or she does not consider that object of worship to be a child of Allāh.

The Fourth Response

TEXT

وكذلك العلماء - أيضا - وجميع المذاهب الأربعة يذكرون في باب «حكم المرتد» أن المسلم إذا زعم أن لله ولدا فهو مرتد، وإن أشرك بالله فهو مرتد، فيفرقون بين النوعين. وهذا في غاية الوضوح.

And yet another proof is that all the scholars, and the four *madh-habs*, mention in the chapter concerning the rules pertaining to the *murtad* (the one who has renounced his faith after accepting Islam) that if a Muslim presumes that Allāh has taken a son, then he is a *murtad*, and if he commits *shirk*, he is also a *murtad*. So they differentiate between the two, and this matter is extremely clear and does not need further elaboration.

EXPL.

In other words, all the scholars of Islām agree that a Muslim becomes an apostate, or *murtad*, if he claims that Allāh has a child. Likewise, they also agree that if a Muslim were to commit *shirk*, he too becomes an apostate. Thus, all the scholars of Islām clearly understand that there is a difference between these two matters, and belief in one of them is sufficient for one to be expelled from Islām.

And the refutation of this argument – that the Arabs of old were considered *kāfirs* only because they believed that the angels were daughters of Allāh – is very simple and clear to any person of intellect.

The Ninth Argument

TEXT

وإن قال: ﴿أَلا إِنَّ أَوْلِيَاء اللّهِ لاَ خَوْفٌ عَلَيْهِمْ وَلاَ هُمْ يَحْزَنُونَ﴾ (سورة يونس، الآية: ٦٢). فقل: هذا هو الحق، ولكن لا يعبدون. و نحن لا ننكر إلا عبادتهم مع الله، وإشراكهم معه. وإلا فالواجب عليك حبهم، واتباعهم، والإقرار بكراماتهم. ولا يجحد كرامات الإولياء إلا أهل البدع والضلالات. ودين الله وسط بين طرفين، وهدى بين ضلالتين، وحق بين باطلين.

Now, if he tries yet another tactic to prove his *shirk* and says: "Verily the friends of Allāh – there is no fear for them, neither will they worry" [Sūrah *Yūnus*; 62] thus trying to prove that such people are worthy of intercession, then respond to him: This is indeed true that they occupy a high place with Allāh, but they are not to be worshipped! And we only deny that they should be worshipped along with Allāh, and that they be taken as partners along with Him. Otherwise we both agree that it is obligatory to love them, and follow them, and to believe in any miracles that might have occurred to them by the blessings of Allāh. And no one except a person of deviation denies the existence of such miracles. But the religion of Allāh is in the middle, between the two extremes; a guidance between the two extremities of falsehood, and a truth between the two extremities of evil.

EXPL.

The essence of this argument is that the *awliyā* of Allāh (the ones whom He has protected) and the prophets have a very high status in Allāh's sight. Thus, the adversary brings forth proofs and evidences which show the high status of these beings, and that Allāh has blessed and favoured them over others. Of these verses is the one quoted by the author, in which Allāh describes the *awliyā* as having no reason to fear, nor any cause to worry. This, states the adversary, shows the high status that they have, which in turn justifies our turning to them.

The response to this argument is that we do not deny this high status. Rather, we affirm it just as you do. However, this status does not entail that they be worshipped along with Allāh.

Additionally, the only reason that they achieved this status in the first place is by their pure worship of Allāh. If this is understood, then in order to truly appreciate them, we should love them for their worship, and imitate their worship of Allāh in order that we ourselves draw closer to Him. Instead of using them as intermediaries to come between us and Allāh, we should use them as examples in order for us to achieve their status as well.

The author mentions the miracles, or *ḳaramāt* (singular: *ḳarāmah*), of these *awliyā*. Many of the opponents of *Ahl al-Sunnah* falsely claim that the *Ahl al-Sunnah* deny the existence of these miracles. However, no true Muslim denies that Allāh blesses some of His servants with supernatural miracles. Such miracles have been affirmed in the Qur'ān, Sunnah and books of history. Additionally, this is a matter which has been affirmed by human experience, for in every age and place there are certain incidents that occur to various people which cannot be explained by the natural, everyday laws of physics.

It is important, however, that the two extremes with regards to these *ḳaramāt* are avoided. The one extreme, which is present in Muslims who seek to rationalise Islām (such as the *Muʿtazilah* of the past) is the outright denial of these miracles. Such people seek to deny everything which the human intellect cannot fathom or understand. The other extreme, which is present in groups which emphasize spirituality and blind emotion (such as the *Ṣūfīs*), is the exaltation of such *ḳaramāt* and the people on whose hands they occur. The fact that a person has been blessed with a *ḳarāmah* does not change the reality of his status – that he is a created being who cannot benefit or harm anyone without Allāh's permission. So if it has authentically been confirmed that a *ḳarāmah* has occurred to a particular person, the true Muslim does not change his relationship with Allāh because of such a *ḳarāmah*.

Additionally, it must be mentioned that it is extremely common for the extreme *Ṣūfīs* to use black magic in order to prove that they have been blessed with *ḳaramāt*. A *ḳarāmah* does not occur by the will of anyone, for it is a pure blessing from Allāh. When a person is obviously flaunting 'miraculous deeds', and producing them at will in order to impress others, then it can be assumed beyond a shadow of a doubt that such a person is a charlatan, or even worse: a black magician. A real *walī* that has been blessed with a *ḳarāmah* will in fact increase in his *īmān*, and try his utmost to hide such a *ḳarāmah*, just as he would try to hide a good deed. Lastly, it should be borne in mind that a *ḳarāmah* is not necessarily a sign of strong faith (*īmān*), for it is possible that a *karāmah* be given to a weak believer in order for him to increase his *īmān*. One of the author's grandchildren wrote, "A *karāmah* is not necessarily a sign of high status or rank (in the sight of Allāh). For verily, a group of people have walked over water, whilst another group that was better than them died of thirst! And these *karamāt* were numerous in the second and third centuries of the *Hijrah*, even though in the first century there existed people far better than the ones whom these miracles occurred to (and yet were not blessed with such *karamāt*)."[159]

This argument that the adversaries put forward clearly proves that it is the common practice of the people of deviation to quote an authentic proof and then use it in order to justify something which has absolutely nothing to do with the proof itself. Thus, they will quote vague and imprecise verses or *aḥādīth*, and then apply them to a specific pre-conceived matter. In the process, they ignore the precise meaning of their evidence, and they also ignore all of the other texts of the Qur'ān and Sunnah which contradict the point that they seek to prove. Even on the supposition that this verse, and others like it, imparted any hint of worshipping the *awliyā* of Allāh, there are many other verses and texts which prove that this interpretation is not valid in the first place.

Once their methodology is understood, and their tactics recognised, then most of the evidences and arguments that they use can be immediately dismissed. This is especially true with regards to the evidences that they present to prove the high status of the Prophet (ﷺ). The status of the Prophet (ﷺ) is a matter which no Muslim can deny, but this status has absolutely nothing to do with directing acts of worship to him.

The *Shirk* of the Modern *Mushrikūn* is More Severe than the *Shirk* of Ancient Times

TEXT

فإذا عرفت أن هذا الذي يسميه المشركون في زماننا «كبير الإعتقاد» هو الشرك الذي أنزل فيه القرآن ، وقاتل رسول الله صلى الله عليه وسلم الناس عليه ، فأعلم أن شرك الأولين أخف من شرك أهل وقتنا بأمرين

When you realise that this concept that those who commit *shirk* in our times call *iʿtiqād*, or creed, is in fact the same *shirk* that the Qur'ān was revealed concerning, and it was this same *shirk* that the Prophet (ﷺ) fought, then know that the *shirk* of the people of the past is less evil than the *shirk* of the people of our times. And this is due to two factors.

---

[159] *Tuḥfat al-Ṭālib wa l-Jalīs*, p. 72.

EXPL. The author points out that the belief of these groups of his time, which they had labeled *'iʿtiqād'* (or, according to other manuscripts of this text, *'Kabīr iʿtiqād'*), is in fact the same as the *shirk* of the *Jāhilīyyah* Arabs of old. The only difference was that those earlier generations went through intermediaries, and clearly understood that this act disqualified them from being Muslims, whereas these people of the author's time claimed to be Muslims, and in fact defended this blatant *shirk*.

By this time, it should be absolutely clear to the reader that a person who directs his *duʿā*, prostrations, feelings of divine love, fear, hope, the sacrifices that he performs, and other religious matters to graves and dead saints cannot be considered a Muslim, even if he claims to be one (except possibly in extreme cases where ignorance might be used as an excuse).

Once a person understands this, the author then points out that the *shirk* of the people of later times is in reality *worse* that the *shirk* of the *Jāhilīyyah* Arabs of old, for two reasons.

TEXT أحدهما: أن الأولين لا يشركون ولا يدعون الملائكة والأولياء والأوثان مع الله إلا في الرخاء ، وأما الشدة فيخلصون الدين لله كما قال تعالى: ﴿فَإِذَا رَكِبُوا فِي الْفُلْكِ دَعَوُا اللَّهَ مُخْلِصِينَ لَهُ الدِّينَ فَلَمَّا نَجَّاهُمْ إِلَى الْبَرِّ إِذَا هُمْ يُشْرِكُونَ﴾(سورة العنكبوت، الآية: ٦٥) و قال تعالى : ﴿وإذا مسكم الضر في البحر ضل من تدعون إلا إياه فلما نجاكم إلى البر أعرضتم وكان الإنسان كفوراً﴾ (سورة الإسراء، الآية: ٦٧) .

وقال تعالى : ﴿قل أرأيتكم إن أتاكم عذاب الله وأتتكم الساعة أغير الله تدعون إن كنتم صادقين، بل إياه تدعون فيكشف ما تدعون إليه إن شاء وتنسون ما تشركون﴾ (سورة الأنعام ، الآيتان: ٤١، ٤٠) .

وقوله تعالى: ﴿وإذا مس الإنسان ضر دعا ربه منيباً إليه﴾ إلى قوله: ﴿تمتع بكفرك قليلاً إنك من أصحاب النار﴾ (سورة الزمر، الآية: ٨) وقوله تعالى:-﴿وإذا غشيهم موج كالظل دعوا الله مخلصين له الدين﴾ (سورة لقمان، الآية: ٢٢) .

فمن فهم هذه المسألة التي وضحها الله في كتابه وهي أن المشركين الذين قاتلهم رسول الله صلى الله عليه وسلم يدعون الله ويدعون غيره في الرخاء ، وأما في الضراء والشدة فلا يدعون إلا الله وحده لا شريك له وينسون سادتهم تبين له الفرق بين شرك أهل زماننا وشرك الأولين ولكن أين من يفهم قلبه هذه المسألة فهما راسخاً ، والله المستعان.

> Firstly: the early people from amongst the pagan Arabs did not commit *shirk*, and call out to the angels and saints and idols, except at times and situations of ease and comfort. However, when they were in extenuating circumstances and were desperate for a response, they would make their religion and prayer sincere to Allāh. Allāh says, "So when they ride in the ships, they call out to Allāh in all sincerity, and when He saves them to the land, they commit *shirk*" [Sūrah *al-ʿAnkabūt*; 65]. And He also says, "And when a problem falls upon you while you are at sea, all those whom you call upon leave you except He (Allāh)" [Sūrah *al-Isrā'*; 67]. And He also says, "Ask them: If the punishment of Allāh were to come to you, or the Day of Judgement, would you call upon other than Allāh if you are truthful. Rather, Him alone would you call, and He will remove what has afflicted you if He wills, and you will forget (those objects) whom you do *shirk* with" [Sūrah *al-Anʿām*; 40-41]. And Allāh says, "And when an affliction touches man, he calls out to his Lord, humbly, and when He exchanges it with a good situation, he forgets what he was calling for before" [Sūrah *al-Zumar*; 8]. And Allāh says, "So when the waves come out to them, like dark clouds, they call out to Allāh, making the religion sincere to Him..." [Sūrah *Luqmān*; 32].
>
> So whoever understands this point – that those whom the Prophet (ﷺ) fought would call out to Allāh, and would call out to other than Allāh only at times of ease, as for times of distress, then they would only call out to Allāh alone, and leave calling out to their leaders – will clearly see the difference between the two types of *shirk*. But where is the person who will understand this matter perfectly...and help is only sought from Allāh!

The first point which proves that the *shirk* of the people of later times is worse than the *shirk* of the people of the past is that the people of the past would only commit *shirk* when they were not in desperate situations. So at times of ease and comfort, when they could afford a delayed response, or when the matter was not urgent, they would call out to their idols. However, at times of distress, or when they urgently needed a response, they would sincerely call out to Allāh alone, ignoring all of their idols. The five verses that the author quotes are all self-explanatory, and clearly prove this point. At times of extreme danger, the *Jāhilīyyah* Arabs would beseech and implore Allāh directly, and due to this sincerity, Allāh would respond to them. However, as soon as they were saved from that situation, they would forget their sincerity to Allāh, and worship their idols along with Allāh. EXPL.

This proves that the *Jāhilīyyah* Arabs were intelligent enough to realise that their gods were not able to help them; thus they would turn directly to Allāh when they were desperate for a response. This meaning is clearly confirmed in the story of Ḥusayn, the father of the famous Companion ʿImrān ibn Ḥusayn. It has been narrated that he came to the Prophet (ﷺ) as a non-Muslim. The

Prophet (ﷺ) asked him, "How many gods do you worship?" He replied, "Seven! Six on this earth, and One in the skies (i.e., Allāh)." So the Prophet (ﷺ) questioned him, "Who do you count on when you are in fear, or hopeful (for a response)?" He said, "The One in the skies!"[160] Thus, the Prophet (ﷺ) demonstrated the foolishness of worshipping other than Allāh when it is Allāh who responds to the one in distress.

The story of ʿIkrimah ibn Abī Jahl also demonstrates this point. ʿIkrimah, like his father, was one of the most severe people in his enmity towards the Prophet (ﷺ). Therefore, when the Prophet (ﷺ) entered Makkah as the victor after the Conquest of Makkah, he issued a general amnesty to all its inhabitants, except for four people, one of whom was ʿIkrimah. ʿIkrimah, knowing that he would not be spared due to the harm that he had caused the Muslims, had already fled. He fled to the sea, and took a boat, hoping to live in a foreign land safely. However, a great storm overtook them while they were at sea, and the people of the boat thought that they would all drown. So they told one another, "Make *duʿā* sincerely to Allāh, for verily all your idols and other gods will be of no help to you now!"

On hearing this, ʿIkrimah said to himself, "By Allāh! If only Allāh can save us in the ocean when we pray sincerely to Him, then He is the only One that can save us when we are on land as well! O Allāh! You have a promise that I make with You, that if You save me from this storm, then I will of a surety go to Muḥammad, and put my hand in his hand, and of a surety I will only find him to be forgiving and generous."

So the ship was saved from drowning, and ʿIkrimah fulfilled his promise and went to the Prophet (ﷺ), and indeed, he found the Prophet (ﷺ) to be as he expected, for the Prophet (ﷺ) forgave him, and treated him with respect. And ʿIkrimah proved to be a brave and courageous Muslim, and died as a martyr in one of the battles.[161]

So this incident demonstrated to ʿIkrimah the foolishness of his enmity to the call of the Prophet (ﷺ), for the call of the Prophet (ﷺ) was *tawḥīd*. When the people of the boat – who were all idol-worshippers – told each other that only

---

[160] Reported by al-Tirmidhī (# 3405), who declared it *ḥasan gharīb*. Al-Albānī declared it weak in *Ḍaʿīf al-Tirmidhī* (# 690). Ibn Ḥajr quoted it in *al-Isābah* (2/77), and did not comment on it. It appears that this wording of the story cannot be confirmed, as there is a weak narrator in the chain; however, Ibn Ḥajr declares that the incident of Ḥusayn meeting the Prophet (ﷺ) and accepting Islām has authentically been narrated. This narration, therefore, gives details of the meeting, but there is a weakness in it. The meaning of the ḥadīth, of course, is correct.

[161] See: *al-Isābah*, 4/443.

thousand of 'pilgrims' congregate around his mausoleum, and perform *tawāf* around it, vowing and sacrificing to it. One incident that this person is known for, and which is mentioned in various books of history, is that he entered the *masjid* before the Friday prayer, urinated inside the *masjid*, and then left without praying the *Ṣalāt*.[171]

The author here mentions these two matters with which he clearly demonstrates that the *shirk* of these pseudo-Islāmic sects of our times is in fact worse than the *shirk* of the *Jāhilīyyah* Arabs. In reality, there is yet a third aspect which shows this fact as well, and that is that these modern groups believe that their Shaykhs and Sayyids (the *awliyā'* of Allāh) have complete control over all matters in this world and the hereafter. In other words, these groups give their leaders powers of *Rubūbiyyah* (Lordship); something which even the *Jāhilīyyah* Arabs did not do!

So, they claim that their Shaykhs can cause the rain to fall, and revive the dead back to life, and grant their followers paradise, and bless whoever they wish with children, and so on. When one ponders over this matter, it becomes clear that the *shirk* of these groups is far worse than the *shirk* of the pagans of old.

We quote some of these incidents – and the fact of the matter is that their books are full of such stories – in order that the reader not presume that this is an exaggeration or lie against them.

Al-Nabhānī writes, "The Shaykh 'Abdallāh, one of the companions of Sayyid 'Umar al-Nabītī, wrote to me that he saw me with the Prophet (ﷺ), and he said to Imām 'Alī ibn Abī Ṭālib:[172] 'Put this cap of mine on 'Abd al-Wahhāb al-Sha'rānī (one of the most famous *Sūfī Sayyids*), and inform him that he can control the entire creation at will, for there is nothing that can prevent him from this.'"[173]

He also writes, 'Ubayd, "one of the companions of the Shaykh Hussain, was blessed with amazing miracles. Of them was that he would command the skies to rain, and they would rain immediately. And anyone that ridiculed him instantly died. Once, he entered (the district of) Ja'fariyyah, and around fifty

---

[171] *Qurrat 'Uyūn al-Muwaḥidīn*, p. 114.

[172] There is a very strong relationship between the *Sūfīs* and the *Shī'ites*, for they both believe in a 'hidden way', and that the Prophet (ﷺ) passed on secret knowledge to chosen people. They both exalt the status of their Shaykhs and spiritual leaders, directing acts of worship to them, and even attributing powers of *Rubūbiyyah* to them. And they both exaggerate the status of 'Alī ibn Abī Ṭālib, may Allāh be pleased with him.

[173] *Jāmi' Karāmāt al-'awliyā*, 2/275. The reader is asked to recall what the modern Noah Ha Mīm Keller has stated concerning the author of this work (mentioned previously).

children followed him, making fun of him. He said, 'O Azrā'il![174] If you do not take their souls, I will remove you from the ranks of the angels!' So they all fell down dead immediately..."[175]

He also writes concerning a certain, "...'Abd al-Raḥmān ibn Aḥmad al-Jāmi': of his miracles is that once he was sitting on the bank of a river, when a dead porcupine floated on the water to him. Our leader al-Jāmi' took it, and wiped his hand over its back, after which the signs of life became apparent on it. When we returned to the city, it followed us back."[176]

In another work, the actions of a certain Shaykh Madyan ibn Aḥmad are described. The author writes, "Once, a woman came up to him and said, 'Here are thirty silver coins, can you guarantee me Paradise?' The Shaykh replied, joking with her, 'This is not enough.' She replied, 'I do not have anything besides this.' So he guaranteed her that Allāh would cause her to enter Paradise. After she died, her inheritors heard of her action, so they went to the Shaykh, asking him to return the silver coins, claiming that this was a guarantee which was not correct (i.e., that the Shaykh had no right taking these coins since he could not guarantee paradise). So she appeared before them in a dream, and said, 'Be thankful to the Shaykh on my behalf, for indeed I entered Paradise.' So they left the Shaykh (without taking the coins)."[177]

The poem of al-Buṣayri also clearly shows this, as the descriptions given to the Prophet (ﷺ) are powers that only Allāh deserves.

These are just a selection of the quotes found in their books. We have intentionally restricted ourselves to quoting books that they consider the best and most authentic in the field, otherwise there are literally thousands of works of this nature which are saturated with beliefs of pure *shirk*.

---

[174] Azrā'il is the supposed name of the angel of death; however, there is nothing authentic from the Qur'ān or sunnah to support this claim.

[175] *Jāmi' Karāmāt al-Awliyā*, 2/286. The author continues to quote the 'miracles' that this man has supposedly performed, but in reality I felt too embarrassed to even quote them (the next one involves him saving a ship from drowning by pulling it with his private part – we seek Allāh's refuge from believing in such madness).

[176] *Jāmi' Karamāt al-Awliyā*, 2/254.

[177] *Tabaqāt al-Kubrā* of al-Sha'ranī, 2/101. It is also reported in al-Nabhānī's work as well (2/436). In reality, this is how the leaders of such deviation eat the people's wealth without any shame.

The Tenth Argument

TEXT

إذا تحققت أن الذين قاتلهم رسول الله صلى الله عليه وسلم ، أصح عقولاً ، وأخف شركاً من هؤلاء، فأعلم أن لهؤلاء شبهة يوردونها على ما ذكرنا وهي من أعظم شبههم ، فأصغ سمعك لجوابها وهي:

Now that you have realised that those whom the Prophet (ﷺ) fought were more intelligent and committed a lesser type of *shirk* than the people of our own times, then know that these people have yet another argument which they use, in addition to all that has preceded, and this is of their greatest arguments, so pay attention to it and to its response.

EXPL.

In other words, once you realise that these modern *mushrikūn* are less intelligent than the pagans of old, due to the two factors mentioned above, then realise that there is another argument that they use in order to refute those who oppose them.

This argument is, in reality, one of the strongest arguments in the eyes of the ignorant masses, even though its falsity and speciousness is clear to those with knowledge. Because this argument is used to deceive many people, the author goes into great detail in refuting it. He brings forth over eight different responses to this one argument.

So what, then, is this argument that they employ?

TEXT

أنهم يقولون: إن الذين نزل فيهم القرآن لا يشهدون أن لا إله إلا الله ويكذبون الرسول صلى الله عليه وسلم ، وينكرون البعث ويكذبون القرآن ويجعلونه سحراً ، ونحن نشهد أن لا إله إلا الله وأن محمد رسول الله ونصدق القرآن ، ونؤمن بالبعث ونصلي ونصوم، فكيف تجعلوننا مثل أولئك؟

This argument is that they say: "The people whom the Qur'ān mentions did not testify *Lā ilāha illa Allāh*; they used to deny the Prophet (ﷺ) and thought that he was a liar. They also used to deny the resurrection, and the Qur'ān, for they claimed that it was merely magic! As for us, we testify *Lā ilāha illa Allāh, Muḥammad Rasūl Allāh*. We believe in the Qur'ān, and in the Resurrection. We pray and we fast. So how can you compare us with those people of old?"

EXPL.

The essence of their argument is that it is not proper to equate them with the *Jāhilīyyah* Arabs of old. They state, "As for the *Jāhilīyyah* Arabs, they denied the Prophet (ﷺ), the Qur'ān, and the resurrection. They did not profess Islām, nor did they pray, or give *zakāt*, or fast. As for us, then we believe in all of this, and pray and fast and do all of these good deeds. How can you compare us with the pagans of old?"

The essence of this argument revolves around their misunderstanding of *kufr*. They believe that a person can only become a *kāfir* if he rejects the entire religion of Islām at once. So they claim that once a person prays, and claims to be a Muslim, there is nothing that can abrogate this claim.

The reason that this argument is so successful amongst average Muslims is that they find it difficult to think evil of a person who fasts, prays, and claims to be a Muslim. Due to the fact that this argument is so popular, the author responds to it in eight different ways.

The First Response

TEXT

فالجواب:-أنه لا خلاف بين العلماء كلهم أن الرجل إذا صدق رسول الله صلى الله عليه وسلم ، في شيء وكذبه في شيء ، أنه كافر لم يدخل في الإسلام ، وكذلك إذا آمن ببعض القرآن وجحد بعضه كمن أقر بالتوحيد وجحد وجوب الصلاة ، أو أقر بالتوحيد والصلاة وجحد وجوب الزكاة ، أو أقر بهذا كله وجحد الصوم ، أو أقر بهذا كله وجحد الحج ، ولما لم ينقد أناس في زمن النبي صلى الله عليه وسلم ، للحج أنزل الله في حقهم ﴿ولله على الناس حج البيت من أستطاع إليه سبيلاً ومن كفر فإن الله غني عن العالمين﴾ (سورة آل عمران، الآية: ٩٧) .

ومن أقر بهذا كله وجحد البعث كفر بالإجماع ، وحل دمه وماله ، كما قال تعالى : ﴿إن الذين يكفرون بالله ورسله ويريدون أن يفرقوا بين الله ورسله ويقولون نؤمن ببعض ونكفر ببعض ويريدون أن يتخذوا بين ذلك سبيلاً أولئك هم الكافرون حقاً وأعتدنا للكافرين عذاباً مهيناً﴾ (سورة النساء، الآيتان: ١٥٠، ١٥١).

فإذا كان الله قد صرح في كتابه : أن من آمن ببعض وكفر ببعض فهو الكافر حقاً زالت هذه الشبهة ، وهذه هي التي ذكرها بعض أهل الإحساء في كتابه الذي أرسل إلينا.

The response to this is to say: There is no difference of opinion amongst scholars – all of them – that if a person believes the Prophet (ﷺ) in one matter, and rejects another matter from him, that he is a disbeliever who has not entered Islām. Likewise, if he believes in part of the Qur'ān, and denies another part then he too is not a Muslim. For example, if a person believes in *tawḥīd*, but claims that he does not have to pray, or if he believes in *tawḥīd*

> and prayer but claims that he does not have to give *zakāt*, or if he believes in all of this but denies the legality of the fast of *Ramaḍān*, or believes in all of this, but denies the Ḥajj, such a person is not a Muslim. And the proof for this is that when a certain group of people were unwilling to do Ḥajj during the Prophet's (ﷺ) time, Allāh revealed concerning them, "And the Ḥajj is a right that is due to Allāh by mankind. But whoever disbelieves then Allāh is self-sufficient of the world" [Sūrah *Āl-ʿImrān*; 97].
>
> And whoever agrees with all of these pillars, but denies the resurrection on the Day of Judgement, then he has disbelieved by unanimous consensus, and his life and property are allowed (for the Islāmic state) to take, as Allāh said, "Those who disbelieve in Allāh and His Messengers, and wish to differentiate between Allāh and His Messengers..." [Sūrah *al-Nisā'*;150]. So if Allāh has clearly mentioned in His Book that a person who believes in a part of it and disbelieves in a part of it is a disbeliever, then this argument is destroyed! And this argument was sent to me in a letter that some people from the city of al-Aḥsā wrote.

The author mentions that this argument was sent to him by some of his EXPL. adversaries from al-Aḥsā. Although the author replied to this argument during his life time, it is sad to note that, to this day, this is one of the primary arguments that is circulated amongst the masses in order to counter-attack the scholars of *Ahl al-Sunnah*.

The first response that he gives to this argument is that *kufr* can occur by rejecting one single matter from the fundamentals of faith. This is a matter that all Muslims, laymen and scholars, have agreed on. So, if a person claims that he is a Muslim, yet states that it is not obligatory for him to pray the *Ṣalāt*, then this statement of his will nullify his profession of Islām. The same applies for the other examples given by the author.

Allāh states in the Qur'ān,

أَفَتُؤْمِنُونَ بِبَعْضِ ٱلْكِتَٰبِ وَتَكْفُرُونَ
بِبَعْضٍ ۚ فَمَا جَزَآءُ مَن يَفْعَلُ ذَٰلِكَ مِنكُمْ إِلَّا خِزْىٌ
فِى ٱلْحَيَوٰةِ ٱلدُّنْيَا ۖ وَيَوْمَ ٱلْقِيَٰمَةِ يُرَدُّونَ إِلَىٰٓ أَشَدِّ ٱلْعَذَابِ ۗ

> "Do you believe in a part of the Book, and disbelieve in a part of it? Then what is the penalty for those who do that among you except disgrace in this worldly life, and on the Day of Judgement they will be returned to the most severe punishment" [Sūrah *al-Baqarah*; 85].

The author also quotes a verse in the Qur'ān, which clearly states that rejecting some of the messengers is tantamount to rejecting all of them:

إِنَّ ٱلَّذِينَ يَكۡفُرُونَ
بِٱللَّهِ وَرُسُلِهِۦ وَيُرِيدُونَ أَن يُفَرِّقُواْ بَيۡنَ ٱللَّهِ وَرُسُلِهِۦ
وَيَقُولُونَ نُؤۡمِنُ بِبَعۡضٖ وَنَكۡفُرُ بِبَعۡضٖ وَيُرِيدُونَ
أَن يَتَّخِذُواْ بَيۡنَ ذَٰلِكَ سَبِيلًا ﴿١٥٠﴾ أُوْلَٰٓئِكَ هُمُ ٱلۡكَٰفِرُونَ
حَقّٗاۚ

"Those who disbelieve in Allāh and His messengers, and desire to differentiate between Allāh and His messengers, and say: 'We believe in some of them, and reject some (others),' desiring to take a path between the two; Verily, they are the disbelievers in truth…" [Sūrah *al-Nisā'*; 150-151].

This verse is meant as a refutation of the Christians and Jews, who claim to believe in some of Allāh's prophets, while rejecting others. Allāh states that there is no 'middle-path' when it comes to believing in His prophets, for a rejection of even one prophet is a rejection of Allāh Himself.

The point that the author is demonstrating from this verse is that a person can become a disbeliever by rejecting one prophet of Allāh, even though he might not reject the others. The opposite also holds true, and that is when a person believes in a false prophet and claims that he is a prophet of Allāh.

So, if a person claims to be a Muslim, and performs all the outward deeds of Islām, yet denies that Jesus Christ was Allāh's prophet, then such a person has negated his profession of Islām.

The Second Response

TEXT

ويقال إذا كنت تقر أن من صدق الرسول صلى الله عليه وسلم في كل شيء وجحد وجوب الصلاة فهو كافر حلال الدم المال بالإجماع ، وكذلك إذا أقر بكل شيء إلا البعث ، وكذلك لو جحد وجوب صوم رمضان وكذب بذلك لا يجحد هذا و لا تختلف المذاهب فيه ، وقد نطق به القرآن كما قدمنا.

فمعلوم أن التوحيد هو أعظم فريضة جاء بها النبي صلى الله عليه وسلم وهو أعظم من الصلاة ، والزكاة ، والصوم ، والحج فكيف إذا جحد الإنسان شيئاً من هذه الأمور كفر ولو عمل بكل ما جاء به الرسول صلى الله عليه وسلم ؟ وإذا جحد التوحيد الذي هو دين الرسل كلهم لا يكفر؟ سبحان الله ، ما أعجب هذا الجهل.

And it can also be said in response to this argument: You admit that a person who believes in the Prophet (ﷺ) concerning one matter, yet denies the *Ṣalāt*, is a disbeliever whose life and property become lawful (for the Islāmic state), and this is by consensus of the scholars. And also you admit that one who believes in everything that the Prophet (ﷺ) came with except the Resurrection, then he too is a disbeliever. The same ruling applies if he denies the fasting of *Ramaḍān*, even if he believes in the Resurrection. There is no difference of opinion amongst the Muslims concerning this, and the Qur'ān is explicit on this point, as we have mentioned previously.

Now, it is well-known that *tawḥīd* is the greatest matter that the Prophet (ﷺ) came with, for it is more important than *Ṣalāt*, and *zakāt*, and fasting, and the Ḥajj. So how is it possible that if a person denies one of these pillars of Islām, he is considered a disbeliever by you – even if he acts upon everything else that came from the Prophet (ﷺ) – but when he denies the reality of *tawḥīd*, which is the message of all the prophets, he is not a disbeliever?

Subḥān Allāh, how strange is this ignorance!

EXPL. This second response is a more specific example of the first one, in that here the author mentions that these people who are worshipping graves and saints are in reality rejecting *tawḥīd*. And it is an established fact that *tawḥīd* is more important than any other pillar of Islām. So, if a person – even in your eyes – has committed *kufr* by rejecting a lesser pillar, then what is so strange about claiming that he has committed *kufr* when he rejects the primary pillar of Islām, which is *tawḥīd*?

Once again, the author is proving that a rejection of one agreed-upon foundation of Islām is tantamount to a rejection of Islām. And since *tawḥīd* is the essence of Islām, and its primary pillar, then it follows that a rejection of *tawḥīd* is a rejection of Islām.

The Third Response

TEXT ويقال أيضاً: هؤلاء أصحاب رسول الله صلى الله عليه وسلم قاتلوا بني حنيفة وقد أسلموا مع النبي صلى الله عليه وسلم الله عليه وسلم وهم يشهدون أن لا إله إلا الله وأن محمداً رسول الله ويصلون ويؤذنون .

فإن قال إنهم يقولون: إن مسيلمة نبي.

فقلنا: هذا هو المطلوب إذا كان من رفع رجلاً إلى رتبة النبي صلى الله عليه وسلم كفر وحل ماله ودمه و لم تنفعه الشهادتان ولا الصلاة، فكيف بمن رفع شمسان أو يوسف أو صحابياً أو نبياً في مرتبة جبار السموات والأرض؟

سبحان الله ، ما أعظم شأنه ﴿ كذلك يطبع الله على قلوب الذين لا يعلمون﴾ (سورة الروم ، الآية ٥٩)

And it can also be said as yet another response: The Companions of the Prophet (ﷺ) fought the tribe of Banu Ḥanīfah, even though they accepted Islam with the Prophet (ﷺ), and they testified *Lā ilāha illa Allāh* and that *Muḥammad* is His Messenger and Worshipper. And they used to pray, and give the *adhān*.

Now, when he responds, "But they testified along with all of this that Musaylmah the false prophet is in reality a prophet!", then tell him, "This is exactly the point! If raising a person to the level of the Prophet (ﷺ) causes a person to disbelieve, and makes his life and property lawful (for the Islāmic state), and his testimony of faith and prayer is useless, then how about the one who raises Shamsān, or Yūsuf, or any companion or prophet to the level of the Exalted, the Lord of the Heavens and earth?"

Exalted is He, how great is His Glory! But few will understand for, "This is how Allāh seals up the hearts of those who do not know" [Sūrah *Al-Rūm*; 59].

EXPL. In this response, the author proves that even the Companions fought and killed groups of people who claimed to be Muslims. He gave the example of the tribe of Banu Ḥanīfah. This tribe accepted Islām during the Prophet's (ﷺ) lifetime, and for a period of time followed the other Muslims in their beliefs. However, soon there arose a person by the name of Musaylamah who claimed that he too was a prophet along with the Prophet (ﷺ). Because of this claim, he was given the title *'al-Kadhāb'*, meaning, the Liar. His people followed him, not because they believed in him, but because they preferred to have a prophet from their own tribe rather than from the tribe of Quraysh.

The Companions dealt with them as apostates and did not consider them to be Muslims because they had believed in a matter which nullified their Islām.

The sect known as the Qadianis are not considered as Muslims by any Muslim in the world. It is one of the few sects which the entire Muslim world has unanimously agreed is outside the fold of Islām. Yet, it is amazing that practicing Qadianis pray five times a day, fast the month of *Ramaḍān*, give charity, perform Ḥajj, and do other religious acts. They are active in reciting the Qur'ān, and calling others to their religion. So why are they considered non-Muslims? The reason being that they believe Mirza Ghulam Aḥmad was a prophet of Allāh, after the Prophet (ﷺ).

If a person can become a non-Muslim by believing that a certain person is a prophet of Allāh, then what is the case of a person who believes that another object is worthy of worship, and thus raises it to the level of Allāh? The author mentions the names of Shamsān and Yūsuf, who were two 'saints' that the people of his time worshipped. They sacrificed to them, made *du'ā* to them, and visited their mausoleums with the intent of worshipping them.

The Fourth Response

TEXT

ويقال أيضاً الذين حرقهم علي بن أبي طالب رضي الله عنه بالنار كلهم يدعون الإسلام وهم من أصحاب علي رضي الله عنه وتعلموا العلم من الصحابة ولكن اعتقدوا في علي مثل الاعتقاد في يوسف وشمسان وامثالهما، فكيف أجمع الصحابة على قتلهم وكفرهم؟ أتظنون أن الصحابة يكفرون المسلمين؟ أم تظنون أن الاعتقاد في تاج وأمثاله لا يضر والاعتقاد في علي بن أبي طالب يكفر؟

And it can also be said to them as another response that 'Alī ibn Abī Ṭālib burnt to death people that testified that they were Muslims. They used to be of his companions and followers, and they learnt their religion from the Companions. But they believed 'Alī to have an exaggerated status just like you believe in Yūsuf and Shamsān and others like them. So how was it possible that the Companions agreed to kill them, and considered them disbelievers even though they professed Islam? Do you accuse the Companions of pronouncing the Muslims to be *kāfirs*? Or do you differentiate between believing in Tāj and others like him, claiming that such a belief is not harmful, but belief in 'Alī ibn Abī Ṭālib as having certain supernatural powers causes one to disbelieve?

EXPL.

Here the author gives another example which proves his earlier points. During the time of 'Alī ibn Abī Ṭālib, a certain group of people – who are the precursors of the modern Shi'ites – claimed that 'Alī was in fact Allāh impersonified. The leader of this group was 'Abdullāh ibn Saba', a Yemenite Jew who professed Islām but was in reality a heretic who wished to destroy it. 'Alī captured many of his followers, but could not capture 'Abdullāh ibn Saba', for he fled to another country and continued to preach his doctrines. Although his actual followers eventually died out, he was the one who first planted the seed of 'Alī's veneration, and this seed gave sprout to many different sects, all of which had this one theme in common. So some of them believed that 'Alī was in fact god-incarnate, whereas others felt that he was a prophet. The main sect that still remains is that of the Twelver Shi'ites, who are predominantly in Iran and parts of Iraq. They believe that 'Alī was the undisputed Successor of the Prophet (ﷺ), and they give him and his progeny after him powers of Lordship (*Rubūbiyyah*). Additionally, grave worship is rampant amongst them, for they worship all of their Imāms, and have built large mausoleums over their graves.

When ʿAlī ibn Abī Ṭālib was informed of this group, he called them to his presence and debated with them. But they refused to change their views that he was god-incarnate. Since the ruling in Islāmic law for apostates is death, he had no choice but to execute them – a decision which all of the Companions agreed to. ʿAlī decided to burn them alive, which he did, but some of the Companions did not agree that this was the appropriate death penalty.

Al-Bukhārī reports in his *Ṣaḥīḥ* that a group of heretics were brought to ʿAlī ibn Abī Ṭālib, and he burnt them alive. When Ibn ʿAbbās heard of this, he said, "Had it been I (who was responsible), I would not have burnt them…"[178]

The point that the author makes is that the Companions agreed to execute a group of people who professed Islām, prayed, fasted, and did all the other acts that they were required to do. The one matter that made their life and property lawful for the Muslims to take was that they raised ʿAlī ibn Abī Ṭālib, a pious Caliph and Companion of the Prophet (ﷺ), to the level of a god.

So if the Companions did this to a group of people who exaggerated the status of ʿAlī, then what is the difference between them and those who exaggerate the status of Yūsuf, Shamsān, and Tāj, who are nowhere near the status of ʿAlī ibn Abī Ṭālib? What is the difference between those who worship these 'saints' and claim that they control all matters, and between those who worshipped ʿAlī?

In fact, the 'saint' called Tāj was a person who claimed to have a high religious status, and would demand that his followers pay him money in order to pray for them. He would collect regular stipends from the people of surrounding areas and tribes. He had guards that were greatly feared by the people, and who would extract this money from them. Many stories and miracles were falsely attributed to him. After his death, his grave became a place of worship, to the extent that *tawāf* was performed around it. Despite this professed high status, Tāj was notorious for his evil life-style. So in reality the followers of Ibn Saba' had more sense than the followers of Tāj did, for at least they exalted a pious man who in actuality did have a high status with Allāh, whereas the followers of Tāj exalted a person notorious for his evil.

These three names (Tāj, Yūsuf and Shamsān) appear to be the three icons that were the most famous objects of worship during the time of the author, for he mentions them in other works as well.

---

[178] *Ṣaḥīḥ al-Bukhārī*, 6/151. The details of these heretics, and that they were the followers of Ibn Saba', are found in the books of history, such as al-Ṭabarī's *Tarīkh*.

TEXT

ويقال أيضاً : بنو عبيد القداح الذين ملكوا المغرب ومصر في زمن بني العباس كلهم يشهدون أن لا إله إلا الله وأن محمداً رسول الله ، ويدعون الإسلام، ويصلون الجمعة والجماعة فلما أظهروا مخالفة الشريعة في أشياء دون ما نحن فيه أجمع العلماء على كفرهم وقتالهم ، وأن بلادهم بلاد حرب ، وغزاهم المسلمون حتى أستنفذوا ما بأيديهم من بلدان المسلمين.

And it can be said to them as yet another response that the Banu 'Ubayd al-Qaddāḥ (the Fatimids), the family that controlled the territory from Morocco to Egypt during the time of the 'Abbāsids used to testify *Lā ilāh illa Allāh Muḥammad Rasūl Allāh*, and they used to pray the Friday prayer, and the other congregational prayers. But when they demonstrated that they opposed the Islamic Law in certain matters – matters that are less evil than what we are discussing now – the scholars unanimously agreed that they were disbelievers who should be fought. They considered their country as enemy territory, and so the Muslims fought them until they saved the lands that were in their hands and returned them to Muslim hands.

EXPL.

Here the author gives yet another example to prove his point.

During the fourth and fifth centuries of the *Ḥijrah*, there existed a powerful extremist Shī'ite dynasty that controlled – at the peak of its power – Northern Africa in its entirety. Although they professed Islām, they were in reality a group of heretics who claimed that the Qur'ān had an esoteric hidden meaning, which was known only to them. Thus, they interpreted the *Ṣalāt* as a spiritual remembrance of Allāh, and the fasting as a fasting from sins, and the Ḥajj as visiting their leaders, and so on. They venerated their caliphs, and considered them to have supernatural powers. In addition, they introduced the innovation of *mīlād* (celebrating the Prophet's (ﷺ) birthday), which was unknown to the Muslims before that time. History books are filled with the details of their *kufr*, and their injustices to the Muslims.

Because of their obvious disbelief, the Muslims of their times declared them to be unbelievers, and fought against them. Salāh al-Dīn al-Ayūbi, the famous general who fought the Christian armies in the Crusades, was the one who finally managed to destroy their empire, and thus re-captured Egypt for the Muslims.

The point that the author makes is that these people also declared their Islām, and some of them, albeit not their leaders, even fasted and prayed. However, due to their extreme aberrations in faith and practices, all the Muslims of their times declared them to be enemies of Islām, and considered their country as enemy territory, thus justifying an attack against them.

So if this is the case with an entire country, then what about a tribe or a small group of people who openly practice idolatry? Is it not even more imperative for an Islāmic state to stop them?

The Sixth Response

TEXT

ويقال أيضاً إذا كان الأولون لم يكفروا إلا لأنهم جمعوا بين الشرك وتكذيب الرسول والقرآن ، وإنكار البعث وغير ذلك فما معنى الباب الذي ذكر العلماء في كل مذهب : (باب حكم المرتد) وهو المسلم الذي يكفر بعد إسلامه ، ثم ذكروا أنواعاً كثيرة كل نوع منها يكفر ويحل دم الرجل وماله ، حتى أنهم ذكروا أشياء يسيرة عند من فعلها ، مثل كلمة يذكرها بلسانه دون قلبه ، أو كلمة يذكرها على وجه المزح واللعب.

And it can also be said as another response: If you claim that the *Jāhilīyyah* Arabs only disbelieved due to the fact that they combined in them many factors, such as *shirk*, and rejecting the prophets and the Qur'ān, and denying the Day of Judgement, and other matters, then how do you explain the existence of the chapter that all scholars mention in books of law entitled, "The Chapter Concerning the Ruling of the *Murtad*?" For the *murtad* is a Muslim who commits disbelief after his Islām. And these scholars mention many matters that cause a person to disbelieve. Any one of these matters causes one to disbelieve, and makes his life and property lawful. In fact, they even mention certain matters that may appear to be trivial by the one who performs them, such as making a statement without actually intending what was said, or saying something jokingly or in jest.

EXPL. Here the author re-iterates that scholars of *fiqh* all have chapters in their books entitled, '*Bāb al-Murtad*,' or, 'The Rulings on the Apostate.' In this chapter, they discuss who is considered an apostate, and how to deal with such a person. These scholars mention many matters, any one of which is sufficient for a person to be considered an apostate. It is not necessary according to *any* scholar of Islām that all these matters be combined in a person for him to be considered a *murtad*. It is even possible that a Muslim be considered a *murtad* because of a single sentence that he says by way of jest. For example, if a person curses Allah, or ridicules the Prophet (ﷺ), then even if he intended by it to crack a joke or make other people laugh, and did not actually intend with his heart to curse them, this excuse would not be accepted. And this is a matter which all the schools of Islāmic *fiqh* have agreed upon.

Once again, the author proves that it is possible for a person to become a *murtad* even if he fasts, reads the Qur'ān, and there are marks of fatigue on his face due to his long prostrations! The criterion here is not whether a person merely fasts and prays, but rather that a person believes in the fundamental principles of Islām. If at any time someone rejects a matter which is an agreed-upon principle of Islām, he has in fact rejected the entire religion. And without a doubt, the most fundamental of all fundamentals of this religion is that only Allāh be worshipped – nothing else.

The Seventh Response

TEXT

ويقال أيضاً: الذين قال الله فيهم ﴿يحلفون بالله ما قالوا ولقد قالوا كلمة الكفر وكفروا بعد إسلامهم﴾ (سورة التوبة الآية: ٧٤) أما سمعت الله كفرهم بكلمة مع كونهم في زمن رسول الله صلى الله عليه وسلم ويجاهدون معه ويصلون معه ، ويزكون ، ويحجون، ويوحدون ، وكذلك الذين قال الله تعالى فيهم: ﴿قل أبالله وآياته ورسوله كنتم تستهزؤن لا تعتذروا قد كفرتم بعد إيمانكم﴾(سورة التوبة الآية: ٦٦-٦٥). فهؤلاء الذين صرح الله أنهم كفروا بعد إيمانهم – وهم مع رسول الله صلى الله عليه وسلم في غزوة تبوك – قالوا كلمة ذكروا أنهم قالوها على وجه المزح.

And yet another response to this is to say, "Do you not see that Allāh said regarding a group of people who used to perform *jihād* with the Prophet (ﷺ), and pray with him, and give *zakāt*, and perform Ḥajj, and believed in *tawḥīd* that they, "...swear by Allāh that they did not say (what they said), even though they said a statement of disbelief, and became disbelievers after their Islām" [Sūrah *al-Tawbah*; 74]? Do you not see that Allāh pronounced them disbelievers because of this one statement that they made, even though they performed all of these other good deeds? Likewise, Allāh said regarding some people, "Say: Do you jest with Allāh, and His signs and His Prophet? Do not give excuses, you have indeed disbelieved after your faith" [Sūrah *al-Tawbah*; 65-66]. These people whom Allāh refers to committed disbelief after having *īmān*. They were fighting alongside the Prophet (ﷺ) during the Battle of Tabūk, and they made a certain statement of disbelief which they later claimed was meant as a joke and idle-talk. Nonetheless, this excuse was not accepted from them.

EXPL.

In this seventh response, the author mentions an incident that occurred during the Battle of Tabuk. During this Battle, many of the hypocrites of Madīnah also accompanied the army. One of them said, "I have never seen reciters (of the Qur'ān) like our companions here (referring to the Prophet (ﷺ) and the Companions) who are more eager (to fill) their bellies, or are more prone to lying, and are more cowardly during battle." Hearing this, one of the Companions by the name of 'Awf ibn Mālik immediately retorted, "You have lied! Rather, you are a hypocrite, and of a surety I will inform the Prophet (ﷺ) of your affair." So

'Awf went to the Prophet (ﷺ), but discovered that a revelation from Allāh had preceded him, and that the Prophet (ﷺ) was already aware of their statements. Allāh had revealed verses of the Qur'ān concerning this incident (Sūrah *al-Tawbah*, verse 64 and those after it). The narrator of this incident states, "It is as if I am seeing the person who made that statement, holding on to the stirrup of the Prophet's (ﷺ) saddle, and the stones are dragging his feet, while he is saying, 'We were only joking and playing,' and the Prophet (ﷺ) is replying to him, 'Do you jest with Allāh, and His signs and His Prophet?'"[179]

So these people, who were in fact accompanying the Messenger of Allāh (ﷺ) during a battle, fell into *kufr* merely by uttering a statement that they said was in jest. Here, Allāh Himself proclaimed their disbelief, for He states,

لَا تَعْتَذِرُوا قَدْ كَفَرْتُم بَعْدَ إِيمَانِكُمْ

"Do not give excuses, you have indeed disbelieved after your faith" [Sūrah *al-Tawbah*; 66].

Once again, a group of people have been declared disbelievers, despite their profession of Islām, and their acts of prayer and *jihād*, due to one statement that they uttered. So is not a person who constantly worships other than Allāh more liable to be considered a disbeliever?

TEXT

فتأمل هذه الشبهة، وهي قولهم «تكفرون المسلمين أنا سا يشهدون ألا إله إلا الله، ويصلون ويصومون»! ثم تأمل جوابها؛ فإنه من أنفع ما في هذه الأوراق.

So ponder over their argument, and their saying, "You consider Muslims who testify *Lā ilāh illa Allāh* and fast and pray to be disbelievers!" And also ponder over the response to this argument, for it is perhaps the most beneficial point in this tract.

EXPL.

It has always been the practice of the enemies of *tawḥīd* to try to slander the followers of *tawḥīd* in any way possible. And this slander, that the *Ahl al-Sunnah* in general, and Shaykh Muḥammad ibn ʿAbd al-Wahhāb in particular, used to declare all Muslims besides his own group to be disbelievers is without a doubt one of the worst slanders against the people of truth.

Rather, the fact of the matter is that the author, based upon the clear principles of the Qur'ān and Sunnah, proclaimed certain peoples and tribes as outside the fold of Islām, and did not claim that the entire Muslim *ummah* had committed *kufr*. Additionally, even when he made such a ruling upon certain specific groups, it was done *after* the evidences had been clearly presented to them and they persisted in their *shirk*. He himself clearly and unequivocally states (as has been mentioned earlier) that he does not consider any Muslim to become a *kāfir* until the evidence has been firmly established against him. As

[179] Reported by Ibn Jarīr in his *Tafsīr* (10/119) with an authentic chain of narrators.

for people who commit such acts out of sheer ignorance, and who do not have recourse to knowledgeable people, then without a doubt they are excused as long as they really and truly were ignorant, believing that these acts were a part of Islām.

However, these points that the author brings clearly justifies the principle of declaring any Muslim who has committed a clear act of *kufr* or *shirk* a disbeliever (as long as the other conditions for pronouncing *takfīr* are met). Additionally, it is important to differentiate between a general ruling, and specifying that ruling on a particular person. Here, the author is mentioning general rulings and examples, and is not applying them to specific people.

In order to emphasise the importance of these responses, the author mentions that they might in fact be the most beneficial matter in this book.

The Eighth Response

TEXT

ومن الدليل على ذلك أيضاً ما حكى الله عز وجل عن بني إسرائيل مع إسلامهم وعلمهم وصلاحهم أنهم قالوا لموسى: ﴿اجعل لنا إلهاً كما لهم آلهة﴾ (سورة الأعراف، الآية: ١٣٨) وقول أناس من الصحابة: «اجعل لنا – يا رسول – ذات أنواط» فحلف رسول صلى الله عليه وسلم ، أن هذا مثل قول بني إسرائيل اجعل لنا إلهاً.

And of the proofs for what we have mentioned is contained in the description that Allāh gave to the Children of Israel, even though they were Muslims, and had knowledge and piety. For they asked Moses, "Make for us a god" [Sūrah *al-Aʿrāf;* 138]. Also some of the Companions said, "Make for us, O Messenger of Allāh, a *Dhāt Anwāṭ*," so the Prophet (ﷺ) swore that their statement was similar to that of the Children of Israel, "Make for us a god."

EXPL.

Here, the author brings the last response to this argument, and that is the story that Allāh mentions in the Qur'ān concerning the Children of Israel. Once, they passed by an idol-worshipping nation, so, in their ignorance, they asked Mūsa, 'Make for us a god, just like they have a god.' And such a request, without a doubt, is a request of *shirk*.

In a similar incident, Abū Wāqid al-Laythī reports, "We went with the Prophet (ﷺ) to Hunayn, and we had newly left disbelief (i.e., we had just recently embraced Islām). The pagans had a tree that was called *Dhāt Anwāṭ* that they would seek blessings from, and they would hang their weapons on it (as a good-luck charm before battle). So we too passed by a tree, and said, 'O Messenger of Allah! Make for us a *Dhāt Anwāṭ* just like they have a *Dhāt Anwāṭ*!' So the Prophet (ﷺ) said,

> "*Subḥān Allāh!* Verily it is the practice (that you are going to follow those before you). You have said – by Him in Whose hands is my soul – just like the Children of Israel said to Mūsa,

اَجْعَل لَّنَآ إِلَـٰهًا كَمَا لَهُمْ ءَالِهَةٌ
قَالَ إِنَّكُمْ قَوْمٌ تَجْهَلُونَ ﴿١٣٨﴾

'Make for us a god, just like they have a god. He (Mūsa) responded: You are an ignorant nation' [Sūrah *al-Aʿrāf;* 138].

You will of a surety follow the practices of the peoples before you."[180]

These Companions who were new to Islām, and thus not fully aware of the implications of what they were doing, asked the Prophet (ﷺ) to make for them a tree that they could seek blessings from. The Prophet (ﷺ) equated this with the request of the Children of Israel, since the seeking of blessings is an act of worship that can only be done with Allāh's permission. Thus, to seek blessings from any object that is not sanctioned by Sacred Law is an act of *shirk*. Another reason why such an act is considered *shirk* is that the person trying to obtain 'good luck' from an object begins to venerate that object. They respect it, entertain hopes from it, and fear its rejection. And, as has been discussed previously, these acts make such an object an *ilāh* that is worshipped besides Allāh.

The point here is that the Prophet (ﷺ) equated this request with the request of the Children of Israel, and thus proclaimed that they were asking something of *shirk*.

However, there is a counter-argument used by justifiers of *shirk* with regards to the story of the Children of Israel, and the incident of *Dhāt Anwāṭ*.

TEXT ولكن للمشركين شبهة يدلون بها عند هذه القصة وهي أنهم يقولون: إن بني إسرائيل لم يكفروا بذلك، وكذلك الذين قالوا للنبي صلى الله عليه وسلم اجعل لنا ذات أنواط لم يكفروا.

But the *mushrikīn* have an argument that they use to try to refute the proper understanding of this story, and that is that they say: the Children of Israel did not become disbelievers by this action of theirs, and neither did the Companions when they asked the Prophet (ﷺ) to make for them a *Dhāt Anwāṭ*.

EXPL. So they claim that the use of these two incidents as proof is in fact unjustified, as the people that were involved did not actually *become* disbelievers. Therefore, there is no basis for using these incidents to justify the initial point.

---

[180] Reported by al-Tirmidhī (# 2180), who declared it *ḥasan Ṣaḥīḥ*.

TEXT

فالجواب: أن نقول إن بني إسرائيل لم يفعلوا ذلك، وكذلك الذين سألوا النبي صلى الله عليه وسلم ، لم يفعلوا ، ولا خلاف أن بني إسرائيل لو فعلوا ذلك لكفروا، وكذلك لا خلاف أن الذين نهاهم النبي صلى الله عليه وسلم لو لم يطيعوه واتخذوا ذات أنواط بعد نهيه لكفروا وهذا هو المطلوب.

So we respond by stating: the Children of Israel did not actually do the act, and likewise nor did the Companions. And there is no difference of opinion that if the Children of Israel went ahead with the act they would have become disbelievers. Likewise, there is no difference of opinion that, had the Companions disobeyed the Prophet (ﷺ) when he prohibited them, and instead taken a *Dhāt Anwāṭ* after his prohibition, they would have become disbelievers. And this is the point.

EXPL.

Even though the two groups did not actually *become* disbelievers due to their respective requests, the point is that they would have had they actually implemented them. And the initial thesis that has been proven over and over again, and can be proven with these incidents as well, is that it is possible for a believer to become a disbeliever by committing one act of *kufr* intentionally and without coercion.

Another benefit to be obtained from their counter-argument is that this is exactly what our own position is as well: that a Muslim who commits an act of *kufr* out of sheer ignorance will in all likelihood be forgiven.[181] Such a person will only be held accountable if he intended to commit an act of *kufr*, knowing full well the status of such an act, and not having physically been coerced into it.

So these are eight responses for the seventh argument that the author mentions in this tract. Before moving on to the next argument, the author draws our attention to some important points that we can benefit from also.

Four Benefits from These Incidents

TEXT

ولكن هذه القصة تفيد أن المسلم بل العالم قد يقع في أنواع من الشرك لا يدري عنها

But this story has a number of benefits that we can derive from it, the first of

[181] There is an exception to this general ruling, and that is for those acts which are known by necessity and common sense to be acts of *kufr*, such as cursing Allāh or the Messenger (ﷺ), or showing disrespect to the Qur'ān, or other similar behaviour, in which even ignorance cannot be used as an excuse.

these is that a Muslim – even a scholar – might fall into certain types of *shirk* while he is unaware of it.

EXPL. The proof for this is that the Companions of the Prophet (ﷺ), and those of Mūsa, were obviously not aware that they were asking for matters of *shirk*. So it becomes even more imperative upon us that we fear this great evil, and that we be ever cautious of falling into the trap of *Shayṭān*.

This is especially true when a person might have studied a certain branch of Islām, but not others. So it is possible to find some scholars of Islamic law, or Arabic grammar, falling into certain aspects that constitute *shirk*, simply because they have never specialised in the study of *tawḥīd* and *shirk*. And such is the case with many of the opponents of *Ahl al-Sunnah* who wrote refutations against the author, and it is also the case of those before him who refuted scholars such as Ibn Taymiyyah. Such opponents might actually have reached a very high level of knowledge, but only in fields unrelated to the fundamental sciences of *tawḥīd* and *shirk*.

Therefore, it should not come as any surprise that throughout the centuries, in particular the last few centuries, there have existed scholars who have tried to justify acts of *shirk* and innovation. These scholars might have achieved great fame or status in their respective fields, and might be well-respected by the masses. They might even have written books proving these acts of *shirk* and innovation, seeking to justify them from the Qur'ān, Sunnah, and statements of other scholars.

In the incident of *Dhāt Anwāṭ*, some of the Companions themselves asked the Prophet (ﷺ) for an act which was clear *kufr* (even though they were ignorant of the status of this act, and were thus excused). So if someone were to try to justify this same action (of seeking blessings through a tree) by using the behaviour of these Companions, he would be mistaken. So what then is the case of someone who tries to justify acts of *shirk* by quoting a person who lived a thousand years after the Prophet (ﷺ), and is nowhere near the status of these same Companions?

The religion of Islām is not based upon the statements of scholars, no matter who they might be. It is based upon the Qur'ān and Sunnah, and the understanding of the early generations of Islām. Every scholar's statements must be weighed with the texts of the Qur'ān and Sunnah; whatever is in conformity with it can be taken from him, and whatever goes against it must be rejected, no matter who he is.

TEXT فتفيد التعلم والتحرز ومعرفة أن قول الجاهل (التوحيد فهمناه) أن هذا من أكبر الجهل ومكائد الشيطان.

A second benefit is to teach and warn us, so that we realise that an ignorant person's statement, "We understand *tawḥīd*," is of the greatest types of ignorance! Rather, it is a plot of *Shayṭān*.

EXPL.

Indeed, one of the most successful ways in which *Shayṭān* misguides Muslims is that he makes them feel confident of their own knowledge of *tawḥīd*. If a person believes that he is fully aware of *tawḥīd* and *shirk* while he has never studied them, how can he feel confident that he will not fall into *shirk*? In the incidents described above, we have the Prophet's (ﷺ) Companions and those of Mūsa, respectively asking their prophets for matters which are *shirk*. So if even such noble people and pious followers might accidentally ask something so evil, then what about the average Muslim?

When one tries to discuss *tawḥīd* with the average Muslim, a typical response is, "Everyone knows what *tawḥīd* is. Allāh is one, how much more is there to *tawḥīd*?" The same applies to the concept of *shirk*. The average Muslim only thinks of *shirk* as idol-worship, and does not realise that it is of many types and categories.

Yet, when one examines the biography of the Prophet (ﷺ), one finds that this was always the constant theme of his call. For the thirteen years that he was in Makkah, this was in fact the *only* matter that he called to, for at that point in time the Sacred Laws of Islām had not been revealed. And even in Madīnah he continued emphasising this most important fundamental. The incident of *Dhāt Anwāṭ* in fact occurred during the later part of his time in Madīnah. And one of the last phrases that came out of his mouth, hours before his death, was the warning, "Allāh has cursed the Jews and the Christians, for they took the graves of their prophets as places of worship. Verily do not do so, for I forbid you from it."[182]

TEXT

وتفيد أيضاً أن المسلم المجتهد إذا تكلم بكلام كفر وهو لا يدري فنبه على ذلك وتاب من ساعته أنه لا يكفر كما فعل بنو إسرائيل والذين سألوا رسول الله صلى الله عليه وسلم.

A third benefit is that if a Muslim strives to understand the truth, and utters a statement of disbelief, without realising that it is disbelief (*kufr*), then when this is pointed out to him, and he repents immediately, such a person has not committed disbelief. And this is what occurred with the Children of Israel, and the Companions when they asked the Prophet (ﷺ).

EXPL.

This is a matter which many people fail to understand. It is possible that a person falls into an act or belief of *kufr* without knowing the reality of his action.

---

[182] Reported by al-Bukhārī (1/427) and others.

If such a person was sincerely trying to please Allāh, and did not know the ruling on that action, then he will not be held accountable for such a mistake as long as he repents when it is pointed out to him. Proof for this is that the Companions, and the Children of Israel, did not become disbelievers by asking for these matters, for they were excused because of their ignorance.

This ruling is even more applicable to new Muslims, or those living in areas where there are no scholars to explain the essence of what they are doing.

This explicit statement by the author clearly proves that he did not unconditionally consider all those who fell into *shirk* as *mushriks*, nor did he consider the majority of Muslims to be *kāfirs*. And this clearly refutes the slander that is propagated by his opponents concerning this matter.

TEXT وتفيد – أيضا – أنه لو لم يكفر فإنه يغلظ عليه الكلام تغليظاً شديداً كما فعل رسول الله صلى الله عليه وسلم.

A final benefit is that even if such a person does not enter into disbelief, then he should be rebuked and reprimanded severely, as the Prophet (ﷺ) did.

EXPL. Even if a person does not actually become a *kāfir* because of his ignorance, this does not warrant that we overlook this ignorance. Rather, such a person needs to be taught immediately, and in fact severely reprimanded, so that he does not fall into such error again.

So, for example, the Prophet (ﷺ) responded severely to the incident of *Dhāt Anwāṭ*. Firstly, by saying *Subḥān Allāh*, which was usually said by him at times of amazement, and to glorify Allāh and exalt Him above any evil. Secondly, by his equating their request with that of the Children of Israel. Thirdly, by stating that they would follow the path of those before them, and that path led to misguidance.

Of course, severity should only be shown if the person that is so reprimanding has authority, or is well-respected by the one that is being reprimanded. The father can be strict with his family, and the leader with his followers. However, if a person is a stranger in the community, or does not occupy a position of leadership with them, then he needs to proceed wisely, and ensure that whatever steps he takes will be beneficial in order to impart the correct knowledge that he has.

The Eleventh Argument

TEXT

وللمشركين شبهة أخرى يقولون: إن النبي صلى الله عليه وسلم أنكر على أسامة – رضي الله عنه – قتل من قال « لا إله إلا الله» ، وكذلك قوله: «أمرت أن أقاتل الناس حتى يقولوا لا إله إلا الله»، كذلك وأحاديث أخرى في الكف عمن قالها ، ومراد هؤلاء الجهلة أن من قالها لا يكفر، ولا يقتل ولو فعل ما فعل.

People who commit *shirk* in our times employ another argument similar to the one that has gone before, which they use to try to refute their opponents. They say: The Prophet (ﷺ) reprimanded Usāmah ibn Zayd when he killed the person who said *Lā ilāh illa Allāh*, and he told him, "Did you (dare) to kill him after he said *Lā ilāh illa Allāh?*" And they also use the ḥadith, "I have been commanded to fight mankind until they testify *Lā ilāh illa Allāh...*" and similar *aḥādīth*, that prohibit harming the one who testifies *Lā ilāh illa Allāh*. The point that these ignoramuses try to prove with all of these *aḥādīth* is that whoever says it will not become a disbeliever, and neither should he be killed, no matter what he does.

EXPL.

This argument is similar to the one that has preceded, except that there is an added point that they seek to prove. In the last argument, they sought to show that the one who claims to be a Muslim and outwardly adheres to the Sacred Law cannot become a disbeliever. So the author proved that this is the case only if he refrains from believing or committing an act that nullifies his Islām.

In this argument, they now try to prove that it is impermissible to fight those who claim to be Muslim, and testify *Lā ilāha illa Allāh*. This is because the author, since he had established an Islāmic state in Arabia during his time, would undertake military action against those who committed major *shirk* and refrained from desisting even after evidence had been established against them. Therefore, his opponents objected to his actions, and considered them to be impermissible. They quoted various *aḥādīth* to prove their point. Of them is the ḥadith of Usāmah, who narrates, "The Prophet (ﷺ) sent us on an expedition. When we surprised the enemy, we defeated them. I caught a person amongst them, but when I was about to over-power him (to kill him), he said, '*Lā ilāha ilāh Allah*.' But I killed him anyway. When we returned, the Prophet (ﷺ) was informed of my action. He asked me, 'O Usāmah! Did you (dare) to kill him after he testified *Lā ilāha illa Allāh*?' I said, 'O Messenger of Allāh, he was only trying to save himself!' But he responded, "Did you open his chest (to verify this information)? What will you do with *Lā ilāha illa Allāh* on the

Day of Judgement?" And he kept on repeating it, until I wished that I had only embraced Islām that day (so that I would have an excuse for my actions)."[183]

Another ḥadīth they quote is that whereby the Prophet (ﷺ) said,

> "I have been commanded to fight the people until they say '*Lā ilāha illa Allāh*'. Once they say it, their lives and properties become prohibited for me, except with due cause, and their reckoning is with Allāh."[184]

So the author shows, once again, that indeed these evidences are all correct, but they must be understood in light of other evidences – evidences that clearly show that there are certain conditions in which it is allowed to fight against people who profess Islām.[185]

TEXT

فيقال لهؤلاء المشركين الجهلة: معلوم أن رسول الله صلى الله عليه وسلم قاتل اليهود وسباهم وهم يقولون : لا إله إلا الله ، وأن أصحاب رسول الله صلى الله عليه وسلم قاتلوا بني حنيفة وهم يشهدون أن لا إله إلا الله وأن محمداً رسول الله ويصلون ويدعون الإسلام، وكذلك الذين حرقهم علي بن أبي طالب – رضي الله عنه – بالنار.

وهؤلاء الجهلة مقرون أن من أنكر البعث كفر وقتل ولو قال لا إله إلا الله. وأن من أنكر شيئاً من أركان الإسلام كفر وقتل ولو قالها، فكيف لا تنفعه إذا جحد شيأ من الفروع ، وتنفعه إذا جحد التوحيد الذي هو أساس دين الرسل ورأسه؟ .

So it should be said to these ignorant people who commit *shirk*: It is well known that the Prophet (ﷺ) fought the Jews, and took them as captives, even though they testified *Lā ilāh illa Allāh*. And also the Companions

---

[183] Reported in al-Bukhārī and Muslm with various wordings; one of which is in al-Bukhārī (# 4269).

[184] Reported by al-Bukhārī (# 6924).

[185] It must be borne in mind that there is no direct relationship between an Islāmic state fighting a specific group, and that group being outside the fold of Islām (*kāfir*). For example, if a certain group or tribe is guilty of highway robbery and spreading unruliness in the land, then the Islāmic state must fight them, but they are not ruled to be *kāfirs*. On the other hand, it is also possible that a certain group be considered disbelievers, yet the Islāmic state sees some benefit in not fighting them for a period of time. So the author, with the aid of Muḥammad ibn Sa'ūd, would fight Muslim tribes of his time that were openly practicing *shirk* and *kufr*, but did not consider every single group that he fought to be disbelievers (*kāfir*). And this fact has been mentioned and proven from his own writings in the previous sections.

fought the tribe of Banu Ḥanīfah, even though they testified *Lā ilāh illa Allāh Muḥammad Rasūl Allāh*, and they used to pray, and profess to be Muslims. Likewise, the people whom 'Alī ibn Abī Ṭālib burnt used to testify to the same matter.

And these ignorant people agree that a person who denies the Day of Judgement becomes a disbeliever and should be killed, even if he testifies *Lā ilāh illa Allāh*, as does the one who denies one of the pillars of Islām – he too becomes a disbeliever and should be killed, even if he testifies. So how is it possible that this testimony is of no benefit to him if he denies something of the subsidiary issues, but is of benefit when he denies *tawḥīd*, which is the essence of the religion of all the prophets.

EXPL. All these examples have already been given as a refutation of the previous argument. Therefore, here, the author merely mentions them in passing, since they have all been previously explained.

The point that he is making is that the Prophet (ﷺ) and his Companions fought against certain peoples that testified *Lā ilāh illa Allāh*. This fact in and of itself clearly shows that there are certain situations in which it is permissible to fight such people, as he goes on to explain.

TEXT ولكن أعداء الله ما فهموا معنى الأحاديث : فأما حديث أسامة – رضي الله عنه – فإنه قتل رجلاً إدعى الإسلام بسبب أنه ظن أنه ما ادعاه إلا خوفاً على دمه وماله ، والرجل إذا أظهر الإسلام وجب الكف عنه حتى يتبين منه ما يخالف ذلك ، وأنزل الله تعالى في ذلك ﴿يا أيها الذين أمنوا إذا ضربتم في سبيل الله فتبينوا﴾ (سورة النساء، الآية: ٩٤) أي تثبتوا ، فالآية تدل على أنه يجب الكف عنه والتثبت فإن تبين منه بعد ذلك ما يخالف الإسلام قتل لقوله : ﴿فتبينوا﴾ ولو كان لا يقتل إذا قالها لم يكن للتثبيت معنى.

But the enemies of Allāh did not understand the proper meaning of these *aḥādīth*. As for the ḥadīth of Usāmah, then it must be understood that the reason he killed the man who professed Islām is that he presumed that he only pretended to accept Islām, in order to protect his life and wealth. However, when a person apparently accepts Islām, it becomes obligatory to hold back from fighting him, unless some matter appears that contradicts his profession. And so Allāh revealed because of this, "O you who believe! When you travel in the way of Allāh (for *jihād*) then verify.." [Sūrah *al-Nisā'*; 94], meaning make sure that the person you are fighting is not a Muslim. This verse shows that it is obligatory to refrain from fighting a person who declares himself a Muslim, and that verification is needed. So, if after this declaration something becomes apparent from him that contradicts his Islām, he is to be killed. Proof for this is the condition, '...verify,' for if he were not killed after he professes Islām no matter what he did, then there would be no point in verifying his claim.

EXPL. The reason that the Prophet (ﷺ) rebuked Usāmah was that Usāmah had no reason not to believe the person when he testified the *shahādah*. Hence, the Prophet (ﷺ) asked him angrily, 'Did you open his heart?' meaning, 'How do you know he only testified in order to save his life?'

Once a person accepts Islām, even if it is on the battlefield, it becomes prohibited to harm or kill him, as long as he really and truly has accepted Islām. And that is why Allāh Himself commands the believers to verify the Islām of one who gives the Muslim greeting of *salām*. So the whole point of verifying his Islām is that, if it becomes clear due to some external factors that the one pretending to be a Muslim is in reality not a Muslim, then this ruling is lifted from him. In our case, the author is showing that even if certain tribes of his time professed Islām, the fact that they openly worshipped idols (such as graves and trees), and made *duʿā* to other than Allāh, proved that in reality they had *not* accepted true Islām.

In fact, this understating can be obtained from the very ḥadīth that these adversaries quote, whereby the Prophet (ﷺ) said,

> "I have been commanded to fight the people until they say '*Lā ilāha illa Allāh*'. Once they say it, their lives and properties become prohibited for me, except with due cause, and their reckoning is with Allāh."[186]

The Prophet (ﷺ) stated that a Muslim's life and property is sacred unless and until that Muslim does something to abrogate this sanctity. So, for example, if he steals, then his hand is cut off, and if he drinks, then he is lashed, and so forth. Likewise, if he openly engages in acts of *shirk*, then he lifts this sanctity from his persona due to his own actions, and this is what the author is saying.

TEXT وكذلك الحديث الآخر وأمثاله معناه ما ذكرناه أن من أظهر الإسلام التوحيد وجب الكف عنه إلى أن يتبين منه ما يناقض ذلك والدليل على هذا أن رسول الله صلى الله عليه وسلم ، قال : «أقتلته بعد ما قال لا إله إلا الله» وقال : «أمرت أن أقاتل الناس حتى يقولوا لا إله إلا الله» هو الذي قال في الخوارج «أينما لقيتموهم فاقتلوهم لئن أدركتهم لأقتلنهم قتل عادٍ» مع كونهم من أكثر

---

[186] Reported by al-Bukhārī (# 6924).

الناس عبادة وتهليلاً، حتى إن الصحابة يحقرون أنفسهم عندهم، وهم تعلموا العلم من الصحابة فلم تنفعهم لا إله إلا الله ، ولا كثرة العبادة ، ولا ادعاء الإسلام لما ظهر منهم مخالفة الشريعة .

And likewise, all of these other *aḥādīth* that were mentioned must be understood in the same light. Whoever professes Islām, and claims to be following *tawḥīd*, then it becomes obligatory to stop harming him, except if some matter becomes apparent which contradicts his claim. And another proof for this is that the Prophet (ﷺ) – the same person who said, "Did you kill him after he said *Lā ilāh illa Allāh*?" and, "I have been ordered to fight mankind until they testify *Lā ilāh illa Allāh*," – also said concerning the *Khawārij*, "Wherever you find them, kill them," and he said, "If I were to meet them, I would kill them the way Ād was killed." This verdict was given even though they were of those who worshipped Allāh fervently, and used to praise Allāh frequently. In fact, the Companions would feel humbled in front of them due to their extreme worship, even though the *Khawārij* learnt from the Companions. Their profession of *Lā ilāh illa Allāh* did not benefit them, and neither did their worship, or their claim to be Muslims, because they openly showed through other matters their rejection of Islāmic Law.

EXPL.

The author once again proves this point by mentioning other incidents and *aḥādīth* which show that it is permissible to fight groups that claim to be Muslim, if there is evidence to show that their claim is not true. For example, the Prophet (ﷺ) himself instructed the Muslims to kill a group known as the *Khawārij*. This was the first sect to break away from the beliefs of the Muslims, and, even though they did not appear until after the Prophet's (ﷺ) death, the Prophet (ﷺ) warned the Muslims against them, and described them in many different *aḥādīth*. He mentioned that even the Companions would humble themselves looking at them, for the *Khawārij* were extreme fanatics in their worship of Allāh. They would pray long hours, fast regularly, and constantly recite the Qur'ān. Thus, outwardly, it seemed as if they were more practicing than even the Companions were. Yet, due to their extreme heretical beliefs, they proclaimed that the majority of the Companions were disbelievers, and considered it permissible to kill them. And so, when the *Khawārij* exceeded the limits of the Sacred Law, ʿAlī ibn Abī Ṭālib himself took part in attacks against them, and the Companions fought them in the Battle of Nahrawān, killing most of them.

So here, we find that the claim of the *Khawārij* that they were Muslims, and their extreme worship of Allāh, did not prevent the Companions from fighting them. And this was due to their exceeding the bounds of the *Sharīʿah*, and their killing of innocent people. So when they exceeded the bounds that the Sacred Law set, the sanctity of their lives and property was lifted. And so too is the case of a group of people who openly worship other than Allāh, for their claim to be Muslim holds no weight when they are engaged in such blatant *shirk*.

The two *aḥādīth* quoted by the author are both reported by al-Bukhārī and Muslim. The first ḥadīth, narrated by ʿAlī, states,

> "There will come, toward the end of time, a group of people who are young in age, foolish in intellect. They (appear) to be saying the best speech (ever to come from) mankind. But they will pass through this religion just like an arrow passes through its target. Faith (*īmān*) will not go past their throats. So wherever you find them, kill them, for there will be a reward for whoever kills them on the Day of Judgement."[187]

The second narration describes them as,

> '...they will kill the people of Islām, but leave the people (that worship) idols. If I were to catch them, I would of a certainty kill them like ʿĀd was killed.'[188]

One point of benefit to be derived here is that the author is clearly freeing himself from the beliefs of the *Khawārij*, and defending the Companions' decision to fight them. This in itself is clear proof that the author did not consider himself of the *Khawārij* – how could he, when his whole call was the same as that of the Companions? Yet, perhaps the greatest slander that he and those who followed him were charged with was that they were a faction of the *Khawārij*. In reality, any person who makes such a claim is ignorant of the true beliefs of the *Khawārij*, and of the teachings of the author.

Another point of benefit is that a person's worship of Allāh does not make him correct in all that he does or says. One of the most convincing proofs that adversaries to *tawḥīd* bring forth (the tenth argument above) is that these people who are worshipping saints and grave are 'pious' people who constantly pray, fast, read the Qur'ān, and do many good deeds. So they ask how can such people be considered *kāfirs*? The response is that even the *Khawārij* were fervent worshippers of Allāh. They would pray, fast and recite the Qur'ān more than the Companions of the Prophet (ﷺ) would. Yet, they deviated from the religion of Islām, and, as the Prophet (ﷺ) said,

> '...they will pass through this religion just like an arrow passes through its target. Faith (*īmān*) will not go past their throats.'[189]

---

[187] Reported by al-Bukhārī (# 3611) and Muslim (# 1066).

[188] Reported by al-Bukhārī (# 3644) and Muslim (# 1060).

[189] Scholars of the past (and present) have differed about the status of these *Khawārij* whom ʿAlī fought: were they disbelievers (*kāfirs*) or not? A discussion of this question is outside the scope of this work, however, the opinion of the majority of scholars (as also that of ʿAlī ibn Abī Ṭālib himself) is that they were sinful Muslims, not disbelievers.

The proof of a person being correct does not come from the amount of worship that he does, rather, it comes from his conformity to the Qur'ān and Sunnah.

TEXT

وكذلك ما ذكرناه من قتال اليهود ، وقتال الصحابة رضي الله عنهم بني حنيفة ، وكذلك أراد النبي صلى الله عليه وسلم أن يغزو بني المصطلق لما أخبره رجل أنهم منعوا الزكاة حتى أنزل الله تعالى: ﴿يا أيها الذين أمنوا إن جاءكم فاسق بنبأ فتبينوا﴾ (سورة الحجرات، الآية : ٦). وكان الرجل كاذباً عليهم، فكل هذا يدل على أن مراد النبي صلى الله عليه وسلم في الأحاديث الواردة ما ذكرناه .

And another proof is the fact that was just mentioned concerning the fighting against the Jews, and that the Companions fought against Banu Ḥanīfah. Furthermore, the Prophet (ﷺ) intended to attack the Banu al-Muṣṭaliq when a person informed him that they refused to pay *zakāt*, until Allāh revealed, "O you who believe! If an evil person comes to you with some news, then verify it..." [Sūrah *al-Ḥujurāt*; 6], so it was discovered that the person had lied against them. So all of these evidences show what the Prophet (ﷺ) intended with these *aḥādīth* is the explanation that has been given.

Here the author gives three more examples to prove his point.

EXPL.

As for the first two, then they have already been given above, namely, that the Prophet (ﷺ) fought the Jews, even though they believed in *Lā ilāh illa Allāh*. But because they denied the prophethood of the Prophet (ﷺ), their testimony was of no value. Likewise, the Companions fought the tribe of Banu Ḥanīfah since they believed in the prophethood of Musaylamah the Liar. This belief of theirs negated their claim to be Muslims.

The third example relates to the story of the tribe Banu al-Muṣṭaliq. The Prophet (ﷺ) sent an emissary to collect the *zakāt* from the tribe of Banu al-Muṣṭaliq. This emissary, however, came back with a false story, and claimed that he had been prevented from collecting their *zakāt*, and that they had tried to kill him. Acting upon this false story, the Prophet (ﷺ) ordered that the Companions attack them, for the refusal to pay *zakāt* to the Islāmic state is treachery. However, it was then discovered that the emissary had not told the truth, and that the Banu al-Muṣṭaliq had not received him in the first place. Due to this incident, Allāh revealed,

يَٰٓأَيُّهَا ٱلَّذِينَ ءَامَنُوٓاْ إِن جَآءَكُمْ فَاسِقُۢ بِنَبَإٍ فَتَبَيَّنُوٓاْ
أَن تُصِيبُواْ قَوْمًۢا بِجَهَٰلَةٍ فَتُصْبِحُواْ عَلَىٰ مَا فَعَلْتُمْ نَٰدِمِينَ

"O you who believe! If an evil person comes to you with some news, then verify it, perchance you might ignorantly afflict a group of people (with some evil), then feel guilty for what you have done" [Sūrah *al-Ḥujurāt*; 6].

In this verse, Allāh instructed the Muslims to verify any information that they receive before taking an important course of action.[190]

The point here is that the Prophet (ﷺ) organised an attack against the Banu al-Muṣṭaliq, thus indicating that the sanctity of their lives and property had been lifted because of actions they were mistakenly believed to have taken.

This clearly shows that the *aḥādīth* which mention the sanctity of one who professes *Lā ilāha illa Allāh* must be understood in light of other ḥadīth. So it is impermissible to harm or attack any group which professes Islām *until there exists clear evidence to show that they have reneged on their claim*. It is not necessary that they actually *claim* they are not Muslims, for the *Khawārij*, and the Banu al-Ḥanifah, and the Banu al-Muṣṭaliq, all claimed that they were Muslims. What is required for this sanctity to be lifted is that they believe or perform an act that flouts their claim to Islām. And without a doubt, worshipping graves and performing *shirk* with saints are acts that clearly go against the teachings of Islām.

The Twelfth Argument

TEXT

ولهم شبهة أخرى : وهي ما ذكر النبي صلى الله عليه وسلم أن الناس يوم القيامة يستغيثون بآدم ، ثم بنوح ، ثم بإبراهيم ، ثم بموسى ، ثم بعيسى فكلهم يعتذرون حتى ينتهوا إلى رسول الله صلى الله عليه وسلم. قالوا: فهذا يدل على أن الإستغاثة بغير الله ليست شركاً.

And those who justify *shirk* have yet another evidence, which is the fact that the Prophet (ﷺ) mentioned that on the Day of Judgement people will seek help from Adam, and then from Nūḥ, then from Ibrāhīm, then from Mūsa, and then from 'Īsa, and all of them will give some type of excuse, until finally they reach the Prophet (ﷺ). They say that this is clear evidence that seeking help from other than Allāh is not considered *shirk*.

EXPL. Here the author introduces yet another argument that is used by the justifiers of *shirk*. This argument uses a ḥadīth that describes the intercession that will occur on the Day of Judgement.

The Prophet (ﷺ) stated,

> "I am the leader of mankind on the Day of Judgement, and do you know how that is the case? Allāh will gather all of mankind, from the first of them to the last of them, on one plain...and the sun will come close to them, so much so that the people will be afflicted with grief and pain, and sufferings that they cannot bear. So some of the people will say to others: 'Do you not see what situation you are in? Do you not see what has occurred? Why do you not find people who will intercede on your behalf with your Lord?' So some of

[190] For more details of this incident, see *Tafsīr al-Ṭabarī* 14/182.

them will say to others, 'Let us go to Adam.' They will go to Adam, and say, 'O Adam! You are the father of mankind. Allāh created you with His Own hands, and blew into you His spirit, and commanded the angels to prostrate to you. Intercede on our behalf with Allāh, for do you not see the situation we are in?' So Adam will respond, 'My Lord has become angry today, an anger that He has never had before, nor will He ever have again. And He prohibited me from the tree, but I disobeyed Him. I am only worried about myself, myself! Go to someone else besides me, go to Nūḥ.' So they will go to Nūḥ, and say, 'O Nūḥ! You are the first of the messengers that were sent to earth, and Allāh has described you as a thankful servant. Do you not see the situation we are in?' So he will respond, 'My Lord has become angry today, an anger that He has never had before, nor will He ever have again. And I had one request that I (already used) when I prayed against my people (that Allāh destroy them).[191] I am only worried about myself, myself. Go to Ibrāhīm.' So they will go to Ibrāhīm, and say, 'You are the prophet of Allāh, and His Chosen Friend amongst the creation. Intercede with Allāh on our behalf, do you not see the situation we are in?' But Ibrāhīm will say, 'My Lord has become angry today, an anger that He has never had before, nor will He ever have again.' And he will remember the lies that he said,[192] and say, 'I am only worried about myself, myself. Go to someone else, go to Mūsa.' So they will go to Mūsa, and say, 'O Mūsa! You are the messenger of Allāh. Allāh favoured you with his prophethood and His speaking directly to you. Intercede on our behalf with Allāh, do you not see the situation we are in?' But Mūsa will respond, 'My Lord has become angry today, an anger that He has never had before, nor will He ever have again. And verily, I killed a person whom I had not been commanded to kill.[193] I am only worried about myself, myself. Go to 'Īsa.' So they will go to 'Īsa, and say, 'O 'Īsa! You are the messenger of Allāh, you spoke to the people while you were still in the cradle. You are the Word of Allāh that He gave to Maryam, and a Spirit proceeding from Him. Intercede for us with our Lord, for do you not see the situation we are in?' But 'Īsa will respond, 'My Lord has become angry today, an anger that He has never had before, nor will He ever have again.' And he will not mention any sin, but will say, 'I am only worried about myself, myself. Go to Muḥammad (ﷺ).' So

[191] According to other narrations, Nūḥ will express his regret for asking Allāh to save his disbelieving son, and thus feel too embarrassed to ask Allāh now.

[192] These 'lies' were not actually lies, but due to the severity of the Day of Judgement, Ibrāhīm will consider them to be sins, even though they were not. Of these 'lies' is that he told the evil king that his wife was his sister (intending that she was his sister in faith), since the king would otherwise have killed them. And of his 'lies' is that he told his people that the one who had destroyed their idols was the largest idol; this he said in order to show them the foolishness of their deeds, and to call them to the worship of Allāh. For further details, see *Fatḥ al-Bārī* (6/391).

[193] Referring to the accidental death of one of the Egyptians who was abusing one of the Children of Israel. Mūsa in his anger struck and unintentionally killed him.

they will come to me, and say, 'O Muḥammad (ﷺ)! You are the Messenger of Allāh, and the Seal of the Prophets. Allāh has forgiven all of your sins. Do you not see the situation we are in? Intercede for us with our Lord.' So I will proceed to the Throne of Allāh, and will fall down in prostration in front of my Lord. Then, Allāh will inspire me, and reveal to me words of praise to Him, and His glorification, which no one before was ever given. It will then be said to me, 'O Muḥammad! Raise your head. Ask, and you shall be given. Intercede, and your intercession shall be accepted.'"[194]

This long ḥadīth is the famous ḥadīth known as 'The ḥadīth of Intercession.'

In this ḥadīth, according to the adversary, is clear proof from the Prophet (ﷺ) where he mentions, and thus sanctions, the seeking of help from other created beings. Since people will ask various prophets on the Day of Judgement for such help, what is the problem with asking them for help in this world as well? After all, according to our adversary, they are asking the Prophet (ﷺ) for intercession, and so are we? So what is the difference?

TEXT

والجواب: أن نقول سبحان من طبع على قلوب أعدائه فإن الإستغاثة بالمخلوق فيما يقدر عليه لا ننكرها ، كما قال الله تعالى في قصة موسى: ﴿فاستغاثه الذي من شيعته على الذي من عدوه﴾ (سورة القصص، الآية:١٥). وكما يستغيث الإنسان بأصحابه في الحرب و غيره في أشياء يقدر عليها المخلوق، ونحن أنكرنا استغاثة العبادة التي يفعلونها عند قبور الأولياء، أو في غيبتهم في الأشياء التي لا يقدرعليها إلا الله.

إذا ثبت ذلك فاستغاثتهم بالأنبياء يوم القيامة يريدون منهم أن يدعوا الله أن يحاسب الناس حتى يستريح أهل الجنة من كرب الموقف وهذا جائز في الدنيا والآخرة ، أن تأتي عند رجل صالح حي يجالسك ويسمع كلامك تقول له: ادع الله لي، كما كان أصحاب رسول الله صلى الله عليه وسلم ، يسألونه في حياته، وأما بعد موته فحاشا وكلا أنهم سألوه ذلك عند قبره ، بل أنكر السلف الصالح على من قصد دعاء الله عند قبره فكيف بدعائه نفسه؟

The response to this is to say, "How exalted is the One Who has sealed the hearts of His enemies! For we ourselves don't deny the legality of seeking help from a created object in matters that it is capable of. Allāh says, 'So [the one who was being victimised] sought help from [Moses], his tribesman, against his enemy' [Sūrah *al-Qaṣaṣ*; 15]. And the person in battle, or any other situation, seeks help from another in matters that he can do and are

[194] Reported by al-Bukhārī (8/10) and Muslim (3/53).

> not supernatural or beyond the normal capabilities of man. But we do object to the supernatural help that is sought – the religious seeking of help that is done at the graves of the righteous, or in their absence, concerning matters that none except Allāh has power to do."
>
> Once this is understood, then realise that the help that is sought from the prophets on the Day of Judgement is that they want them (the prophets) to pray to Allāh to hasten the Reckoning so that the people of Paradise can be relieved from the agonies of that Day. This type of asking is allowed in this world and in the Hereafter; that you go to a righteous person that is in front of you, and listens to you, and then you ask him to pray for you. And this is just as the Companions used to do with the Prophet (ﷺ) while he was alive. After his death, however, then by no means did they ask anything from him, or even ask at his graveside. Rather, scholars of the early generations would rebuke those who used to pray to Allāh at his grave, so what would be their response to someone who actually prayed to him?

So the response to this argument is very simple, and that is that no one denies the permissibility of asking a created object to do something which he or she is physically capable of doing. If one were to ask a person to help one carry a heavy object, then this does not entail *shirk* in the very least! However, if one were to ask this very person to grant one a child, or forgive all one's sins, then this is the very essence of *shirk*! EXPL.

It is essential, therefore, to differentiate between asking a person in front of you (or can otherwise hear you) a matter that he is physically capable of doing, and asking someone or something for a matter that is beyond their normal capabilities.

The asking of intercession that will be done on the Day of Judgement is similar to the asking that is done in this world when the prophets were alive. Some of the Companions would ask the Prophet (ﷺ) to pray to Allāh to fulfill something on their behalf. After he died, however, there is not a single report to the effect that any of them asked him for anything. The Companions understood that the life that the Prophet (ﷺ) was in (known as *barzakh*) was totally different from this life, and thus it was not possible to ask him to pray for them. However, once they too have entered into this life, and are similar to the Prophet (ﷺ) in the type of life that he is in, then it will become permissible to ask him to pray to Allāh for a matter, just as it was permissible in this life. So on the Day of Judgement all of mankind will be in a state of life similar to that of the prophets, hence it will be permissible for them to ask for their intercession before Allāh.

One of the most fundamental principles of the beliefs of *Ahl al-Sunnah* is that the Companions are the best and most knowledgeable generation of Muslims. This fundamental, which many of the adversaries to *tawḥīd* verbally agree to, can be invoked here to prove the error of those that use this ḥadīth to justify *shirk*. Even though the Companions loved the Prophet (ﷺ) more than any other generation, and were more knowledgeable of the religion of Islām, it has never been reported that any of them ever asked the Prophet (ﷺ) for a matter after his death. So the question arises, if they did not do it despite their *īmān* and knowledge, then on what basis do these later generations of grave-worshippers justify their actions?

In fact, the opposite has been narrated from them. The early generations of Muslims would criticise those who used to pray to Allāh at the grave of the Prophet (ﷺ), so what would be their reaction had they seen people actually praying *to* the Prophet (ﷺ)? One of the descendants of the Prophet (ﷺ), ʿAlī ibn al-Ḥusayn ibn ʿAlī ibn Abī Ṭālib, saw a person frequenting the Prophet's (ﷺ) grave in order to make *duʿā* to Allāh (it appears that he believed that his *duʿā* had a greater chance of being accepted at the grave). So ʿAlī said to him, "Should I not narrate to you a ḥadīth that I heard from my father, who narrated from his father, that the Prophet (ﷺ) said,

> "Do not take my grave a place of frequent visitation (*ʿeed*), nor make your houses like graves (i.e., by abandoning prayer in them), for your salutations (upon me) reach me wherever you are."[195]

In another incident, al-Ḥasan ibn Ḥasan ibn ʿAlī ibn Abī Ṭālib, another of the Prophet's (ﷺ) descendants, saw a person visiting the Prophet's (ﷺ) grave every single day, standing in front of it. He asked him, "Why do you stand in front of it?" He replied, "I stand to give my salutations upon the Prophet (ﷺ)." So he said, "When you enter the *masjid*, send your salutations upon him[196], for the Prophet (ﷺ) said,

> 'Do not make my grave a place of worship. And pray in your houses, and do not make them like graves. Allāh's curse is on the Jews, for they took the graves of their prophets as places of worship. And send your salutations upon me, for your salutations reach me wherever you are.'

Verily, you (standing in front of the grave), and a person at Andalus (Spain), are equivalent!"[197] In other words, the fact that you are standing in front of the grave does not give you any special privilege, and you are in the same position as a person who is at the farthest corner of earth. Since the Prophet's (ﷺ) life in the grave is a special life, distance does not matter when it comes to sending *salāms* upon him, for even if a person is in front of the grave, or far from it, an angel will

---

[195] Reported with an authentic chain in Ismāʿīl ibn Isḥāq al-Qāḍī's *Faḍl al-Ṣalāt ala al-Nabī* (# 20). As for the actual ḥadīth, it is reported in al-Bukhārī and others.

[196] Referring to the *duʿā* that one should state when entering any mosque, "*Bismillah Allāhuma Ṣalli ʿAla Muḥammad*, O Allāh! Open for me the gates of Mercy."

[197] *Faḍl al-Ṣalāt ʿala al-Nabī* (# 30); and also in the *Sunan* of Saʿīd ibn Manṣūr. The actual text of the ḥadīth is reported in al-Bukhārī and Muslim (with a slightly different wording).

convey the greetings to the Prophet (ﷺ), and he will not hear it himself.[198] On another occasion, al-Ḥasan saw people congregating around the Prophet's (ﷺ) grave. He prohibited them from doing so, and said,

> "The Prophet (ﷺ) said: Do not make my grave an ʿ*eed* (regular place of worship)."[199]

So in these incidents, we see that the early generations – even descendants of the Prophet (ﷺ) himself – disliked worship next to the grave. This was due to the prohibition that the Prophet (ﷺ) gave of taking his grave as a place of worship, for this is one of the primary roads that leads to *shirk*. One can only imagine what they would have said if they saw people actually worshipping the grave itself, as is common in our times! One finds people frequently raising their hands *to* the grave, and making *duʿā* to the Prophet (ﷺ) himself, asking *him* to fulfill their needs, which is pure *shirk*. Others seek his intercession, praying to him to make a *duʿā* to Allāh for their requests, and this act too is prohibited, and leads to *shirk*. In fact, the extremists amongst such people actually perform *tawāf* around the Prophet's (ﷺ) grave, and prostrate to it, which, without a doubt, are forms of major *shirk*.

Another point of benefit here is that these prohibitions are mentioned for the Prophet's (ﷺ) grave, which is without a doubt the most noble and holy of all graves. So if it is prohibited to take the Prophet's (ﷺ) grave as a regular place of worship, then what about the graves of those far below his status, such as the graves of the thousands of 'saints' which Muslims all over the world venerate?

To conclude this section, this argument – that mankind will seek intercession from the prophets on the Day of Judgement – is totally irrelevant to the point that these adversaries seek to prove. No one denies the permissibility of asking someone for help in a matter that they are physically capable of doing. However, asking dead saints and prophets to help one in the affairs of this life is simply beyond their capabilities, even supposing that they could actually hear these requests.

---

[198] There are a number of fabricated narrations which praise the one who sends *salāms* upon the Prophet (ﷺ) in front of the grave, but none of them are even close to being authentic.

[199] Reported by ʿAbd al-Razzāq in his *al-Muṣannaf* (# 6726).

The Thirteenth Argument

TEXT ولهم شبهة أخرى وهي : قصة إبراهيم عليه السلام لما ألقي في النار اعترض له جبريل في الهواء فقال: ألك حاجة؟ فقال إبراهيم : أما إليك فلا، قالوا: فلو كانت الإستغاثة بجبرائيل شركاً لم يعرضها على إبراهيم ؟

And those that justify *shirk* have yet another evidence, and that is the story of Ibrāhīm. When he was thrown in the fire that Nimrūd built for that purpose, the angel Jibrīl came flying to him, and asked him, "Do you have any need?" So Ibrāhīm responded, "From you, no!" They opine from this story that had the seeking of help from Jibrīl been considered *shirk*, then he would not have offered Ibrāhīm any help.

EXPL. In this argument, the adversary uses a story narrated in certain books of *Tafsīr*, which states that when the tyrannical King Nimrūd threw the prophet Ibrāhīm into the fire that he had built, the angel Jibrīl appeared before him, offering his help. However, Ibrāhīm responded that he had no need of Jibrīl's help, implying that he would instead rely upon Allāh's Mercy to save him.

So the proponents of *shirk* extract from this story the permissibility of asking angels, saints, and prophets for help. Since Jibrīl offered his help to Ibrāhīm, this shows that it is permissible for angels to help men, and if this is so, then it is permissible to ask for such help. Similarly, if this is the case with angels, then the same applies to prophets and pious saints as well.

TEXT فالجواب: أن هذا من جنس الشبهة الأولى: فإن جبرائيل عليه السلام عرض عليه أن ينفعه بأمر يقدر عليه، فإنه كما قال الله تعالى فيه: ﴿شديد القوى﴾ (سورة النجم، الآية:٥) فلو أذن الله له أن يأخذ نار إبراهيم وما حولها من الأرض والجبال ويلقيها في المشرق أو المغرب لفعل، ولو أمره أن يضع إبراهيم في مكان بعيد لفعل ، ولو أمره أن يرفعه إلى السماء لفعل، وهذا كرجل غني له مال كثير يرى رجلاً محتاجاً فيعرض عليه أن يقرضه ، أو أن يهبه شيئاً يقضي به حاجته فيأبى ذلك الرجل المحتاج أن يأخذ ويصبر إلى أن يأتيه الله برزق لا منة فيه لأحد. فأين هذا من إستغاثة العبادة والشرك لو كانوا يفقهون؟! .

The response to this is that this is the exact same as the previous story, because Jibrīl offered to help him in a matter that he was capable of, for Allāh describes him as being, "...of great strength" [Sūrah *al-Najm*; 5]. So if Allāh had given him permission to take the fire of Ibrāhīm, and even all that was surrounding it of the earth and mountains, and to throw it all into the far corners of the east or west, he could have done so. And if Allāh had commanded him to transport Ibrāhīm to a far away place, he could have done so. And if He had commanded him to raise him up to the skies, he could have done so. The example of this story is like the example of a rich, wealthy person who sees a poor person in need and offers to help him, either by giving him a loan, or a gift with which he can fulfill his needs. Instead of accepting any help, the poor person refuses his help, and is content at being patient until Allāh provides him with a means of sustenance in which he will not owe anyone a favour. Such is Ibrāhīm's example when he relied on his Lord instead of any other being. So where is this example for seeking religious help or committing *shirk*, if they only understood?

EXPL.

Here the author refutes the argument by pointing out that the help that Jibrīl offered Ibrāhīm concerned a matter that Allāh gave him the power to do. Allāh describes Jibrīl as an angel of great strength, so if Allāh had given Jibrīl permission to help Ibrāhīm, Jibrīl could easily have saved him by transporting him to another location.

The author further illustrates this concept by the example of a rich person offering to help a poor person. The poor person, if he has strong faith in Allāh, would rather rely upon the Mercy of Allāh than humiliate himself by taking help from someone else.

Another example which explains this story is that of a weak person being victimised by a thief. If he were to call out to someone stronger for help, there would be no *shirk* involved whatsoever, for this is a matter that they are physically capable of doing.

Here, the author assumes that this story is authentic, and replies to it as if it were an established story. However, the fact of the matter is that this story has absolutely no basis to it, for it is not narrated – even with a fabricated chain – in any book of ḥadīth. Rather, this story is found in a few books of *Tafsīr* without any chain of narrators. Therefore, this story cannot be used as evidence in the first place. In fact, scholars of ḥadīth have clearly stated that this story is a fabrication, and thus has absolutely no basis in Islām.[200]

So in reality this argument is proven false by its non-existence. And this is an important point to note: that all of these groups rely heavily upon fabricated or very weak narrations, seeking to prove acts that go against clear verses in the Qur'ān, or *aḥādīth* in *Ṣaḥīḥ al-Bukhārī*! One of the first matters that any student of knowledge needs to do when presented with an evidence from these groups is to verify the authenticity of that evidence. This is especially true with regards to the *aḥādīth* of the Prophet (ﷺ). It is imperative to verify the authenticity of any narration before attempting to respond to it, for if a narration is weak then, by unanimous consensus of all scholars of Islām, it cannot be used in deriving laws

---

[200] See *Silsilat al-Ḍa'īfah*, # 21.

and beliefs. And if this is the case with weak narrations, then how about very weak or fabricated narrations?

Conclusion: Acting upon this Knowledge

TEXT

ولنختم الكتاب بذكر مسألة عظيمة مهمة تفهم مما تقدم ، ولكن نفرد لها الكلام لعظم شأنها، ولكثرة الغلط فيها فنقول: لا خلاف أن التوحيد لا بد أن يكون بالقلب واللسان والعمل ، فإن أختل شيء من هذا لم يكن الرجل مسلماً، فإن عرف التوحيد و لم يعمل به فهو كافر معاند كفرعون وإبليس و أمثالهما.

Let us conclude this book by mentioning an important matter that will clarify what has previously been said. We will discuss it separately because of its importance, and because many people fail to understand it correctly. So we say: there is no difference of opinion that *tawḥīd* must exist and be manifested with the heart, and tongue, and outer deeds. If one of these matters is missing, a person will not be a Muslim. So if a person knows *tawḥīd*, but does not act upon it, then he is an arrogant disbeliever, as was the case with the likes of Pharaoh, and Iblīs, and others like them.

EXPL.

In this last section, the author concludes by discussing an extremely important matter. Namely, that knowledge of *tawḥīd* alone is insufficient for a person to be saved from Allāh's punishment. Even if a person memorises the types of *tawḥīd*, and fully believes in them, unless and until he *acts* upon that belief, there is no benefit that his knowledge will give him.

The reason that the author concludes with this matter is that many people during his time (and even in our times) acknowledge these matters that the author seeks to prove. They believed that it was major *shirk* to make *duʿā* to other than Allāh, or call out to dead saints, or perform *ṭawāf* or prostrate at graves. They knew that those who committed such acts willingly, after having the evidences established against them, were outside the fold of Islām. Yet, despite this knowledge and belief, they themselves refused to do anything to change the situation of their society. They silently acknowledged and tacitly supported these acts, despite having the status and power to prohibit them. They feared that, if they were to try to change the *status quo*, they would face the enmity of their own peoples. They might lose their prestige, or salaries, or even their kingdoms.

Thus, in order to advise such people, the author concludes this work with an explanation of the dangers that such people expose themselves to.

The scholars of *Ahl al-Sunnah* have unanimously agreed that *tawḥīd* (and *īmān*) consist of three matters: beliefs of the heart, statements of the tongue, and actions of the limbs. Thus, believing in the existence of Allāh is a necessary component of *tawḥīd*. Likewise, the verbalisation of the testimony of faith (*shahādah*) is a necessary component of *tawḥīd* as well. And the worshipping of Allāh with the limbs (such as by performing the *Ṣalāt*) is also a necessary component of *tawḥīd*.

If, for any reason, a person does not act upon his beliefs, then in reality he is in the same league as Iblīs and Pharaoh. Both of them knew that Allāh was their Lord and Creator, and that only Allāh is worthy of worship. Yet, due to their arrogance, and love for this world, they refused to submit themselves to His worship, choosing instead to enjoy the pleasures of this temporal life over the permanent pleasures of the Hereafter.

TEXT

وهذا يغلط فيه كثير من الناس يقولون : هذا حق ونحن نفهم هذا ، ونشهد أنه الحق، ولكنا لا نقدر أن نفعله ولا يجوز عند أهل بلدنا إلا من وافقهم ، وغير ذلك من الأعذار .

و لم يدر المسكين أن غالب أئمة الكفر يعرفون الحق، و لم يتركوه إلا لشيء من الأعذار كما قال تعالى: ﴿اشتروا بآيات الله ثمناً قليلاً﴾ (سورة التوبة، الآية: ٩). وغير ذلك من الآيات كقوله: ﴿يعرفونه كما يعرفون أبنائهم﴾ (سورة البقرة، الآية:١٤٦).

And this is a matter that many people misunderstand. They say, "This matter of what you have explained is true, and we fully understand it, and testify to its veracity. However, we are not able to do it and put it into practice, and it is not allowed by our countrymen to act upon these matters unless it agrees with them and their beliefs and customs". And they give other excuses so that they do not act upon correct beliefs.

However, such a wretched person does not realise that most of the leaders of falsehood know the truth, and they only leave acting upon it due to some excuse, as Allāh mentions, "They purchased with the signs of Allāh a miserable price" [Sūrah *al-Tawbah*; 9]. Other verses also explain this point, such as: "They recognise him (the Prophet (ﷺ)) as well as they recognise their own sons" [Sūrah *al-Baqarah*; 146].

EXPL.

So the reality of the matter is that the majority of people who reject the message of Islām do so, not because they are in doubt as to its truthfulness, but because they have ulterior motives and desires which prevent them from accepting the worship of Allāh. Such was the case with Iblīs, who only refused to submit to Allāh's command out of sheer arrogance.

قَالَ أَنَا۠ خَيْرٌ مِّنْهُ خَلَقْتَنِى مِن نَّارٍ وَخَلَقْتَهُۥ مِن طِينٍ ﴿١٢﴾

> "He said: 'I am better than him. You created me from fire, and created him from dust'" [Sūrah *al-Aʿrāf*; 12].

And so too Pharaoh,

وَجَحَدُواْ بِهَا وَٱسْتَيْقَنَتْهَآ أَنفُسُهُمْ ظُلْمًا وَعُلُوًّا

> "And they (the Pharaoh and his people) rejected it (the prophethood of Mūsa), and their souls were certain of it, (but out of) injustice and arrogance" [Sūrah *al-Naml*; 14].

As for the Jews, and some of the Christians, they knew that the Prophet Muḥammad (ﷺ) was indeed the very prophet that they were waiting for, and they recognised him just like they recognised their own children. Yet, out of sheer arrogance and disdain, they refused to subject themselves to believing in a prophet from amongst the Arabs.

Even before the coming of the Prophet (ﷺ), the Jews would sell their religion for a miserable price. So the money they earned by selling their religion was in fact the reason why they refused to worship Allāh.

Despite the clarity of this matter, the author states that you will find many people who claim: "All of your arguments are correct. I believe in them, and fully understand them. I believe that only Allāh is worthy of worship, and that it is *shirk* to direct one's *duʿā* or any other acts of worship to the Prophet (ﷺ), saints, or graves. Yet, I cannot go against the culture of my people. I cannot oppose my leaders and Shaykhs, for it will cause too many problems for me. I simply cannot give up the prestige, or the acceptance, or the money, that my community gives me. Therefore, even though I believe you and your points, I must follow my people in their actions."

Here the author now refutes this mentality: the mentality of he who has recognised the truth but fails to follow it.

TEXT

فإن عمل بالتوحيد عملاً ظاهراً وهو لا يفهم ، و لا يعتقده بقلبه فهو منافق، وهو شر من الكافر الخالص كما قوله تعالى: ﴿إن المنافقين في الدرك الأسفل من النار﴾ (سورة النساء، الآية: ١٤٥) .

وهذه المسألة كبيرة طويلة تتبين لك إذا تأملتها في ألسنة الناس ترى من يعرف الحق ويترك العمل به لخوف نقص دنياه، أو جاهه ، أو ملكه ، وترى من يعمل به ظاهراً لا باطناً فإذا سألته عما يعتقد بقلبه إذا هو لا يعرفه.

Now, if he acts upon *tawḥīd* with his outward actions while he does not understand nor believe in his heart, then he is a hypocrite who is more evil

cases, a person who willingly commits acts of *shirk*, or is in a position of authority and encourages his subordinates to do so, has actually fulfilled *none* of these three conditions. To compound the problem, such a person willingly obliges in these acts, for his heart and soul do not feel any guilt or hatred towards these deeds.

الثانية : قوله تعالى ﴿ذلك بأنهم استحبوا الحياة الدنيا على الآخرة﴾ فصرح أن هذا الكفر والعذاب لم يكن بسبب الاعتقاد و الجهل، و البغض للدين ، أو محبة الكفر وإنما سببه أن له في ذلك حظاً من حظوظ الدنيا فآثره على الدين. TEXT

Secondly, the phrase, '..that was because they preferred the life of this world over the life of the Hereafter ' [Sūrah *al-Naḥl*;107]. So it is clearly mentioned that the reason for their *kufr* and punishment was not due to any heartfelt belief, or because of ignorance, or a hatred of religion, or a love of disbelief. Rather, the reason for their eternal punishment of the Hereafter was due to the fact that he achieved some benefit in this world, preferring this benefit over religion.

The second evidence is that, in the very next verse, Allāh gives a description of those who perform *kufr*, and states that they are those who have preferred the life of this world over the Hereafter. This description applies perfectly to those leaders, religious and otherwise, who exhort their followers to commit acts of *shirk*, merely in order to obtain some physical benefits of this life. Such people are not ignorant of the truth, nor do they actually deny the validity of *tawḥīd*. Rather, they merely refrain from *acting* upon what they truly believe because they prefer the pleasures of this world over Allāh's Pleasure. EXPL.

Therefore, whoever willingly engages in acts of *shirk* in order to benefit from this life has in fact rejected Islām and accepted *kufr*, even if his heart firmly believes in *tawḥīd*.

والله أعلم TEXT

And Allāh knows best.

With this phrase, the author ends his work, thus signifying his humility, and seeking forgiveness for any mistakes that he might have inadvertently made. Verily, man is only human, and it is only the Divine Who never makes mistakes. EXPL.

What has been presented here is correct to the best of our knowledge and abilities, and if any lapse has occurred, than it is a mistake from ourselves, and from the whisperings of *Shayṭān*.

May Allāh bless us to be amongst those who worship Him purely. May He save us from all types of *shirk*, the major and the minor of it. And may He make us callers to His path, calling to the worship of Allāh alone, based upon the Sunnah of His Messenger (ﷺ). *Amīn!*

So Exalted is your Lord
– the Lord of Honour (and Glory) –
over what they ascribe to Him.
And Peace (and Mercy) be upon the Messengers.
And all praise is due to Allāh alone,
the Lord of all creation.
[Sūrah al-Ṣāffāt; 180-182]

14. Glossary of Terms

Adhān: The call to prayer which informs Muslims of the times of the prayer, and summons them to the mosque.

Aḥādīth: See ḥadīth

Ashʿarīs: An Islāmic sect which was founded in the third century of Ḥijrah. Of their beliefs is that *īmān* is only belief (i.e., actions are not a part of *īmān*); that *īmān* does not increase or decrease; that *tawḥīd* is restricted to affirming the perfect nature of Allāh (i.e., *Rubūbiyyah*); and that most of the Attributes of Allāh are metaphorical.

Asmā wa l-Ṣifāt: One of the categories of *tawḥīd*; it signifies that Allāh has the Most Perfect and Beautiful Names, and Exalted Attributes.

Awliyā: See *walī*.

Barelwi: A pseudo-Islāmic sect that exaggerates the status of the Prophet (ﷺ) to levels beyond those allowed by Islām, directs acts of worship to him, and claims that he has divine powers.

Duʿā: A plea or call for supernatural help.

Īmān: Belief in Allāh and the fundamental pillars of Islām

Fiṭrah: An innate instinct that Allāh has placed in all men which enables them to differentiate right from wrong.

Ḥadīth (plural: *aḥādīth*): A statement of the Prophet Muḥammad (ﷺ).

Ḥajj : The Muslim pilgrimage which is required from every capable adult once in a life-time.

Iblīs: the proper name of the leader of the devils.

ʿIbādah: An act of worship. Any act, belief, or statement that Allāh commands the Muslims to do is an act of worship.

Ilāh: Usually translated in English as 'deity,' however, the Islāmic meaning is broader: any object, real or imagined, that a person turns to for supernatural help. Once a person's heart becomes spiritually attached to an object, hoping the best from it, and fearing rejection, then this object becomes an *ilāh* to him.

Jāhilīyyah: The time-frame before the advent of Islām; it translates as 'Ignorance,' signifying the sheer ignorance of Allāh that existed before the advent of the Prophet (ﷺ).

Jahmiyyah: An early sect which denied that Allāh has any Names and Attributes. The scholars of their time were unanimous in the fact that this group was outside the fold of Islām.

Ka'bah: The House of Allāh at Makkah.

Kāfir: One who is not a Muslim.

Karāmah (plural: *ḳarāmāt*): A miracle attributed to a follower of a prophet.

Khawārij: The first sect to split ranks with the Muslims. They believed that any person who committed a major sin, such as stealing, lying, or fornicating, became a disbeliever due to that sin. They considered most of the Companions as disbelievers, and as such fought them.

Kufr: A belief, statement, or act, which negates one's claim to be a Muslim; it is a rejection of the religion of the Prophet (ﷺ).

Madh-hab: A school of thought.

Murtad: A person who professed Islām, then reneged and became an apostate.

Mushriḳ: One who associates partners with Allāh (i.e., is guilty of *shirḳ*).

Rāfiḍah: The name applied to the Twelver Shī'ite sect, so called since they believe in twelve *Imāms*. They ascribe powers of lordship to these Imāms, perform *tawāf* around their graves, and direct their *du'ās* to them.

Rubūbiyyah: One of the three categories of *tawḥīd*; it signifies that Allāh is the Supreme Lord, Creator and Sustainer of the universe.

Ṣalāt: The five daily prayers obligatory upon Muslims.

Shafā'ah: The concept of intercession in Islām, where one asks another being to act as an intermediary between oneself and Allāh in order that one's request be fulfilled.

Shahādah: The Muslim testimony of faith, 'I testify that only Allāh is worthy of worship, and that Muḥammad is his Messenger.'

Shī'ite: A name given to a collection of different sects, all of whom exaggerate the status of ʿAlī ibn Abī Ṭālib. The most common group amongst them are the *Rāfidah* 'Twelver' *Shī'ites*.

Shayṭān (plural: *Shayāṭīn*): Satan.

Shirk: The act of associating partners with Allāh, either in lordship, or in aspects of worship, or in names and attributes.

Sūfīs: A name given to a collection of different sects, some more extreme than others, all of whom emphasize the concept of spirituality, but reach it through innovated means. They exaggerate the status of pious people (*awliyā*), and believe that every single person must take a particular path of Sūfism if he wishes to attain success. They are characterised by an indifference to studious learning, and veneration of saints.

Sunnah: The practice of the Prophet Muḥammad (ﷺ).

Tawāf: the circumambulation (going around) the *Kaʿbah*; some deviant groups also perform *tawāf* around other objects, which is an example of major *shirk*.

Tawḥīd: The Islāmic concept of monotheism; it consists of unifying Allāh in His Lordship (*Rubūbiyyah*), His right of worship (*Ulūhiyyah*), and His Names and Attributes (*Asmā wa al-Ṣifāt*).

Ulūhiyyah: One of the three categories of *tawḥīd*; it signifies that all of one's actions of worship must be directed to Allāh alone.

Wali (plural: *Awliyā*): A 'friend' of Allāh, meaning one whom Allāh has protected. Although the term is used in the Qur'ān, the *Sūfīs* have abused this term, and used in order to justify acts of *shirk*.

15. Select Bibliography

- *al-Dalā'il wa l-Ishārāt alā Kashf al-Shubuhāt*, Ṣāliḥ ibn Muḥammad al-Asmari. Aḍwaa al-Salaf, Riyādh. 1420 AH.
- *Kashf al-Shubuhāt*, ed. Abū Anas al-Hussay ibn Umar Mazūzi. Foreword by Dr. Safar al-Ḥawalī. Dār al-Watan lil Nashr. Riyādh, 1413 AH.
- *Kashf al-Shubuhāt*, ed. ʿAbdullāh ibn ʿIyāḍ al-Qaḥtānī. Foreword by Dr. ʿAbd al-Raḥmān ibn Ṣāliḥ al-Maḥmūd. Dār al-Suma'yee, Riyādh. 1418 AH.
- *Sharḥ Kashf al-Shubuhāt*, Ṣāliḥ Āl al-Shaykh (Audio Cassettes; Dār Ibn Rajab, Riyādh).
- *Sharḥ Kashf al-Shubuhāt*, Muḥammad ibn Ibrāhīm Āl al-Shaykh. Riyādh, 1419 AH.
- *Sharḥ Kashf al-Shubuhāt*, Muḥammad ibn Ṣāliḥ al-ʿUthaymīn. Dār al-Thurayā, Riyādh, 1416 AH.
- *Taʿliqāt ʿala Kashf al-Shubuhāt*, ʿAbd al-ʿAzīz Āl ʿAbd al-Latīf. Dār al-Watan, Riyādh. 1418 AH.